KOSHER
CUISINE

Helen Nash

KOSHER CUISINE

ILLUSTRATIONS BY PAT STEWART

Random House
New York

*Grateful acknowledgment is made to the following for permission
to reprint previously published material:*

Simon & Schuster, Inc.: listing of Kosher symbols from
How to Run a Traditional Jewish Household by Blu Greenberg.
Copyright © 1983 by Blu Greenberg. Reprinted by permission of
Simon & Schuster, Inc.

Workman Publishing Co., Inc.: recipe for "Chocolate Soufflé Cake,"
from *Cooking the Nouvelle Cuisine in America*.
Copyright © 1979 by Michele Urvater and David Liederman.
Workman Publishing, New York. Reprinted with permission
of the publisher.

Library of Congress Cataloging in Publication Data

Nash, Helen, 1935–
Kosher cuisine.

Includes index.
1. Cookery, Jewish. I. Title.
TX724.N36   1984   641.5'676   83-43183
ISBN 0-394-52788-7

Manufactured in the United States of America

2 4 6 8 9 7 5 3

FIRST EDITION

Book design by Carole Lowenstein

To Jack, Pamela, Joshua and George

Acknowledgments

The advice and encouragement of many people made this book possible.

First, I extend my deepest gratitude to Lilly Joss Reich for her guidance, patience and unwavering support.

I thank my editor, Jason Epstein, for believing in me.

My thanks to Leon Levy for his irrepressible enthusiasm and good cheer.

Millie Chan, Michael Field, Lydie Marshall and Perla Meyers were all generous teachers to whom I am indebted for their encouragement and inspiration.

Finally, my heartful appreciation to family, friends and the wonderful people at Random House: Ida Babad, Ruth Bowman, Dody Edmands, Shula Eisner, Tamara Elia, Rosa Englander, Caryl Englander, Inez Glucksman, Beverly Haviland, Inez Krech, Amanda Larrick, Carole Lowenstein, Mildred Marmur, Rachel Nash, Sonia Shalam, Lusia Sheinbaum, and Paul Steiner.

Contents

Introduction

My interest in food awakened only after I was married. My childhood was far from conducive to developing an interest in cooking.

I was born in Cracow, Poland, in 1935 into a dynastic family of Rabbis and merchants that included Talmudic scholars and commentators. We can trace my mother's family back to the fourteenth century. Our family, very well known and respected, had lived in Poland for many generations. I have no recollection of our life prior to the outbreak of World War II, but my mother tells me that she worked in the family textile business, leaving my sister, my brother, myself, and all the household responsibilities to the servants.

This way of life ended in September 1939. My earliest memory is of being awakened by the sound of my mother sobbing. She threw a few articles into a suitcase and dressed us as Russian soldiers held us at gunpoint. What I remember next is a long, uncomfortable train journey to Sverdlovsk, Siberia. There we lived in a prison labor camp, several families crammed into a small space. We stayed in Russia for only two years and from there traveled to Samarkand and other cities in Central Asia, where we were able to remain until the war ended. Throughout these years, we lived in mud houses and attended Russian schools, finding it extremely difficult to adjust to a culture which to us seemed so primitive and alien. I cannot remember what we ate, but I do know that we observed Jewish dietary laws, which we continue to do to this day.

After the war, we returned to Poland, where we found my maternal grandparents but no other trace of our families or property. The prospect of rebuilding a life in Poland was too painful for my parents to bear, so they resolved to come to the United States. To obtain a visa we traveled to Prague, and there for the first time I saw an orange and a banana. The memory of the striking fragrance and beauty of those fruits is still with me.

I was fourteen years old when we arrived in the United States and settled in Brooklyn, into what was for me a totally strange environment. I attended a religious all-girls high school and then Hunter College. During my adolescence, since I was Orthodox, I was conscious of feeling quite apart from the American culture of the 1950s. I ate only at home or at the homes of equally observant friends. We ate simple traditional Eastern European Jewish food: gefilte fish, chicken soup, kreplach, and so on.

The first time I set foot in a restaurant was on my first date with the man who would later become my husband, and then only to drink a cup of coffee. I was young, eager to please, and defensive about the supposed lack of variety and undistinguished preparation of kosher food. I will never forget an incident which occurred a year after we were married. My husband invited a friend home for dinner. I served roast duck. Our guest, aware that he was eating in a kosher home, jokingly asked if the duck was circumcised. I was so taken aback by this question that I ran into the kitchen and burst into tears. Perhaps it was then that I decided to prove that kosher food could be as varied, light, elegant, and exciting as one wished to make it. My husband, who loves good food and whose background is less traditional than mine, was most encouraging and supportive of my desire to develop my natural sense of taste, smell, and aesthetics.

I bought many cookbooks, studied them, experimented with recipes that did not require any special technique and whose nonkosher ingredients could be replaced with kosher ones. I began to attend cooking classes, where I watched food being prepared, but did not eat it. Instead, I then tried the same recipes at home using kosher ingredients.

The late Michael Field, pianist, restaurateur, author of many cookbooks, and one of the great cooking teachers, taught me all the basics, encouraged me to experiment, and complimented me on my courage.

Lilly Joss Reich, author of *The Viennese Pastry Cookbook*, became my pastry teacher and a devoted friend and mentor.

Lydie Marshall, author of *Cooking with Lydie Marshall*, and one of the most accomplished teachers of French cuisine, was wonderful and inspiring.

Perla Meyers, author of several cookbooks, taught me to have confidence in my own cooking.

Most importantly, a friend presented me with an exciting gift—Chinese cooking lessons with Millie Chan, teacher at the China Institute and at the Spanish Portuguese Synagogue. Learning about Chinese cooking was an absolute revelation. Discovering how compatible Chinese and kosher ingredients and seasonings could be opened up for me whole new areas of taste, smell, texture, and decoration.

After learning, experimenting, and cooking for twenty-five years, I have developed an eclectic repertoire of recipes, techniques, and style of entertaining. Now I enjoy having small sit-down dinners and luncheons of eight to ten people. I like to do it in an elegant yet relaxed manner, with fine linens, china, flowers, good food, and a mixture of people of different backgrounds and interests. Most of the time our guests do not keep kosher and often are not even Jewish.

The market dictates what the menu will be. I prefer to serve small portions and many courses, often mixing different ethnic foods. For example, I often serve wontons with cocktails, begin dinner with a hot soup, to be followed by chicken or veal with a vegetable and starch, a salad to follow as a separate course, and end the meal with a refreshing fruit sorbet or poached fruit and an assortment of cookies.

A typical luncheon may be a cold soup; pasta, fish, or a salad; and a light dessert of fresh fruit and cake or cookies.

I like my food honestly and simply garnished, emphasizing its harmony of colors.

I always read the recipe carefully to familiarize myself with it. I select the best and freshest ingredients; if they are unavailable, I do not compromise, but make something else.

I organize my menu so as to prepare several dishes in advance, which makes entertaining so much more relaxing.

Palates differ. Some people like food spicy, some mild, some sweet. Styles of cooking differ; some cooks have a lighter hand and some a heavier. I have often made the identical dish with different results on different occasions. I urge you to experiment, trust yourself, have confidence, and use your imagination.

KOSHER

The word *kosher* means "fit" or "proper." It is often taken to mean "clean" when applied to food, that is, not soiled or spoiled. But the true meaning is "clean" in an ethical sense: prepared in accordance with religious law.

Kosher food need not be in any particular ethnic style. After all, Jews have lived and continue to live all over the world, making use of the ingredients and spices of all the places they live. The selections they make and their methods of preparation are in accordance with the law, regardless of the culinary styles around them. It is a common mistake to think that kosher food must be the food of Eastern Europe, which was heavy and sustaining for populations living in cold climates in unheated houses.

The laws of *kashruth* (the Hebrew word that refers to the dietary laws) may appear to outsiders to be arcane health regulations. Observance of the laws may well have a positive effect on one's health, but that is not the true purpose of the dietary laws. Their purpose, rather, is to teach reverence for life. Their observance should serve as an affirmation of faith.

Jewish tradition strives to orient every aspect of our daily life toward holiness. Food is that which gives us the physical sustenance to fulfill God's will.

Consider the prohibition against eating pork. Jews do not avoid pork because of pigs' dirty habits. After all, in the days of primitive husbandry, herds did not live in clean stables, and the pig was probably no dirtier than other animals. The difference was that pigs were used for sacrifice by heathen cultures and were thus ethically unfit for consumption by God-fearing people.

In order to avoid cruelty to animals and underscore the importance of compassion and respect for all living things, special humane methods of slaughter were required. The method was designed for a quick and painless death. Not just anyone could do the slaughtering; it had to be done by someone especially trained for it, one who had the proper spiritual orientation.

There are two important rules regarding meat—in Deut. 14:21 and Ex. 23:19 and 34:26 ("You shall not boil a kid in its mother's milk") and in Lev. 7:26–27 and 17:10–14 ("You must not consume any blood, either, in fowl, or animal, For the life of the flesh is in the blood").

From the first rule has come the separation of meat and milk, not just at meals but in their preparation and even in the cleaning and drying of pots and dishes. Specific time intervals are observed between the eating of meat and the eating of dairy meals. (Some foods are neutral, neither meat nor dairy. These "pareve" foods can be eaten in conjunction with either, but care must be taken in their preparation so that meat utensils are not used for dairy foods or vice versa.)

The second rule about meat, which forbids the consumption of blood, affects the preparation of meat from the moment of slaughter on. First, in addition to the speed and painlessness of the method of slaughter, the law requires complete and rapid draining of the blood. Following this, meat must be "kashered" to remove any remaining blood. While today kashering is generally performed by kosher butchers, it is possible to do it at home by an easy sequence of rinsing and salting the meat.

The rule against consumption of blood also applies to eggs. If you crack open an egg and it has a spot of blood, you must discard it. It is therefore important to open eggs one at a time, over a separate bowl from the one that contains the rest of the eggs.

Only meat from animals with cloven hooves that chew their cud may be eaten. All others are forbidden, such as camel, horse, hare, pig, and donkey, which were often eaten or offered as sacrifice by idolatrous races.

Certain cuts of meat, those taken from the hindquarter, are also forbidden because the sciatic nerve, which runs through the hindquarter, is forbidden. While historically kosher butchers removed this and its accompanying blood vessels (as they do in Israel today), it is too time-consuming for the American meat industry, and there are too few butchers skilled enough to do it. Instead, hindquarters are sold to nonkosher butchers.

Kosher rules apply to all foods, not just to meat. Only fish with fins and scales are permitted. All types of shellfish, which are scavengers, are forbidden. But even so, there are at least seventy-five different species of fish allowed, a large enough variety.

Poultry that are permitted include the usual domestic birds—chicken, turkey, duck, goose, dove. Wild birds and birds of prey are not allowed, nor are the eggs from those birds. Anything creeping or crawling is forbidden—insects, snakes, amphibian snails. The prohibition also applies to insects that attack fruits and vegetables. In a kosher kitchen, care is taken to examine all produce for worms and to examine dried beans and peas for weevils. Food that is contaminated in this way is not kosher.

Neutral foods (parve or pareve) include all fruits and vegetables, nuts, spices, sugar, salt, tea, coffee, the permitted fish, and eggs from permitted poultry. These can be eaten with either meat or dairy dishes. When buying packaged foods, look for a symbol that indicates that the contents were prepared under rabbinic supervision. Some symbols are the following:

Ⓤ—the Union of Orthodox Jewish Congregations, New York, New York. (Inasmuch as the   is under the aegis of a large communal organization, this is the best known and most widely used symbol of kashruth.)

Ⓚ—O.K. (Organized Kashrut) Laboratories, Brooklyn, New York.

Ⓜ—(K.V.H.) Kashrut Commission of the Vaad Horabanim (Rabbinical Council) of New England, Boston, Massachusetts.

Ⓚ—Rabbi J. H. Ralbag, New York, New York.

Ⓚ—Kosher Supervision Service, Hackensack, New Jersey.

Ⓚ—Kosher Overseers Association of America, Beverly Hills, California.

Ⓥ—Vaad Hoeir of Saint Louis, Saint Louis, Missouri.

Ⓦ—Board of Rabbis, Jersey City, New Jersey.

☆—Vaad Hakashrus of Baltimore, Baltimore, Maryland.

If you are thinking of setting up a kosher kitchen, you should seek rabbinic advice on how to proceed. You may also wish to consult one of the many excellent books on the subject, such as Blu Greenberg's *How to Run a Traditional Jewish Household* (Simon and Schuster, 1983), through whose courtesy I have reproduced the symbols in the preceding paragraph.

The following is simply a brief overview.

A kosher kitchen can be set up in any space. You will require separate cooking vessels and utensils for meat and dairy foods, as well as separate serving dishes for meat and dairy. Similarly, you will need separate bowls and blades for the food processor, as well as separate blender bowls. If you have two sinks and two dishwashers, you can designate one for meat and one for dairy, as meat and dairy dishes and utensils may not be washed or kept together. Most of us, however, have only one sink and one dishwasher; we use two sets of dish drainers, two sink liners, and two separate dishwasher racks. If you do not want to bother with two separate dishwasher racks, simply use the machine for meat dishes and utensils and wash your dairy set by hand. Use kosher detergents for dishwashing and designate different towels and sponges for dairy and milk dishes. To simplify, use different colored items for meat and dairy.

In addition, Passover requires the use of two completely separate sets of dishes and utensils. Elaborate as all this sounds, keeping kosher becomes quite manageable once you begin living it.

Needless to say, this is a book of kosher recipes and not a book on kashruth. In setting up your kosher kitchen, and when in doubt as to any kashruth-related matter, you should seek out proper rabbinic advice.

INGREDIENTS

The proverbial expression "what you put in, you get out" applies very much to cooking and baking. Menu planning comes *after* the choice of ingredients, not before it. That is, you should design your menu on the basis of what food is fresh and of top quality. When selecting foods, learn to touch them, smell them, observe them, and select wisely. Find a friendly butcher, fishman, and greengrocer, even in supermarkets. At the same time, experiment freely with the recipes, as every palate is individual.

Before you start to cook or bake, make sure you read and understand the recipe. Assemble all the ingredients and utensils. As you cook, learn to taste, smell, improvise, and above all have fun.

Beets   Pick small- to medium-size beets with the tops on. Larger ones are often tasteless. Fresh beets without the tops keep very well refrigerated in a plastic bag.

Butter   I always use sweet, unsalted butter. Sweet butter is essential for baking. Salted butter has a greater water content and a less-delicate flavor. Sweet butter is purer, but is also more perishable. If you don't plan to keep it more than a week or so, freeze it.

CLARIFIED BUTTER   Melt butter in a small saucepan over low heat. Cool it a bit, then skim off the white froth on top. Carefully pour the rest into a small jar, leaving the watery dregs, or whey, in the saucepan.

Clarified butter keeps for weeks refrigerated. It is used for sautéeing, since it won't burn as quickly as unclarified butter. It is also used for baking when butter flavor is required, as in Genoise and crepes. *See also Margarine.*

Carrots   Buy small- to medium-size carrots with green tops. Discard the tops and store the carrots in a plastic bag in the refrigerator.

Cream   Buy plain old-fashioned heavy cream, not the new ultra-pasteurized variety. If a recipe calls for light cream and you cannot find it in your market, use half and half instead.

TO WHIP CREAM   Day-old cream whips better than fresh cream.

Chill a metal bowl in the freezer for 15 minutes or longer. Pour in the chilled cream and beat it with either an electric or a rotary hand beater, moving the beaters around the bowl to whip the cream evenly.

Dried Beans and Lentils Try to buy dried beans or lentils in health food or specialty stores. Dried beans last a long time, and it is hard to distinguish long-stored ones from the newer ones; therefore, after the beans are soaked, discard those that seem very hard.

Eggs All the recipes call for large eggs.

SEPARATING EGGS I crack one egg at a time on the edge of a bowl and empty the whole egg into my hand, letting the white drip into the bowl and leaving the yolk dry, then drop the yolk into another bowl.

EGG WHITES Egg whites will have greater volume when beaten if they are at room temperature. Both bowl and beater or whisk should be very clean. Egg whites should be beaten until they are stiff. To test whether the eggs have been beaten sufficiently, turn the bowl upside down; if they have been beaten enough, the foam will not fall out.

Egg whites cannot be beaten ahead of time; they will lose air if allowed to stand. They must be folded into the other ingredients as soon as they are beaten.

Egg whites freeze well in glass jars, either individually or several together.

HARD-COOKED EGGS Place the eggs in a saucepan filled with cold water. Bring the water to a boil over high heat and continue boiling for 1 minute. Cover the pan, remove from the heat, and let rest for 20 minutes. Remove the eggs and let them cool. If you are in a hurry, rinse them with cold water.

Flour Unless otherwise specified, all recipes using flour were tested with all-purpose unbleached flour (Hecker's).

TO MEASURE FLOUR Scoop it out with a dry measuring cup and level off the top with a straight-edged knife. Do not shake or bang the cup.

TO SIFT FLOUR Place a dry measuring cup on a sheet of wax paper. Fill the flour sifter. Hold it at least 1 inch above the measuring cup and sift the flour into the cup. Do not bang the cup. When it is full, level it off with a knife. Excess flour left on the wax paper can be reused.

CAKE FLOUR This is a fine flour for cakes. I use Swans Down.

WHOLE WHEAT AND RYE FLOUR These flours can be found in health food or specialty stores.

Garlic Try to buy loose (not packaged) heads of garlic. They should be large and full, not dry or wrinkled. I store garlic in a plastic bag in the refrigerator.

TO MINCE GARLIC Press down on the clove with the flat side of a large knife blade, or with your hand, to split the skin. Peel off the skin and mince the garlic.

Gingerroot   Look for fresh young roots with an off-white color inside. As the root ages, it becomes gray, stringy, and has a stronger flavor. I keep gingerroot refrigerated, wrapped in foil, then placed in a plastic bag. When ready to use, trim off any discolored part, cut off the needed amount, peel, and mince.

Herbs   The delicious flavor of fresh herbs will enhance any dish.

Basil is available in summer and fall. Discard the stems, wash, and dry. Then wrap it in a paper towel, place in a plastic bag, and refrigerate.

Bay leaves are always dried, but the fresher they are the better. Freshly dried leaves are pale green and have a fresh scent; after long storage they become brown and brittle.

Bouquet garni is a little bundle of herbs tied in a double layer of cheese-cloth with a string and is used for flavoring sauces, soups, and stews. The usual ingredients are parsley sprigs, dried thyme, and bay leaf, but there are many other combinations. You can make your own or buy them ready-made in specialty stores.

Chives should not be washed, but should be kept dry to prevent spoilage. Snip them off with a scissors.

Fresh dill is available all year round, so never use it dried. Do not wash dill either. Rather wrap it in a paper towel, place it in a plastic bag, and refrigerate until needed. Snip it to bits with a scissors, like chives.

Parsley is also available all year round. There are two types: curly and flat leaf. I prefer to use the flat leaf, which is also known as Italian parsley, because it is more flavorful. Discard all or some of the stems. Wash the leaves, then dry them in a salad spinner, wrap in a paper towel, place in a plastic bag, and refrigerate. It will keep for several days.

Rosemary, tarragon, and *thyme* are available fresh for part of the year. When not available, buy good-quality whole dried herbs (not ground). When ready to use, rub the dried herb between your palms to release more flavor.

Margarine   I use 100 percent corn-oil margarine (Mazola), unsalted and pareve.

Mushrooms   When using fresh mushrooms, choose those that are white and firm, with no opening between the stems and caps. Simply wipe them with a damp paper towel to remove any specks of soil. Trim the base of the stems if needed.

DRIED MUSHROOMS   Imported dried mushrooms come mostly from Poland, Czechoslovakia, France, Italy, and China. They have a wonderful flavor and are indispensable for many dishes. They are expensive because of the expense of drying and exporting them, but only a small amount is usually needed. Look for large pieces and avoid buying them in packages.

TO RECONSTITUTE DRIED MUSHROOMS   Soak them in boiling water; the necessary amount of water and the time needed will be listed in each recipe. Lift out the softened mushrooms and squeeze out as much of the soaking liquid as possible. Wash the mushrooms, since they are generally quite sandy. Strain the soaking liquid through a fine sieve lined with a damp paper towel. The liquid will add flavor to the dish.

Nuts   I buy shelled nuts preferably in health food stores or specialty markets, as they seem to be fresher.

All nuts freeze well, but should be brought to room temperature before using. Nuts keep better whole. If you need them chopped or grated, process only the amount you need. For small amounts use a small nut grater or Mouli grater. For large amounts the food processor will do.

TO BLANCH ALMONDS   In a saucepan bring water to a boil. Drop in shelled almonds and let the water return to the boil. Let boil for 1 minute, drain, and slip off the skins. Place on paper towels to dry. (Do not leave the almonds in the water.) If some of the almond skins cannot be removed, repeat the process.

TO BLANCH HAZELNUTS   Spread shelled hazelnuts on a baking sheet in a single layer and roast in a preheated 350° F oven for about 15 minutes, or until the skin darkens and begins to flake off. Wrap the nuts in a coarse towel and rub the towel against a hard surface. Most of the skins will come off. Do not worry if some skins remain on a few nuts.

TO ROAST PINE NUTS OR PIGNOLI   Roast the nuts in the oven for about 10 minutes, or sauté them quickly in very little oil. Watch them carefully, since they burn easily.

Oils   In salad dressings I use a light, pale, odorless olive oil, such as Olio Sasso, from Oneglia, Italy, or safflower oil or a combination of the two.

I use corn and peanut oils for deep frying, stir frying, and sautéeing.

Pasta   Most of the time I use fresh pasta, which is available in many specialty shops. It is lighter and more delicate than dried pasta, and it freezes very well.

My favorite dried pasta is the DeCecco brand, imported from Abruzzo, Italy. If you can't find it, be sure to select a brand made with durum wheat.

Phyllo   Both fresh and frozen phyllo dough can be found in specialty stores. Fresh phyllo comes in 18-by-14-inch sheets; frozen phyllo in 16-by-12-inch sheets. I prefer to work with fresh phyllo; it is less fragile. Fresh phyllo can be kept refrigerated for several weeks. If you use frozen dough, follow the instructions on the package to defrost.

Salad Greens   A choice of salad greens is available all year, varying according to the season. There is no need to feel limited to using iceberg lettuce all the time.

Alfalfa sprouts are sold in plastic containers and bags. Make sure they are dry and look fresh. They make a nice crunchy addition to a salad.
Bibb lettuce is a small, tender head, with dark green leaves. The limestone-grown lettuce has a distinctive flavor.
Endive, called Belgian endive or witloof, is small and elongated. It is blanched for marketing and therefore requires very little cleaning. Usually all that is needed is to wipe off the heads with a damp paper towel, remove any discolored outer leaves, and trim the base. They keep fresh for many days in a plastic bag. *To serve endive:* Cut into crosswise round slices, or separate the leaves and cut them into long julienne strips. This green is delicious mixed with watercress, arugula, bibb lettuce, or fresh baked beets. It is also good by itself.
Rugula, or arugula, is a loose head of dark green leaves with pungent or bitter flavor. This green should be eaten after you buy it; the leaves are fragile. Wash this green well.
Watercress is a small sprig with small round dark green leaves with a peppery taste. Delicious as a salad, alone or with other greens; a fine garnish to many dishes; a good ingredient for soups and sauces.

Salt   I use only kosher salt, except for baking. It has a coarse texture, but it is pure salt, containing no additives. To my taste, it is less "salty" than other kinds of table salt. For baking, I use table salt, since the finer grind makes it dissolve more readily.

Shallots   Another relative of the onion, with a flavor more pungent than onion but more delicate than garlic. Shallots grow in clusters of small bulbs. Store in a plastic bag and refrigerate.

Soy Sauce   All recipes requiring soy sauce were tested with Chinese, not Japanese, sauce. There are several varieties of soy sauce; the most familiar are thin (also called light) and black (also called dark). Thin soy sauce is saltier than dark soy sauce.

Spices   Aside from gingerroot, most spices are sold in dried form: black and white peppercorns, cinnamon sticks, black mustard seeds, caraway seeds, nutmeg, and saffron threads. These will keep their flavor better whole. Buy them in small quantities and grind them, if possible, just before you plan to use them. Curry powder, a mixture of ground spices, is available in various degrees of pungency. I use Sun Brand imported Madras curry powder. It keeps a long time.

Tomatoes   One of the most popular of foods, but seldom as tasty as they should be, because the commercial variety has been bred to retain their firmness, for the purposes of shipping, at the expense of flavor. Unripe tomatoes can be ripened by placing them in a brown paper bag and keeping them in a dark place. Be sure to check on them daily.

TO PEEL AND SEED TOMATOES   Bring a large pot of water to a boil. Drop in the tomatoes and let the water return to the boil. Drain tomatoes, then loosen the skin and pull it off. (Do not let tomatoes remain in the boiling water, or the flesh will soften and you will lose some in peeling.) Cut out the tomato core, cutting them in half crosswise. Holding each half cut-side-down, gently press with your hand and the seeds will fall out.

If fresh, well-ripened tomatoes are not available, use canned peeled tomatoes, such as Vitelli brand from San Marzano, Italy, or other Italian tomatoes.

Tomato paste is found in the familiar 6-ounce can and in tubes, good when small amounts are needed. The tubes are imported from Italy and keep for a long time, refrigerated.

Yeast   Today one can buy yeast in several forms: compressed fresh yeast, which comes in 2-ounce blocks; loose granular; and packaged granular of ¼ ounce (7 grams), approximately, 1 tablespoon. An individual package of granular yeast is equivalent to ½ ounce fresh yeast. Fresh yeast should be light, moist, and unblemished. It keeps very well for weeks wrapped in foil and refrigerated. I prefer loose granular yeast without any preservatives, such as El Molino brand sold in health food stores or the Red Star packages sold in some supermarkets. When buying packages, check the expiration date; inactive yeast can ruin a baking recipe.

To start active development of the yeast cells, you need warm water. For granular yeast (100° to 115°F), and for compressed fresh yeast (80° to 90°F). To be accurate, use a (candy) thermometer to test the water.

If you are buying yeast in large bulk in health food stores, the packages are not always dated, and you should "proof" the yeast before using it to find out if it is still active. You do that by adding sugar to the liquid, which provides food for the yeast and speeds the growth.

The rising time of dough is difficult to gauge. It will vary with the temperature of the room, how active the yeast is, and what other ingredients (fats, sugar, types of flour) are used in the recipe. Your best guide for determining that the dough has risen completely is the increase in its bulk. Dough needs a warm, undrafty atmosphere in which to rise, ideally 80° to 100° F. If you have a gas oven, the pilot light will provide warmth; so would a food warmer. If you have an electric oven, preheat it to the lowest temperature, shut it off, then leave the door ajar to let the temperature cool somewhat.

METHODS

Beat   To agitate with a whisk, a rotary hand beater, or an electric mixer so as to break up the ingredients and create a homogeneous mixture. When eggs are beaten, air is added so that the volume is increased. This air is important in baking, because it expands in the oven heat, giving a lighter texture to cakes.

To test if egg whites have been sufficiently beaten, invert the bowl with the whites; if they stick to the bottom of the pan and do not fall out, they are ready.

Blanch   To plunge a vegetable (such as a tomato) or a fruit (such as a peach) or a nut (such as an almond) into boiling water, and leave it there only until the water returns to the boil, draining it immediately. The moist heat loosens the skin so that it can be pulled off easily. Also, to precook briefly, particularly strong-flavored vegetables, such as spinach.

Boil   To cook any food in water to cover. Pasta is an example; the water must be vigorously boiling to keep the strands from sticking together.

Braise   To cook a food in moist heat in a covered container. The amount of moisture is usually very small, often only the natural juice of the meat or vegetable. An excellent way to cook less-tender meats and a good choice for meats with little natural fat, which become dry and stringy in oven roasting.

Broil   To cook meat, poultry, or fish under radiant heat, either gas or electric.

Clarify   To remove all solid particles or droplets of fat from soups or stock.

Also, to remove casein and whey from butter, leaving absolutely clear butterfat with a pure butter flavor and no milky residue to burn.

Cream   A term that has nothing to do with the ingredient cream, but is a special kind of beating used for butter or margarine. The butter is beaten with a mixer or a food processor or is mashed with a wooden spoon to create a soft, creamy texture. Sometimes sugar and/or eggs are added and creamed with the butter or margarine.

Deep Fry   To cook food in fat deep enough to cover it completely. The fat must be heated to a temperature suited to the food, 350° F or more. When the frying is completed, the inside of the food should be moist and tender, the outside crisp and golden. Small dumplings, vegetables, meats, fish, and even fruits can be deep fried.

Degrease   To skim surface fat with a spoon.

Drain   To pour off liquid from a solid. Usually, the solid is retained, and the liquid is discarded. Typical examples are the draining of pasta and of vegetables after blanching. Sometimes a food cooked in water is lifted out with a skimmer rather than being drained; examples are poached fish and kreplach.

Dress   To prepare fresh fish, poultry, or game for cooking. Specific terms for preparing fish include *whole-dressed*, which means that the scales, gills, and guts have been removed, but the head and fins remain; and *pan-dressed*, which means that the scales, gills, guts, head, and fins have been removed.

Fillet   To remove the flesh from both sides of the whole fish, yielding two boneless pieces, which may be skinned or not.

Fold   To combine beaten egg whites with a heavier mixture, such as egg yolks or batter, without losing the air in the egg whites. First one quarter of the beaten egg whites is folded into the heavier mixture to lighten it. Then another quarter of the egg whites is folded in. The balance of the egg whites is then emptied over the batter, and the two are combined. To fold, use a large spatula and cut down into the center of the mixture; then move the spatula underneath the batter and bring it up to the top, making a motion like a figure eight while turning the bowl with your hand. Fold as quickly as possible. A few specks of egg whites may remain visible, but the batter should be homogeneous.

Julienne   To cut any food into small sticks, ¼ to ⅛ inch wide. First slice the food to the needed thickness, then reduce the slice to matchsticks.

Knead   To stretch and mix the dough for breads and other foods made with yeast. The dough is folded, turned, pushed, and stretched with the heel of your hand in order to develop the gluten that will help provide the texture of the finished food.

When the dough has been kneaded enough, it will be smooth, elastic, and will not stick to hands or board.

Dough can be kneaded by hand or by machine with the dough hook on an electric mixer, then finished by hand. Some people also use a food processor, but I find it difficult to gauge.

Poach   To cook a food in water or other liquid to cover at a temperature lower than boiling. A gentle method, good for tender foods such as eggs, pears, and peaches, since it does not break up the food or toughen it.

Puree   To reduce a food to a smooth, thick mixture. Depending on the consistency of the food, it may be pureed by mashing, by forcing through a sieve, by putting through a food mill, or by processing in a blender or food processor.

Refresh   To plunge fully cooked or partly cooked vegetables into cold water or ice water in order to cool them quickly and set the natural color. As soon as the vegetables are cooled, they are drained. If the vegetable is to be served warm or hot, it can be reheated just before serving.

Sauté   To cook a food in a very small amount of butter, oil, or margarine, or a mixture of fats. The total cooking time is very short, a few minutes only, and the amount of butter, margarine, and oil is just enough to coat the pan. Onions and shallots are often sautéed before being added to sauces or other mixtures.

Sift   To put dry ingredients, such as flour, baking powder, baking soda, cornstarch, and salt, through a sieve in order to remove lumps and to make the ingredients light and airy. A cup of unsifted flour is heavier and contains more flour than a cup of sifted flour.

Simmer   For all practical purposes this method is the same as poaching, although foods being simmered may not be covered with the liquid.

Steam   To cook in the steam rising from a liquid boiling beneath the food. The food may be in a separate steaming basket or on a heatproof dish set on a rack in a wok.

Stir   To mix two or more ingredients in order to combine them. Or to mix a liquid in order to aerate it, speed cooling, or prevent the formation of a skin on the surface.

Stir Fry   To sauté in a small amount of hot oil, tossing the food vigorously as it cooks, to expose all sides to the fat. Stir frying can be done in a skillet, but the best utensil is a wok, because the rounded surface makes the stirring easy and allows oil to drain off the pieces. When done in a wok, stir frying requires very little oil. It is a preferred method for Chinese and Japanese cooking.

Strain   To remove solid particles from a liquid; the liquid is retained, the solids are lifted. We strain stock and soups.

Truss   To tie up poultry for cooking. I use a regular thick sewing needle and double cotton thread, and with this I sew up the skin around the openings. No elaborate trussing is needed, but the wings may be folded under and the ends of the drumsticks may be tied together.

KITCHEN EQUIPMENT

Even though a kosher kitchen requires at least two of everything, I still suggest buying high-quality kitchen equipment made of heavy-gauge materials that do not warp, buckle, bend, or burn. It is well worth the investment.

Baking Pans
   Loaf pans, 9 by 5 inches approximately, made of heavy tin.
   Springform pans, 9 by 2½ inches or 10 by 2¾ inches, made of heavy tin.
   Tube pan, 10 by 4 inches.
   Aluminum muffin pans with small depressions.
   Jelly roll pans, 11 by 16 inches approximately.

Baking Sheets   Measure the depth and width of your oven and buy the largest sheets your oven will hold. I prefer to use black sheet-steel (heavy duty) baking sheets with the smallest rims, ⅜ inch wide, so that you can stack them. You will find these heavy sheets essential for making tulips, tuilles, hazelnut crisps, and many other thin cookies.

Blender   Many people think you can toss out the blender once you buy a food processor, but I find it very useful for most pureeing and for making salad dressings and mayonnaise. There is less spilling when you are blending liquid mixtures, such as any of the cream soups.

Cake Tester   A thin metal skewer for testing cakes, breads, and various desserts for doneness. You can also use a wooden toothpick.

Candy Thermometer   I use the Taylor brand thermometer for making sugar syrup, for testing oil for deep frying, and for testing water temperature when dissolving yeast. When caramelizing sugar, you can leave the thermometer in the saucepan for easier reading.

Carving Board   Choose a thick board with a juice catcher.

Cheesecloth   I use cheesecloth for wrapping quenelle and tuna loaf, and for bouquet garni. Buy cotton cheesecloth, not nylon. Cheesecloth comes folded in four layers. Cut off the desired amount and refold it to the thickness required by your recipe.

Chopping Boards   Even though wooden chopping boards are no longer recommended for sanitary reasons, I still prefer them. There are also synthetic (plastic) boards, which come in many sizes and are dishwasher-proof.

Cleavers   They come in two weights: lightweight stainless for chopping and slicing, and heavyweight stainless for disjointing fowl and chopping through the bones.

Colander   Buy a large aluminum one to drain pasta, spinach, and other vegetables.

Cookie and Biscuit Cutters   You will need stainless-steel cookie cutters of various sizes and shapes, not only for cookies, but to cut out rounds of pastry and bread for canapés.

Copper Saucepan for Sugar Syrup   Turning sugar into caramel is much easier if you have a small unlined copper saucepan. You may think it is extravagant to buy a pan specifically for sugar cookery, but when you consider how quickly an aluminum or tinned saucepan can burn with the intense heat of caramelizing, you will agree that it is well worth the expense to have the right pan.

Crepe Pans   These are made of heavy iron or thick steel and come in different sizes. They should be seasoned before they are used and kept clean afterward with an occasional seasoning as well.

TO SEASON PANS   Pour a very thin layer of vegetable oil into the pan and sprinkle with a very thin layer of kosher salt. Put over high heat for a few minutes, then wipe clean with paper towels. Make sure that the last piece of towel is clean.

Dish Towels   Paper towels have not taken over all the functions of dish towels. Have linen and cotton towels on hand. They are wonderful for keeping vegetables dry, straining stock, keeping pastry moist, and many other uses.

Double Boiler   An essential kitchen pot for melting chocolate, making custards, and warm emulsified sauces. Also useful for keeping things warm over hot water. You will need both a small double boiler and a large one, 1½ to 2 quarts.

Dough Scraper   A metal scraper with a wooden handle is a fine tool for scraping dough off a pastry board and for mixing dough such as puff pastry.

Electric Ice-Cream Maker   There are expensive and inexpensive ice-cream makers on the market. The ultimate in appearance and simplicity is *Il Gelataio,* The Ice-Cream Boy, as well as the larger version, The Ice-Cream Man. This machine has its own freezing mechanism and does not require any ice or salt. It makes wonderful ice creams, sorbets, and frozen yogurts. The drawbacks are that it is a bit cumbersome to clean and it is quite heavy. There is also a traditional electric wooden tub ice-cream maker called White Mountain. It requires ice and rock salt and also makes wonderful frozen desserts. I have both. I use one for dairy desserts and the other for pareve ones.

Electric Mixers   I find the Hobart Kitchen Aid Mixer as indispensable as the food processor. It comes in two models: the K-45-SS, which is slightly smaller and therefore less expensive, and the K-5-SS. I use this machine for beating, whipping, and kneading. One of the special advantages of this mixer is the dough hook, which makes kneading quick and easy. Plan to buy the colander-sieve attachment to make it possible to strain fish mousses in order to make them smooth and light as air. Be sure to buy an extra mixer bowl and wire whisk.

I also have an electric hand mixer, which I use for beating cream and egg whites and for making zabaglioni and sauces.

Flour Sifter   A stainless-steel container with a fine mesh sieve in the bottom and a device like a rotator to speed the sifting. Also used for cornstarch, baking powder, baking soda, and so on.

Foil and Foil Pans   Be sure to have wide sheets of heavy-duty foil on hand, as well as foil pans. They come in many sizes and are useful for storing and freezing pastries, among many other uses.

Food Mill (Mouli)   This is a simple hand-operated machine that comes with three sieving discs. It is wonderful for pureeing, for ricing potatoes, and for straining tomato sauce. Many people prefer it to the blender and food processor.

Food Processor   Learn to use your own food processor. Experiment to find out how much pressure should be applied to items in the feed tube in order to obtain various textures. Learn to use the discs and blades. I chop, grate, and shred almost all my vegetables in the food processor, but I cut them into pieces first to enable the blades to work more quickly and not mutilate them. If, however, I need carefully chopped or sliced vegetables, I do them by hand. Never put green or red peppers into the food processor; they will be mutilated. You will need two bowls and two sets of blades.

Glass Containers   You will need some deep glass bowls or terrines to hold foods for marinating.

Grater   I prefer the four-sided kind that can stand on end. Many of its uses have been taken over by the grating disc of the food processor.

Knives   I recommend buying the best quality stainless-steel knives you can afford and caring for them properly. Choose a comfortable handle of good quality wood and finish. Some of the essential knives are a paring knife, a chopping French chef's knife, a slicing knife, a boning knife, and a bread knife, but there is a knife for every kitchen purpose. *See also Cleavers.*

Marble Slab   Excellent for rolling out pastry. It remains cool, therefore the butter or fat in the pastry does not melt and the right texture of the pastry is maintained. Especially necessary for puff pastry and pâté brisée. It is sold in various sizes in kitchen specialty stores. The only drawback is that it is very heavy.

Measuring Cups   Cups for liquids have a pouring spout. Cups for solids can be leveled by passing a knife over the top.

Measuring Spoons   Look for stainless-steel ones, preferably with long handles; they are easier to scoop out. Buy them in sizes from ⅛ teaspoon to 1 tablespoon.

Meat Pounder   A round, flat, solid disc of stainless steel weighing about 2 pounds, used chiefly for pounding meat, such as boneless chicken breasts.

Mouli Grater   A small hand grater that is perfect for grating a small amount of cheese or nuts.

Nut Grater   The drum grater comes in various sizes and is wonderful for grating nuts finely.

Nutmeg Grater   This device is constructed like a peppermill. The nutmeg is dropped into the top, and a crank powers the grinding mechanism. The difference between freshly grated nutmeg and already ground spice is enormous. For best flavor grate just before you need it.

Pastry Blender   A handy device for combining fats with flour for all pastries and doughs. The working part is a series of stainless-steel wire loops; the handle may be wood or plastic. Many people cut with two knives; this is the method that I prefer.

Pastry Brushes   Nonsynthetic flat brushes are my preference. I have them in various sizes. I use them to brush melted butter or margarine onto phyllo sheets, to coat pie crust with egg white, to butter baking pans, and so on. Brushes should be washed in warm, soapy water, then flicked dry and left to air.

Pastry Racks   They come in various sizes, and I use them for cooling breads, cakes, pastries, and so forth.

Pepper Mill   For best flavor I grind peppercorns as I need them. A mill is inexpensive enough so that you can have one for black peppercorns and one for white peppercorns. I recommend the French Perfex or a wooden Peugeot.

Pie Weights   Aluminum nuggets, available wherever baking supplies are sold, even in some supermarkets. These are a great improvement over the "dried beans or rice" formerly used for prebaking pastry shells. The aluminum weights can be used over and over again. If necessary, they can be washed.

Poultry Shears   Special scissors designed to cut through joints of poultry.

Roasting Pans   These are low heavy-duty uncovered pans. Don't buy tin or aluminum; they will buckle in a hot oven. Have several sizes.

Roasting Rack   An adjustable metal rack shaped like a V, designed to hold meats or poultry so that the meat is kept out of the fat.

Rolling Pin   The straight French rolling pin, 18 inches long and 6 inches around, is a beautiful, balanced, smoothly finished tool. It permits a great variation of touch and is long enough to roll out large sheets of dough. Clean it immediately after use with a slightly damp cloth, then dry it.

Rubber Spatulas   They come in various sizes and are excellent for folding, blending, and combining ingredients. Also useful for scraping the last bit of mixture from bowls and jars.

Salad Spin Drier   This indispensable gadget makes the drying of salad greens, spinach, and parsley very easy. The greens are placed in an inner slotted basket, which is set in a plastic bowl. When the basket spins, the water on the leaves is thrown into the outer bowl. Do not pack too many greens in at one time, and empty the water each time. To make sure that the leaves are absolutely dry, after you have spinned them, place them on a piece of paper towel and expose them to the air for a few minutes. If I am using them right away, I place them in a bowl and refrigerate them uncovered. If I am using them the following day, I wrap them in a paper towel and place them in a plastic bag. They will keep crisp for a day or longer, depending on the freshness and variety of the greens. Salad spin driers are available in most hardware stores. They come in two sizes.

Saucepans There are different kinds with many different virtues. Many people like copper, stainless steel, or aluminum. I like the enameled cast-iron ones because they distribute heat evenly and well, can be used both on top of the stove and in the oven, clean easily, come in various colors, are pretty to look at, and food can be refrigerated in them without fear of its absorbing or changing flavor and color. They also come in many sizes. The disadvantage is that they are heavy to hold and when dropped may chip.

Scales The seesaw balance scale made by Dr. Oetker (a German line of baking and kitchen utensils) is convenient for measuring small amounts of ingredients. It reads both grams and ounces. The scoop end holds about ⅔ cup of ingredients. This scale is available in specialty shops and in many department stores that sell kitchen equipment. For large amounts, I use a beam scale, which reads ounces, grams, pounds, and kilograms (up to 10 kilograms, about 22 pounds).

Scissors An all-purpose kitchen tool that can cut wax paper, foil, string, herbs, artichoke leaves, and even dough. Choose one of good quality that is rustproof.

Sieves and Strainers I use stainless-steel mesh sieves, fine and medium, for straining soups, sauces, sieved pureed fruits, and sorbets. For draining pasta and vegetables I use a perforated metal strainer—a colander.

Skillets I like the enameled cast-iron skillets, the heavy-gauge stainless-steel, and the nonstick ones.

Skimmers and Slotted Spoons A wire mesh skimmer is essential for removing batter-coated foods from hot oil. It can be bought with Chinese cookware. Have a large perforated spoon to lift foods from the liquid.

Soufflé Dish The straight-sided rounded baking dish made of porcelain or glass is designed for soufflés, because it encourages the batter to rise straight up to its maximum height. The same dish can be used for chilled or frozen desserts as well. I very often serve sorbets in glass soufflé dishes to show its beautiful color. Soufflé dishes come in various sizes.

Spatulas Buy the best ones you can afford, made of stainless steel, with wooden handles, 3 to 4 inches wide and about 14 to 16 inches long. They are indispensable for lifting caviar and spinach rolls, for turning fish, and for lifting cakes to serving platters. You should also have many sizes of rubber spatulas on hand for folding, mixing, and scraping.

Steaming Baskets There are several good vegetable steamers on the market, but easier and less expensive are separate expanding stainless-steel baskets that can be put into any saucepan or a wok. They come in two sizes and can be found in hardware stores. I use mine to steam all vegetables.

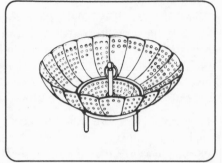

Stockpot I use a large (16 quart) heavy aluminum pot to cook pasta, blanch spinach, and so on.

Storage Jars I use glass jars with glass tops, fitted with a rubber jar ring. They come in many sizes and seal airtight. It is easy to see what is in them, they stack for storage, and they are excellent for freezing soups, stock, and sauces.

Thermometers For testing meat it is useful to have a tiny instant thermometer called Gourmet (it is made by Taylor). It has a very thin point and looks like a body thermometer.

Taylor also makes an oven thermometer, in which the mercury rises in a glass tube as the heat increases. For preheating, place the thermometer in the center of the oven for easier reading, then heat your oven for about 10 minutes before baking.

For testing water temperature to dissolve yeast, I use the same Taylor thermometer that I test fats and sugar syrup with.

Tongs Have cooking tongs in various sizes to pick up foods.

Trivets A well-stocked kitchen should have various trivets on which to rest hot dishes.

Wax Paper Useful in many ways in the kitchen. I use it to roll out dough and to wrap it for chilling, to roll roulades, to pound meat, and to store foods.

Whisks Whisks come in many sizes and qualities. Choose heavy, stainless-steel wire whisks, the best you can afford, and buy at least two sizes. They will not rust or bend.

Wok I like a wok with one wooden handle, instead of two metal ones. The wooden handle is easier to grasp and does not get hot. For gas stoves the wok comes with a metal ring to make it stand firmly. For electric stoves you cannot use the ring, but look for a wok that has a slightly flatter bottom. Buy a cover and a stir-frying spoon along with it. A wok is one of my favorite pots. I use it for stir frying as well as for steaming. It is easy to keep clean; just wash it with soap and water, not detergents or scouring pads. It heats

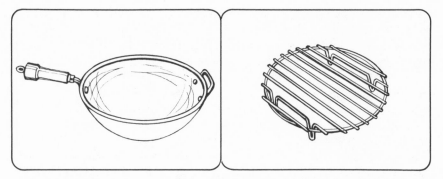

up very quickly, since it is made of rolled tempered steel. Buy a metal rack that fits in it, so that you can rest a heatproof dish on it for steaming.

SEASONING THE WOK   A seasoned wok will keep food from sticking. So, before using it for the first time, wash it thoroughly with soap and dry it well. Then pour a little oil into it and, with a paper towel, keep on rubbing the wok until the paper is clean. After much use, you can oil the wok again.

Wooden Spoons and Spatulas   Their uses are many: for stirring, especially in enameled lined saucepans, since they do not scratch; for mixing ingredients; for rubbing them through a sieve; and for creaming. Whether you use a spatula or a spoon is a matter of personal preference. You can keep them in a decorative container near your stove.

HELPFUL HINTS

· The temperature indicator of your oven may get out of order without your being aware of it. For roasting meats this may not be critical, but for making delicate desserts it is. I therefore always keep an oven thermometer inside the oven to be sure.

· To rescue a dish that has too much salt, add a small peeled raw potato.

· Do not chop dill or chives; rather snip them with a scissors.

· Wash strawberries first, then remove the stems. If you do it in reverse order, the berries will become soggy.

· Green vegetables that are to be dressed or sauced with lemon juice or vinegar should have the acid added just before serving. If you add the acid too far in advance, it will discolor the vegetable.

· To simplify slicing freshly baked bread, first heat the knife under very hot water.

· When scalding milk, first rinse the saucepan with cold water; this will prevent scorching the milk.

· To get more juice out of a lemon, roll it over a hard surface first, pressing down with the palm of your hand until the lemon feels soft; or run hot water over the fruit.

· If tomatoes or other fruits are not sufficiently ripe, place them in a brown paper bag and leave them in a cool, dark place to ripen.

· Refrigerate onions; chilled onions do not irritate the eyes as much when you are cutting them.

· Brown sugar is moist when you buy it; it hardens as it dries after opening. Keep it in the plastic bag that it comes in and store it in the freezer. Take out quantities as needed.

· When sautéeing, use a little oil with either butter or margarine; the oil prevents burning, since it has a burning point twice as high as that of butter.

· When cooking with dried herbs, such as rosemary, thyme, or basil, you will obtain maximum flavor if you will rub them between your fingertips as you add them in.

· You can grate large amounts of Parmesan cheese at one time by using a food processor fitted with the steel blade.

· When using fresh spinach in a recipe, always remove stems and wilted leaves, then wash thoroughly to remove sand.

· Frying oil can be reused. Simply let cool, filter or strain it, then store it in the refrigerator until needed.

· When baking pies, tarts, and quiches, place the filled shell on a thin, flat baking sheet or foil oven liner to prevent any overflow from spilling onto the oven floor.

· Save old cotton pillowcases for straining stock.

· Feta cheese keeps fresh for several weeks, refrigerated in a covered container with some milk or water.

· When a recipe calls for greasing a mold with oil, I find it easier to spread the oil with paper towel.

· Leftover anchovy fillets in oil keep well refrigerated in a covered glass container.

Cocktail Food
& First Course

BROILED CHICKEN LIVERS

A delicious quickie.

6 COCKTAIL
SERVINGS

¾ pound chicken livers
2 tablespoons olive oil
2 tablespoons Dijon-type
   mustard

3 tablespoons unseasoned
   bread crumbs
Kosher salt
Black pepper, freshly ground

Preheat broiler. Cut chicken livers into approximately 1½-inch pieces. Remove any green spots, which are bitter, and any connecting tissues. Pat dry with paper towels.

Beat olive oil and mustard with a fork. Spread bread crumbs on a piece of wax paper.

Line the broiler pan with foil and brush lightly with oil.

Dip livers, one by one, into crumbs and place on foil. Using a brush, coat livers with mustard mixture and sprinkle lightly with salt and pepper. Broil as close to heat source as possible for about 3 minutes, until tops are brown, or to your taste.

Serve immediately with cocktail forks or toothpicks.

CHICKEN LIVERS IN SHERRY SAUCE

A favorite of mine for Friday-night suppers.

4 TO 6
SERVINGS

1 pound chicken livers
¾ package MBT Instant
   Vegetable Broth or ¼
   ounce kosher consommé
   cube
¾ cup boiling water
¼ cup vegetable oil
1 medium onion, chopped
   coarse

¾ cup kosher cream sherry
   (Madeira)
1½ tablespoons unbleached
   flour
Kosher salt
Black pepper, freshly ground
10 sprigs dill, snipped

I suggest you use an enameled cast-iron saucepan large enough to fit the livers in a single layer.

Preheat broiler. Line the broiler pan with foil. Cut livers in half and remove connecting tissue and any green spots, which are bitter.

Place livers on foil and broil as close to heat source as possible, on one side only, until tops are seared, about 3 minutes, or to your taste.

Dissolve vegetable granules or consommé cube in boiling water and set aside.

Heat oil in saucepan until hot. Sauté onions, over medium-high heat until brown. Add sherry (Madeira) and boil over high heat till liquid is reduced to half. Add broth and boil for a few minutes.

Spread flour on a sheet of wax paper. Dip livers, one by one, into flour, shake off excess, then place livers in cooking sauce.

Boil for a few minutes only. Season with salt and pepper. Serve on heated plates, garnished with dill.

◆You can make this dish earlier in the day, stopping at the point where you would place the flour-dipped livers in the sauce.

CHICKEN LIVER PÂTÉ

8 TO 10
SERVINGS
AS A SPREAD

6 TO 8
SERVINGS
AS A FIRST
COURSE

This smooth pâté of chicken livers is wonderful served with thinly sliced, toasted Potato Bread (page 252), toasted French bread, or as a first course garnished with endives. Serve it at room temperature.

1 pound chicken livers	2 tablespoons brandy
¼ cup vegetable oil	(Cognac), heated
1 large onion, chopped fine	½ teaspoon dried thyme
1 small tart apple (greening or	Kosher salt
Granny Smith), peeled,	Black pepper, freshly ground
cored, and chopped fine	

I suggest you use a food processor and an earthenware crock both to refrigerate the pâté in and to serve it from.

Preheat broiler. Line the broiler pan with foil. Cut livers in half, removing any green spots, which are bitter, and any connecting tissue.

Place livers on foil and broil as close to heat source as possible, on each side, until the tops are seared, about 3 minutes, or to your taste.

Heat oil in a skillet until hot. Add onion and sauté over low heat until soft and transparent. Add apple and sauté for a few minutes. Add livers, without any accumulated juices. Raise heat, pour brandy or Cognac over livers, and ignite. When flames have subsided, add thyme. Mix well and sauté for a few minutes.

At once puree until very smooth in a food processor fitted with the steel blade. Season with salt and pepper. Transfer to a crock or dish, let cool, and cover tightly with plastic wrap, foil, or a lid. Refrigerate. (If the pâté is exposed to air, it will change color.)

MARINATED CHICKEN WINGS

An inspiration for this dish came from a Chinese woman I happened to meet at a party. She told me of a wonderful chicken-wing delicacy that had reminded her of the lollipops she used to eat as a child. These easy-to-prepare chicken wings can be served either hot or at room temperature. Allow two lollipops per person.

3 TO 4 SERVINGS AS COCKTAIL FOOD

10 chicken wings

MARINADE:

1 tablespoon thin Chinese soy sauce	½ teaspoon kosher salt
1 tablespoon vegetable oil	¼ teaspoon sugar

COATING:

1 tablespoon thin Chinese soy sauce	1 tablespoon Hoisin sauce
1 tablespoon vegetable oil	1 tablespoon ketchup
	2 to 3 teaspoons sesame seeds

To make it easier to prepare the lollipops, place the chicken wings in freezer for about 30 minutes.

With a knife or cleaver, cut through connecting joint between upper and lower part of each wing (1). Remove wingtips and save for stock. Then, using a sharp, pointed knife, loosen skin, meat, and cartilage from end of wing bone (2). Cut off excess fat and skin with a scissors. Gently pull meat

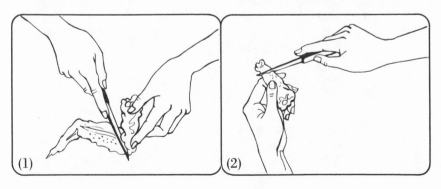

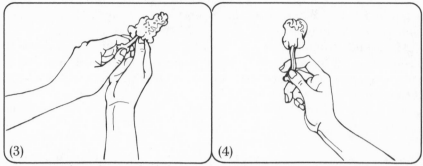

away over the other end of the wing, as if turning a glove inside out (3). You will have a smooth piece of bone with a ball of meat at the other end, skin inside, like a lollipop (4).

Combine marinade ingredients, pour over the wings, and refrigerate for several hours. Combine coating ingredients except for sesame seeds.

Preheat broiler. Line the broiler pan with foil. Place wings on foil and brush with half the coating.

Broil, not too close to heat source, for about 8 minutes. Sprinkle with 1 teaspoon sesame seeds and broil for another few minutes. Turn wings over with tongs, brush with remaining coating, and sprinkle with remaining seeds. Broil for another 10 minutes, or until brown on outside and soft inside.

MRS. KHAZZAM'S
MINIATURE CHICKEN TURNOVERS

ABOUT
6 DOZEN
TURNOVERS

I am indebted to Mrs. Khazzam for sharing this family recipe with me. Her turnovers are crispy, well seasoned, and ideal for large dinner parties, since they freeze very well.

FILLING:

1 approximately 3-pound chicken

½ teaspoon kosher salt

1 large onion

⅓ cup vegetable oil

1 cup canned chick-peas, drained

About 1¼ teaspoons ground cuminseed

¼ teaspoon cayenne pepper

Kosher salt

Black pepper, freshly ground

DOUGH:

⅝ cup warm water (100°F to 115°F)

½ package active dry yeast, about 1½ teaspoons

¼ teaspoon sugar

2¾ cups unbleached flour

1 teaspoon salt

½ cup corn oil

1½ cups peanut oil

I suggest you use the following: a wok with a cover, a metal rack that fits into it, a heatproof dish that fits into the wok, a food processor, an electric mixer with a dough hook, a 3-inch round cookie cutter, and a wire skimmer.

To steam the chicken: Place a metal rack in a wok, add 1 quart water, and bring to a boil over high heat. Place chicken in a heatproof dish and sprinkle with the ½ teaspoon salt. Place on rack in wok, cover, and steam chicken over medium-high heat for 40 minutes. (You may have to add some boiling water to wok.)

Remove dish from wok, pour off accumulated liquid (you will have about 1 cup of strong chicken stock), and let chicken cool.

Skin the chicken, then separate the meat from the bones. Cut meat into pea-size pieces and set aside.

To make the filling: Peel and quarter onion and chop fine in a food processor fitted with the steel blade. Heat vegetable oil in a skillet until hot and sauté onion over medium heat until light brown. Mash chick-peas in food processor until smooth. Add to onion along with chicken. Mix well and season generously.

To make the dough: Pour ½ cup of the warm water into bowl of an electric mixer. Add yeast and sugar, stir lightly, cover with a towel, and leave in a draft-free place for about 10 minutes, or until liquid is foamy.

Add flour, salt, and oil to yeast mixture. Knead with the dough hook at medium speed, gradually adding the remaining ⅓ cup warm water to make a stiff dough. Knead for about 10 minutes, or until dough is smooth, elastic, and not sticking to the bowl.

Cover bowl with a damp towel and leave in a warm, draft-free place (80° to 100°F), such as a food warmer or lightly heated, then cooled-down oven, until double in bulk, about 1 hour.

Punch dough down and cut into six pieces. Roll out one piece at a time, keeping the rest covered, into a very thin, 9-inch circle. With the cookie cutter, cut out circles. Place 1 teaspoon filling in the center of each circle. Fold over into a half-moon shape, pinch edges tightly, then fold slightly. (The dough is elastic and will stretch as you seal the turnovers. Do this carefully, or turnovers may open when they are fried.)

Place finished turnovers on a cookie sheet, with wax paper between layers. Make additional turnovers from leftover scraps of dough.

To deep fry turnovers: Preheat oven to 350°F. Heat wok over high heat. When hot, add peanut oil, and continue to heat until oil reaches 350°F on a frying thermometer. (To test if oil is hot enough without a thermometer, drop a piece of dough into hot oil: If it sizzles, oil is ready; if it burns, oil is too hot.) Deep fry five to six turnovers at a time, turning them with chopsticks until golden, about 2 minutes. Remove with a skimmer to a cookie sheet lined with several layers of paper towels, changing them frequently as needed. Keep warm on a rack set over a cookie sheet in the preheated oven as you continue frying the rest. Serve hot.

NOTE: If you do not have time to deep fry the turnovers after you have filled them, keep them in the refrigerator on the cookie sheet, covered with a towel.

◆If you like, you can steam the chicken the day before and refrigerate it; it is easier to skin when cold. You can also make the filling a day in advance.

To freeze the finished turnovers, wrap them in foil and place in a plastic bag. When needed, place unthawed turnovers on a rack on top of a cookie sheet. Bake in a preheated 450°F oven for about 10 to 15 minutes, or until very hot and crispy.

MEAT BOEREG

ABOUT
7 DOZEN
TRIANGLES

A Middle Eastern specialty made from paper-thin phyllo dough and filled with a well-seasoned meat filling. This crispy finger food freezes well and is marvelous to have on hand for parties.

FILLING:

5 tablespoons vegetable oil	Kosher salt
½ pound lean chuck, ground,	Black pepper, freshly ground
¾ pound lean veal, ground,	Scant ½ teaspoon ground
and then ground together	allspice
twice	¼ bunch Italian flat-leaf
1 large onion, chopped fine	parsley
3 cloves garlic, chopped fine	¼ bunch basil or 1
5 tablespoons pine nuts	tablespoon dried
8 tablespoons (1 stick)	1 pound fresh or frozen phyllo
unsalted margarine, melted	dough

I suggest you use the following: a wok, two damp dish towels, and a pastry brush.

To make the filling: Heat a wok, add 2 tablespoons oil, and heat until hot. Add ground meat and stir fry over high heat until it changes color and separates. Transfer to a bowl. Heat wok again, add 2 more tablespoons oil, heat oil, and stir fry onion and garlic over medium heat until onion is soft and transparent; add to meat. Heat wok again, add remaining 1 tablespoon oil, and stir fry pine nuts over medium heat until golden. (Be careful, because pine nuts burn easily.) Return meat mixture to wok, season with salt, pepper, and allspice, mix thoroughly, and put back into bowl.

Remove parsley and basil stems. Wash leaves, spin dry, and chop fine. Combine with meat and season well. Let mixture cool.

To assemble the boereg: Preheat oven to 375°F. Clear a large work surface and have ready the melted margarine, pastry brush, a knife, damp dish towels, and a foil pan for freezing or refrigerating the boereg.

Remove phyllo sheets from plastic wrapper. Unfold onto one towel, and cover with the other. (Phyllo sheets are very fragile and dry out quickly, so they must be kept covered.) Spread one phyllo sheet on a sheet of wax paper. Brush surface lightly with melted margarine, using a pastry brush, and cover with another sheet (1).

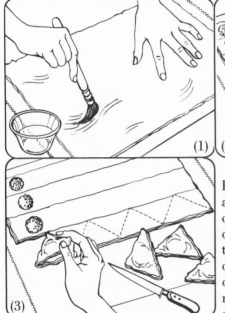

(1) (2)

(3)

Cut sheets into 2-inch strips. Place 1 level teaspoon filling, minus any accumulated liquid, at bottom center of each strip (2) and fold dough to the opposite side to form a triangle (3). Do not fold to the end of the strip, but cut off about 2 inches of the dough before end is reached. (This way they will be less doughy.) Arrange boereg, seam side down, on a foil pan or baking pan. Brush with melted margarine and bake for about 15 minutes, or until crisp and golden. Serve hot.

NOTE: Ask your butcher to do the grinding for you. First to grind both meats separately, then together. It makes the meat fluffier.

You may have some extra phyllo sheets, but I have allowed for that, since often some of them come damaged.

◆If you are not serving the boereg right away and would like to freeze them instead, layer them in the foil pan with wax paper, to prevent the triangles from sticking. Cover with plastic wrap, then foil, and place in a plastic bag. When ready to bake, remove from freezer without thawing. You may have to allow a few more minutes for baking. If you have very little space, freeze them on trays. Then, when they are frozen, wrap in foil and place in a plastic bag.

CURRIED WONTONS

ABOUT
70 WONTONS
A delicacy from Millie Chan's cooking classes. A crispy, well-seasoned finger food, easy to make and delightful to serve.

FILLING:

1 small potato	1½ to 2 teaspoons kosher salt
¼ cup peanut oil	1½ teaspoons sugar
½ pound lean veal, ground, and ½ pound lean chuck, ground, then ground together twice	1 medium onion, chopped fine
	1 tablespoon Madras curry powder
1½ to 2 tablespoons black Chinese soy sauce	

One 1-pound package thin wonton wrappers	2 cups peanut oil

I suggest you use the following: two damp dish towels, a wok, and a wire skimmer.

To make the filling: Wash potato, then, without peeling it, boil in water until done. Let cool, remove skin, and mash till smooth.

Heat wok over high heat and add 3 tablespoons of the oil. When oil is hot, add meat and stir fry over high heat, stirring all the time, until meat changes color and separates. Stir in soy sauce, salt, and sugar. Remove to a bowl.

Heat wok again and add remaining tablespoon oil. When oil is hot, add onion and stir fry over medium heat until soft. Add curry powder, meat, and potato, increase heat, and mix till thoroughly combined. Season generously and transfer to a bowl to cool before filling the wontons.

To fill the wontons: Have a bowl of cold water nearby. Unwrap skins, but keep them covered with a damp towel. Working with one wrapper at a time, place it at an angle on a sheet of wax paper. Put 1 teaspoon filling at the

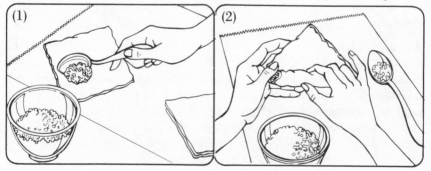

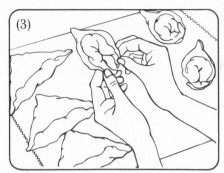

corner nearest you (1). Fold the corner over the filling and roll toward the center but not to the end (2). Leave ½ inch of the opposite corner unrolled. You will have a triangle. Lightly moisten the left-hand corner of the triangle with cold water and bring both ends together to overlap. Moisten and pinch tightly to seal (3).

Place wontons on a cookie sheet, with wax paper between the layers. Cover with a damp towel and refrigerate until ready to fry. If the towel dries in the refrigerator, moisten it.

To deep fry the wontons: Preheat oven to 350°F. Heat a wok over high heat. When hot, add the 2 cups oil and continue to heat until oil reaches 350°F on a frying thermometer. (To test if oil is hot enough without a frying thermometer, drop a piece of wonton wrapper into hot oil: If it sizzles, oil is ready; if it burns, oil is too hot.) Deep fry a few wontons at a time, turning them frequently with chopsticks so that they brown evenly. Fry till golden, about 3 minutes. Remove with a skimmer to a cookie sheet lined with several layers of paper towels, changing them frequently as needed. Keep warm on a rack set over a cookie sheet in the preheated oven as you continue frying the rest. Serve hot.

NOTE: Ask your butcher to grind each meat separately and then grind them together; it makes the meat fluffier.

Wonton wrappers come in approximately 1-pound packages and can be found in Oriental stores. Leftover skins, properly wrapped, freeze very well. Frozen wrappers should be defrosted in the refrigerator.

◆If you fry wontons early in the day, they can be reheated in a preheated 300°F oven.

If you wish to make wontons several days in advance, freeze them, uncooked, on trays. When frozen, transfer them to a plastic bag. Deep fry while still frozen, but allow a little extra time.

SPRING ROLLS (EGG ROLLS) WITH MUSTARD SAUCE

I learned how to make these Chinese delicacies in Millie Chan's class. They can be served as a first course or cut into minisizes and served for cocktails.

20
SPRING ROLLS

½ pound lean veal, boned and without fat or gristle, or
   ½ pound skinned and boned chicken breast

MARINADE:

1 tablespoon black Chinese
  soy sauce

½ teaspoon sugar
1 teaspoon cornstarch

FILLING:

5 Chinese dried mushrooms
Boiling water
½ cup canned bamboo shoots
1 pound Chinese celery
  cabbage

2 scallions, including green
  parts
¼ cup peanut oil
1 tablespoon dry white wine
About ½ teaspoon kosher salt

MUSTARD SAUCE:

¼ cup dried mustard
  (Coleman's brand)
Boiling water

1 tablespoon pale dry sherry
  or dry white wine

1 egg, lightly beaten
1 pound spring-roll (very
  thin nonegg) wrappers,
  about 20

Cornstarch

2 cups peanut oil

I suggest you use a wok and a wire skimmer.

Partially freeze meat or chicken and slice into thin julienne strips. (It is easier to handle when frozen.) Mix well with soy sauce, sugar, and cornstarch.

To make the filling: Place mushrooms in a bowl, cover with boiling water, and leave to soak for 30 minutes. Drain and squeeze dry with your hands. Cut off mushroom stems with scissors and discard. Cut caps into thin julienne strips. Do the same with the bamboo shoots. Separate cabbage leaves, rinse, and pat dry with paper towels. Pile a few cabbage leaves together and cut into julienne strips. Trim scallions, wipe with a damp paper towel, cut into 2-inch pieces, and cut those into julienne strips.

    Heat wok over high heat and add 2 tablespoons of the oil. When oil is hot, stir fry veal or chicken until meat changes color. Add mushrooms and wine and mix well. Transfer to a bowl. Heat wok again, add the remaining 2 tablespoons oil, and heat. Add bamboo shoots, cabbage, and scallions and stir fry over high heat until cabbage is almost wilted. Add meat mixture and season. Transfer to a bowl and let cool.

To make the sauce: Place mustard in a bowl, gradually pour in boiling water, and whisk until smooth (mixture should resemble a thick pancake batter). Stir in sherry or wine; sauce will thicken as it stands.

To assemble the spring rolls: Have beaten egg, pastry brush, and cornstarch ready. Separate spring-roll wrappers and keep covered with a damp towel.

If wrappers cannot be separated easily due to long storage, cover them with a warm, damp towel for a few minutes, then pull apart.

Working with one wrapper at a time, lay it on a flat surface with one corner pointing toward you. Dust very lightly with cornstarch. Spoon ½ tablespoon of the drained filling onto lower corner of wrapper. Roll firmly halfway up the wrapper, making an elongated cylinder. Brush beaten egg over remaining edges. Fold over the left corner and press to seal, then the right corner, making an envelope. Roll tightly to the end and press to seal. Place on a baking sheet with a towel between the layers and keep covered with another towel until ready to deep fry.

To deep fry the spring rolls: Preheat oven to 350°F. Heat a wok over high heat. When hot, add the 2 cups oil and continue to heat until oil reaches 350°F on a frying thermometer. (To test if oil is hot enough without a frying thermometer, drop in a piece of any vegetable: If it sizzles, oil is ready; if it burns, oil is too hot.) Deep fry several spring rolls at a time, turning with chopsticks for even frying until crisp and golden, about 3 minutes. Remove with a skimmer to a cookie sheet lined with several layers of paper towels, changing them frequently as needed. Keep warm in the preheated oven on a rack set over a cookie sheet as you continue frying the rest. Serve hot, with mustard sauce on the side.

NOTE: All ingredients can be found in Oriental specialty stores.

Spring-roll wrappers are not to be confused with egg rolls, which more closely resemble a noodle dough.

To make minisize spring rolls, cut each wrapper into four squares and follow the same procedure.

◆If you want to deep fry spring rolls in advance, you may do so, but they will be a bit soggy. Reheat them in a preheated 450°F oven for about 10 minutes on a rack set over a cookie sheet and turn from time to time until hot and crisp.

The sauce can be made in advance and refrigerated. You may also freeze unfried spring rolls. Deep fry without thawing.

Dairy

BROILED STUFFED MUSHROOM CAPS

6 to 8
COCKTAIL
SERVINGS

4
FIRST-COURSE
SERVINGS

Find firm fresh mushrooms, fill the caps with a well-seasoned mixture, and broil them briefly.

2 scallions, including green
   parts
3½ tablespoons sweet butter
20 small-to-medium firm fresh
   mushrooms (uniform size is
   important)
6 sprigs Italian flat-leaf
   parsley

½ cup freshly grated
   Parmesan cheese
About ½ teaspoon fresh
   lemon juice
Kosher salt
Black pepper, freshly ground

I suggest you use a food processor and an enameled cast-iron skillet.

Preheat broiler. Trim scallions, wipe with a damp paper towel, quarter, and chop fine in a food processor fitted with the steel blade. Heat 1 tablespoon of the butter in a skillet until hot, add scallions, and sauté over low heat until soft.

Wipe mushrooms with a damp paper towel. Remove caps and set aside. Chop stems fine in the food processor.

Add remaining butter to skillet and sauté chopped mushrooms over high heat until they are just coated with butter. Remove from heat.

Remove stems from parsley; wash leaves, spin dry, and chop fine. Add parsley and Parmesan cheese (leaving a bit for garnish) to the mushrooms, and season generously with lemon juice, salt, and pepper.

Line the broiler pan with foil. Fill caps with mushroom mixture, sprinkle lightly with cheese, and place on foil.

Broil mushrooms as close to heat source as possible for about 3 to 5 minutes, or until filling is very hot while caps remain raw.

Serve immediately.

EGGPLANT PARMESAN

A nonoily, light version of a popular dish, for which the eggplant slices are not fried, but broiled, and the entire dish can be assembled in the morning and refrigerated, then heated.

6
FIRST-COURSE
SERVINGS

4
MAIN-COURSE
SERVINGS

2 medium eggplants, about 1
  pound each
3 tablespoons kosher salt
½ bunch basil
½ bunch Italian flat-leaf
  parsley
½ to ⅓ cup olive oil

2 cups Fresh Tomato Sauce,
  very thick and well
  seasoned (page 263)
About ¾ cup coarsely grated
  Parmesan cheese
¾ pound mozzarella, sliced
  thin

I suggest you use a 9-by-14-by-2-inch ovenproof dish.

Peel eggplants and slice into ¼- to ½-inch-thick rounds. Soak for 1 hour in a large bowl of ice water and salt. Drain, then squeeze gently in a dish towel to dry.

Remove basil and parsley stems; wash leaves, spin dry, and chop medium fine.

Preheat broiler. Line the broiler pan with foil. Place eggplant slices on foil and, using a pastry brush, brush lightly with oil. Broil in batches close to the heat source on one side only for about 3 minutes, or until light brown. (Eggplant slices are crisper if broiled on one side only.)

Preheat oven to 350°F. Thinly coat a baking dish with tomato sauce. Arrange eggplant rounds on sauce, sprinkling generously with basil, parsley, and Parmesan cheese. Repeat layers, using up all the tomato sauce, eggplant, basil, parsley, and Parmesan. Top with mozzarella.

Bake, uncovered, in upper third of oven for about 20 to 30 minutes, or until bubbling hot. Broil for a minute in order to brown the top.

TAMARA'S SPINACH GNOCCHI

Making gnocchi seemed a tricky undertaking until a dear friend shared with me her heirloom recipe. It is a wonderful dish, which can also be prepared in the morning and reheated.

4 TO 5
FIRST-COURSE
SERVINGS

APPROXI-
MATELY
50 GNOCCHI

2 pounds fresh spinach

15 ounces whole-milk ricotta cheese

2 eggs plus 1 egg yolk

½ cup freshly grated Parmesan cheese

¾ cup unbleached flour

¼ teaspoon freshly grated nutmeg

About 2 teaspoons kosher salt

Black pepper, freshly ground

SAUCE:

3 cups heavy cream

1 to 2 tablespoons sweet butter, at room temperature

Kosher salt

Black pepper, freshly ground

⅓ cup freshly grated Parmesan cheese

I suggest you use the following: a small enameled cast-iron saucepan, a large pot, and a 9-by-14-by-2-inch ovenproof dish to fit the gnocchi in a single layer.

To make the gnocchi: Discard spinach stems and wilted leaves and wash spinach thoroughly to remove sand. Drop into a large pot of boiling water and let water return to the boil. Drain spinach and refresh with cold water. Take small batches of spinach in your hands and squeeze out as much liquid as possible. Wring out, in batches, in a dish towel to dry very well.

Chop spinach fine and place in a bowl. Stir in ricotta, eggs, egg yolk, the ½ cup Parmesan cheese, and ¼ cup of the flour. Season with nutmeg, salt, and pepper.

Spread the remaining ¼ cup flour thinly on a large sheet of wax paper. Take a heaping teaspoonful of spinach mixture and drop it onto the flour. Roll mixture lightly in flour, forming little croquettes the size of a cork. Remove to a plate as you roll the remainder. (Do not be alarmed if the

croquettes seem very soft; the eggs and flour will hold them together as soon as they are put into the gently boiling water.)

Bring a large pot of salted water to a boil. (Gnocchi need space in which to cook, or do it in batches.) Carefully drop gnocchi, a few at a time, into the gently boiling water and cook only until they rise to the top, about 3 minutes. Remove to a colander with a perforated spoon and proceed with the next batch.

To make the sauce: Boil heavy cream uncovered over medium heat in a small saucepan for about 15 minutes, stirring from time to time to make a thin sauce. Whisk in the butter, and season to taste.

To assemble the gnocchi: Preheat oven to 375°F. Coat an ovenproof dish with the sauce. Place drained gnocchi on top and sprinkle with Parmesan cheese. Cover with foil and heat in oven until bubbling hot, about 10 minutes.

NOTE: Another way of forming the gnocchi is to take a heaping teaspoonful of the mixture in your wet hands and roll it into a croquette.

◆Spinach can be blanched, drained, squeezed dry, and refrigerated a day in advance.
 If you are assembling the gnocchi earlier in the day, refrigerate them, covered with foil, and allow a little more time for heating through.

SPINACH BALLS

These dainty deep-fried miniature spinach balls are easy to serve at large parties.

30 TO 35
MINIBALLS

2 pounds fresh spinach
2 thin slices white bread,
  crusts removed
¼ cup milk
2 tablespoons unseasoned
  bread crumbs
2 eggs plus 2 egg yolks

About ½ cup freshly grated
  Parmesan cheese
⅛ teaspoon freshly grated
  nutmeg
Kosher salt
Black pepper, freshly ground

2 to 3 cups peanut oil

*I suggest you use the following: a food processor, a deep pot, and
a wire skimmer.*

Discard spinach stems and wilted leaves and wash spinach thoroughly to remove sand. Drop into a large pot of boiling water and let water return to the boil. Drain spinach at once and refresh with cold water.
 Soak bread in milk until soft, then squeeze in hands to extract liquid. Take small batches of spinach in your hands and squeeze out as much liquid as possible. Wring out, in batches, in a dish towel to dry very well. Place

spinach, bread, bread crumbs, eggs, and egg yolks into a food processor fitted with the steel blade. Process until semicoarse. Transfer to a bowl. Mix in cheese and nutmeg and season to taste. (The mixture should be a little spicy.)

Shape scant tablespoonfuls of mixture in your hands into little round balls. Place in a single layer on a cookie sheet, cover with plastic wrap, and refrigerate until ready to deep fry.

To deep fry: Heat oil in a pot until it reaches 350°F on a frying thermometer. (To test if oil is hot enough without a frying thermometer, drop in a small amount of mixture: If it sizzles, oil is ready to use; if it burns, oil is too hot.) Deep fry six spinach balls at a time until lightly brown, about 3 to 4 minutes. Remove with a skimmer to a cookie sheet lined with several layers of paper towels, changing them frequently as needed. Serve at once.

◆Spinach can be blanched, drained, squeezed dry, and refrigerated a day ahead of time. Spinach balls can be refrigerated for several hours, but they should be deep fried just before serving. Unfortunately, this oil cannot be reused, because it turns green from the spinach.

SALMON PÂTÉ

12 COCKTAIL SERVINGS Serve this well-seasoned spread on very thin slices of black bread.

1¼ to 1½ pounds fresh salmon, with skin and bone	Black pepper, freshly ground
	¼ cup dry white wine
Kosher salt	1 sprig Italian flat-leaf parsley
4 tablespoons (½ stick) sweet butter, at room temperature	About 2 tablespoons fresh lemon juice, strained
1½ tablespoons cream cheese, at room temperature	1 teaspoon Dijon-type mustard
2 ounces smoked salmon, in small pieces	White pepper, freshly ground
1 small onion, grated fine	4 sprigs dill, snipped

I suggest you use the following: a wok with a cover, a metal rack that fits into it, a heatproof dish that fits into the wok, and a food processor.

To steam the salmon: Place salmon on a heatproof dish that fits into a wok. Sprinkle lightly with salt and pepper. Add wine and parsley.

Place a metal rack in a wok, add 1 quart water, and bring to a boil over high heat. Set dish on rack, cover wok, and steam salmon over high heat for about 10 minutes on each side; it should be well cooked. Remove dish and let cool.

To make the pâté: Skin, bone, and flake fish. Blend butter and cream cheese in a food processor fitted with the steel blade. Add both the steamed and the smoked salmon, onion, and half the lemon juice. Process until very smooth. Transfer mixture to a bowl and season with the remaining lemon juice, the mustard, salt, white pepper, and dill. (Pâté should be well seasoned.)

◆If you like, you can steam the salmon a day in advance and refrigerate on the plate. You can make the entire pâté a day ahead of time and refrigerate it, but serve it at room temperature.

COLD TROUT MOUSSE WITH CUCUMBERS
—>>>

I like the smoky flavor in fish, poultry, meat, or cheese. After eating smoked trout one day, I thought of combining it with freshly poached trout and discovered this delightful cocktail, first-course, or luncheon dish.

8 TO 10
FIRST-COURSE
SERVINGS

8
LUNCHEON-
COURSE
SERVINGS

Make it a day before to chill, but serve it at room temperature.

1 smoked trout, about ½ pound
2 fresh trout, about 1½ pounds altogether

Kosher salt
White pepper, freshly ground
Juice of ½ lemon
¼ cup dry white wine

¼ cup water
1 tablespoon unflavored kosher gelatin
4 scallions, including green parts, chopped fine
1 small onion, grated fine
1 teaspoon dried mustard (Coleman's brand)

2 tablespoons plain yogurt or sour cream
Dash Tabasco
10 sprigs dill, snipped
¾ cup heavy cream, chilled
About 2 teaspoons fresh lemon juice

Vegetable oil
CUCUMBERS:
8 medium Kirby or regular cucumbers
½ cup plain yogurt or sour cream

10 sprigs dill, snipped
Kosher salt
White pepper, freshly ground

I suggest you use the following: a wok with a cover, a metal rack that fits into it, a heatproof dish that fits into the wok, a food processor, and a 5- to 6-cup fish mold.

Skin and bone smoked trout. Cut into small bits and set aside.

To steam the fresh trout: Have the fish man dress trout without removing skin and inside bone. Rinse fish and pat dry with paper towels. Place on a heatproof dish. Season with salt and pepper and sprinkle with lemon juice and wine. Place a metal rack in a wok, add 1 quart water, and bring to a boil over high heat. Set dish on rack, cover wok, and steam fish over high heat for about 5 minutes on each side. Drain and save the liquid in dish. Skin and bone the fish and place in a food processor fitted with the steel blade.

To make the mousse: Combine water and gelatin in a small saucepan and heat slowly, stirring until dissolved. Add reserved fish stock. Pour into food processor and blend with the fish until mixture is very smooth.

Transfer fish puree to a bowl. Add scallions, onion, mustard, yogurt or sour cream, Tabasco, dill, and bits of smoked trout. Whip cream in a well-chilled metal bowl until stiff. Fold into fish puree, using a rubber spatula.

Oil fish mold lightly with vegetable oil, using a paper towel. Spoon in the fish mousse and smooth over the top. Cover tightly with plastic wrap and refrigerate overnight.

To make the cucumbers: Peel cucumbers with a vegetable peeler, trim ends (which may be bitter), and cut in half lengthwise. Scrape out cucumber seeds with a teaspoon.

Slice cucumbers thin in a food processor fitted with the slicing attachment. Place in a sieve, sprinkle lightly with salt, and let drain for 30 minutes.

Pat cucumbers dry with paper towels and combine with the ½ cup yogurt or sour cream. Stir in dill, salt, and pepper and refrigerate. (Do not prepare the cucumbers a day in advance, because they may lose some of their crispness.)

To unmold: Loosen sides of mold with a knife. Dip mold for a minute into hot water. Dry bottom of mold and invert onto a glass or china platter. Tap all along the top and lift the mold gently. If it doesn't work, try a second time.

Just before serving, decorate platter with extra dill sprigs and the drained cucumbers. (If liquid from cucumbers accumulates, pat dry with paper towels.)

PIKE MOUSSE WITH BEURRE BLANC SAUCE

⤜⟫⟫

One of my favorites, which I learned and adapted in Lydie Marshall's cooking class. This silky, airy fish mousse is shaped into a log, wrapped in cheesecloth, and poached in a well-seasoned fish stock. If you own a Kitchen Aid with a colander-sieve attachment (page xxvi), it is very easy to make. The loaf and the sauce can be made earlier in the day or even a day ahead of time.

12 SERVINGS AS COCKTAIL FOOD OR FIRST COURSE FOR BUFFET, CAN SERVE MORE

MOUSSE:

3 pounds pike, filleted to yield
1¼ to 1½ pounds fish
2 egg whites, lightly beaten
2 cups heavy cream, chilled
1 tablespoon brandy (Cognac)

About 1 tablespoon kosher
salt
White pepper, freshly ground
3 cups well-seasoned Fish
Stock (page 258)

SAUCE:

6 medium shallots, minced
very fine
¼ cup tarragon wine vinegar
¼ cup dry white wine
¾ cup fish stock (you may
use stock in which loaf was
poached)

1 cup heavy cream
4 tablespoons (½ stick) sweet
butter, at room temperature
Kosher salt
White pepper, freshly ground

I suggest you use the following: a food processor, an electric mixer with a colander-sieve attachment and a flat spatula, a 16-inch piece of cotton cheesecloth, an approximately 9-by-14-by-2-inch enameled cast-iron oval pan, and an enameled cast-iron saucepan.

To make the mousse and shape the loaf: Have the fish man bone and fillet the pike. (Reserve head and trimmings for stock.) Cube fillets and puree until smooth in a food processor fitted with the steel blade. To further lighten the puree and rid it of bone and gristle, pass it through the colander-sieve attachment of a Kitchen Aid and discard residue.

Attach the flat spatula to the mixer and dribble in beaten egg whites at lowest speed. Put mixer bowl with fish puree into freezer for 15 minutes.

Remove bowl from freezer and, using the same flat spatula, dribble in cream at lowest speed. Do it slowly to allow fish puree to absorb cream. Add brandy (Cognac) and season well.

Unfold cheesecloth and refold in three layers. Wet it and lay it flat. Placing fish mousse in center of cloth, shape it with a knife into a smooth 10-by-5-inch log. Fold cheesecloth to cover log and tie both ends tightly with a string.

To poach the loaf: Bring 3 cups stock to a boil in an oval pan. Lower loaf into stock, reduce heat, and baste top very well with stock.

Cover pan with heavy foil and simmer for 20 minutes, basting frequently. Slide a wide spatula under loaf to see that it is not sticking. When ready, drain loaf on a rack set over a baking pan for a few minutes. Unwrap and flip loaf onto a heated platter. Cover with foil and keep warm in a food warmer or over hot water while you make the sauce.

To make the sauce: In a saucepan, boil shallots, vinegar, and wine until almost dry. Add fish stock and heavy cream. Boil slowly, uncovered, until sauce is thick enough to coat a spoon heavily. Strain sauce through a mesh sieve, pressing hard on solids to extract all flavor. Discard residue. Return sauce to saucepan, heat, and whisk in butter, 1 tablespoonful at a time, until smooth. Season and keep warm.

Coat loaf lightly with sauce and decorate platter before serving. (Shredded endives are nice, for example, because they keep everything in a pale tone.) Pour the rest of the sauce into a sauceboat.

NOTE: If you do not have a colander-sieve attachment, strain puree in batches through a fine-mesh sieve, pushing on the solids with a wooden spoon.

Leftover fish stock can be frozen in a tightly covered glass container.

◆If you poach the loaf a day ahead of time or earlier in the day, cover with foil and refrigerate. Also cover and refrigerate the sauce. Before serving, heat loaf lightly in a low oven, a food warmer, or over hot water. Sauce can be boiled gently.

TUNA LOAF
⫷⫷⫷

6 ᴛᴏ 8
SERVINGS
AS A FIRST
COURSE

6 SERVINGS
AS A
LUNCHEON
COURSE

I find dishes such as Tuna Loaf very useful for summer luncheon entertaining. Decorate this smooth, well-seasoned pâté with olives, tomatoes, cucumbers, and watercress, and serve it with thin buttered toast.

Serve it at room temperature.

2 slices white bread, crusts removed
3 tablespoons milk
3 anchovy fillets
14 ounces Italian light tuna (Genova or Pastene brand), drained
2 eggs
1 tablespoon capers

6 sprigs Italian flat-leaf parsley
About ¼ cup freshly grated Parmesan cheese
Juice of about ¾ lemon, strained
Kosher salt
Black pepper, freshly ground

1 small onion, peeled and
   sliced

1 clove garlic, sliced
¾ cup dry white wine

I suggest you use the following: a food processor, an 18-inch piece of cotton cheesecloth, and a 2-quart pan about 11 inches long to fit the loaf.

Sprinkle bread with milk, then squeeze dry with hands. Rinse anchovy fillets and pat dry with paper towels. Place bread, anchovies, tuna, and eggs in a food processor fitted with the steel blade and puree until smooth. Transfer mixture to a bowl.

Rinse capers, pat dry with paper towels, and chop fine. Remove parsley stems; wash, spin dry, and chop leaves fine. Mix capers, parsley, and cheese with tuna mixture. Season with lemon juice, salt, and pepper.

Unfold cheesecloth and refold in two layers. Wet it, and lay it flat. Placing tuna in center of cloth, shape it with a knife into a log. Fold cheesecloth to cover log and tie both ends tightly with a string.

Place onion, garlic, wine, and the loaf in a pan, adding enough water to cover loaf by ¼ inch. Bring to a boil over high heat. Reduce heat and simmer, covered, for 30 minutes. Uncover and let cool.

Lift loaf and place on a sheet of heavy foil. Unwrap and let cool for a short time (the loaf will darken if exposed to air too long). Wrap in foil and refrigerate.

To serve, cut into ½-inch slices and decorate.

NOTE: If Italian tuna is unavailable, use American tuna.

MUSHROOM CREPES

For years I was afraid to make crepes, which I was sure were difficult to produce. When I finally tried, it proved to be easy.

Crepes can be made several days in advance and refrigerated, or they can be made whenever you have time, and frozen.

I allow about 2 crepes per person for a first course. For luncheon, make them larger.

2 DOZEN
5-INCH
CREPES

4 TO 6
SERVINGS
FOR
LUNCHEON

CREPE BATTER:

½ cup cold water
½ cup milk
⅛ teaspoon salt
2 eggs

2 tablespoons clarified sweet
   butter, cooled (page xvi)
1 cup sifted unbleached flour

½ tablespoon sweet butter

½ tablespoon vegetable oil

FILLING:

6 medium shallots

4 tablespoons (½ stick) sweet butter

1 pound to 18 ounces firm fresh mushrooms

¼ cup kosher cream sherry (Madeira)

1 tablespoon unbleached flour

¼ cup heavy cream

⅓ cup freshly grated Parmesan cheese

Kosher salt

Black pepper, freshly ground

8 sprigs dill, snipped

SAUCE:

2 cups half and half

¾ cup heavy cream

2 tablespoons sweet butter

About 1 tablespoon fresh lemon juice

Kosher salt

Black pepper, freshly ground

1 tablespoon sweet butter, melted

⅓ cup freshly grated Parmesan cheese

I suggest you use the following: a blender, a 5-inch crepe pan or pans (or a heavy nonstick pan of the same size), an enameled cast-iron skillet, a small enameled cast-iron saucepan, and two 9-by-14-by-2-inch ovenproof dishes.

To make the crepe batter: Place water, milk, salt, eggs, and clarified butter in a blender. Process at high speed until thoroughly combined. Sift flour directly into measuring cup, add to blender, and process again. With a rubber spatula, scrape sides of blender and combine until batter is very smooth. Transfer to a measuring cup, since it is easier to pour from.

Cover and refrigerate for several hours or overnight to allow the gluten in the flour to relax and make a light pancake.

To make the crepes: Bring batter to room temperature and mix well.

Melt butter and oil. Heat pan or pans and lightly brush on butter mixture with a pastry brush. To test if pan is hot enough, sprinkle it with a few drops of batter: they should cling to the pan, not draw into a ball. Lift crepe pan and pour in about 2 table-spoonfuls of batter, just enough to coat the bottom of the pan when you swirl it around. Immediately tilt the pan over the measuring cup to pour off any excess batter, no matter how small. Cook till set and flip over into 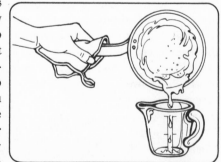 the same pan. If you wish to save time, flip crepe into another heated, lightly buttered pan. You can easily work with two pans at the same time. Do not worry if crepes are not perfectly round, because they will be rolled. Do not butter pans each time. Stack crepes on a plate as they are finished.

To make the filling: Peel, quarter, and chop shallots fine in a food processor fitted with the steel blade. Heat 2 tablespoons of the butter in a skillet until hot. Add shallots and sauté over low heat until soft and transparent. Wipe mushrooms with a damp paper towel. Quarter them and chop coarsely, in batches, in the food processor. Remove each batch before processing the next. Add the remaining 2 tablespoons butter to the skillet and add all the chopped mushrooms. Sauté over low heat, stirring constantly with a wooden spoon, until mushrooms are coated with butter. Stir in sherry (Madeira) and cook until dry. Off the heat, stir in flour. Return to heat and stir in cream. Cook until liquid is absorbed. Remove from heat and add cheese, salt, pepper, and dill.

To make the sauce: Bring half and half and heavy cream to a boil in a small saucepan. Boil, uncovered, until liquid is reduced to about half and has the consistency of a thin sauce. Stir in butter and season with lemon juice, salt, and pepper.

To assemble the crepes: Preheat oven to 375°F. Butter an ovenproof dish or dishes with the melted butter. Lay crepes, darker side up, on a sheet of wax paper. Place 1 tablespoon filling at the lower third of the crepe and roll loosely to the end. Place in pan, seam side down and not too close to one another. Pour sauce across center of crepes only, leaving ends dry. Sprinkle with Parmesan cheese. Cover with foil and heat in oven for 10 minutes. Uncover and bake for another 10 minutes, or until bubbles appear and crepes are very hot. Slide under the broiler, not too close to the heat source, to brown lightly.

NOTE: In order to save time, I prefer to use two pans at the same time. I heat and butter both pans, cook the crepe in the first pan, and flip it over to the second.

◆ If you wish to make crepes a day before, refrigerate them with wax paper between the layers to prevent them from sticking to each other. For freezing, wrap them in foil and place in a plastic bag. Do not thaw, but defrost them in a preheated 200°F oven for about 30 minutes, or until they separate easily. The entire dish can be assembled a day ahead of time, covered with foil, and reheated. You may have to allow a little extra time for heating it through.

RICOTTA CHEESE CREPES

〈〈〈

2 DOZEN
5-INCH
CREPES

Another filling for the master crepe recipe on page 23.

FILLING:

3 ounces cream cheese
8 ounces farmer cheese
15 ounces whole-milk ricotta
cheese
1 scallion, including green
part
¼ bunch Italian flat-leaf
parsley

1 teaspoon Dijon-type
mustard
1 clove garlic, minced fine
¾ cup freshly grated
Parmesan cheese
Kosher salt
White pepper, freshly ground

SAUCE:

1 cup heavy cream
1 cup Fresh Tomato Sauce
(page 263)

Kosher salt
Black pepper, freshly ground

1 tablespoon sweet butter,
melted

⅓ cup freshly grated
Parmesan cheese

I suggest you use a food processor and an enameled cast-iron saucepan.

To make the filling: Place cream cheese, farmer cheese, and ricotta in a food processor fitted with the steel blade and combine for a second. Stop processing before it becomes smooth and transfer to a bowl. Trim scallion, wipe with a damp paper towel, and chop fine. Add to cheese. Remove parsley stems; wash leaves, spin dry, and chop fine. Add to mixture along with mustard, garlic, and Parmesan cheese. Blend thoroughly and season with salt and pepper.

To make the sauce: Boil cream, uncovered, in a saucepan until reduced by about half. Strain tomato sauce through a mesh sieve, pushing on the solids with a wooden spoon. Discard solids and add strained sauce to cream. Simmer for a few minutes and season.

To assemble and heat the crepes: Follow the master recipe.

◆This dish can be assembled a day ahead of time, refrigerated, and reheated.

CAVIAR ROULADE

->>>

This festive flat soufflé is filled with sour cream and caviar and served with more caviar sauce on the side. It makes an elegant brunch or luncheon main dish. It can be made in advance and served at room temperature.

12 TO 14
COCKTAIL
SERVINGS

10 TO 12
FIRST-COURSE
SERVINGS

5 tablespoons sweet butter
9 tablespoons unbleached flour
2 cups milk

FILLING:
3 ounces cream cheese
¾ cup sour cream
10 sprigs Italian flat-leaf
 parsley
2 scallions, including green
 parts

SAUCE:
10 sprigs dill, snipped
1¼ cups sour cream
About ½ teaspoon fresh
 lemon juice
½ teaspoon dried mustard
 (Coleman's brand)

4 eggs, at room temperature,
 separated
½ teaspoon kosher salt

About 1 teaspoon fresh lemon
 juice
½ teaspoon dried mustard
 (Coleman's brand)
⅛ teaspoon cayenne pepper
4 ounces natural red salmon
 caviar

About ¼ teaspoon kosher salt
2 ounces natural red salmon
 caviar

I suggest you use an 11-by-16-inch jelly roll pan and an enameled cast-iron saucepan.

Melt 1 tablespoon of the butter and brush half evenly over bottom and sides of a jelly roll pan. Line with a 21-inch sheet of wax paper, which should extend several inches beyond short ends of pan. Brush paper with remaining melted butter and dust evenly with 1 tablespoon of the flour. Then, holding on to the paper, invert pan and tap to shake off excess.

Melt remaining 4 tablespoons butter in saucepan. Off the heat, mix in remaining 8 tablespoons flour until well combined. Vigorously whisk in milk until flour is dissolved. Return saucepan to heat and continue whisking until mixture is very thick, the consistency of very heavy pudding. Boil gently for a minute or two. Remove from heat and whisk in egg yolks, one at a time. Season with salt and let cool till lukewarm.

Preheat oven to 325°F. Beat egg whites at high speed until stiff. With a rubber spatula, fold one quarter of the whites into the yolk mixture until well combined. Now reverse the process, pouring batter over the remaining whites. Gently fold the two mixtures together, using a motion like a figure eight, until all the whites have disappeared. Be careful not to overfold, or roulade will be heavy. Transfer batter to the prepared pan, spreading it evenly and smoothing the top (1).

Bake in center of oven for 50 to 60 minutes. Test with a cake tester in the center; it should come out dry, and top should be golden. Let cool on a rack.

To make the filling: Combine cream cheese and sour cream well. Remove parsley stems; wash leaves, spin dry, and chop fine. Trim scallions, wipe with a damp paper towel, and chop fine. Mix in parsley, scallions, and remaining ingredients (except caviar) into cream mixture. Adjust seasoning (the filling should be fairly spicy). Finally add caviar and combine gently to avoid breaking eggs.

To make the sauce: Combine all ingredients except caviar in a glass or ceramic dish. Adjust seasoning (the sauce should be less spicy than the filling). Finally, fold in caviar.

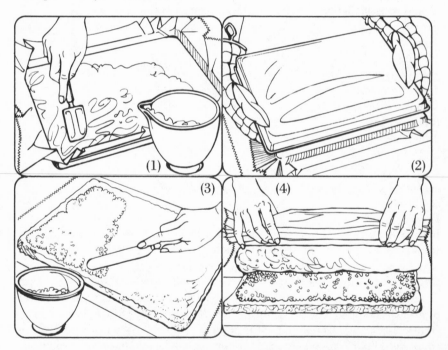

To assemble the roulade: Spread out a double fold of wax paper about 2 feet long. Invert cooled roulade onto wax paper (2). Remove pan, then gently peel off wax paper. Trim cracked edges slightly. Spread filling evenly over roulade (3). With the help of the long side of the wax paper, lift edge and roll it up loosely like a jelly roll (4). Adjust the log shape with wax paper. If roll cracks, don't worry about it. Slide two long, wide spatulas under short ends of roll and carefully lift it from the wax paper to a serving platter. Trim the two short ends slightly. If the roulade is not to be served at once, cover it with foil in order to retain the log shape.

Cut into pieces 1 to 1½ inches wide and serve, with the sauce on the side, at room temperature.

SPINACH ROULADE

A festive way to serve spinach at cocktails or for brunch. It is delicious served either warm or at room temperature.

10 TO 12 SERVINGS AS COCKTAIL FOOD OR FIRST COURSE

1 tablespoon sweet butter, melted
1½ tablespoons unseasoned bread crumbs
4 pounds fresh spinach
FILLING:
4 medium shallots
½ pound firm fresh mushrooms
4 tablespoons (½ stick) sweet butter
8 ounces farmer cheese
3 ounces cream cheese

5 eggs, at room temperature, separated
About 1 teaspoon kosher salt
Black pepper, freshly ground
Nutmeg, freshly grated

8 ounces sour cream
About ½ cup freshly grated Parmesan cheese
4 sprigs dill, snipped
1 tablespoon kosher salt
Black pepper, freshly ground

I suggest you use the following: an 11-by-16-inch jelly roll pan, a food processor, an enameled cast-iron skillet.

Preheat oven to 400°F. Use half the melted butter to brush evenly over bottom and sides of a jelly roll pan. Line with a 21-inch sheet of wax paper, which should extend several inches beyond short ends of pan. Brush paper with remaining melted butter and dust evenly with bread crumbs. Then, holding on to the paper, invert pan and tap to shake off excess.

Discard spinach stems and wilted leaves and wash spinach thoroughly to remove any sand. Drop into a large pot of boiling water and let water return to the boil. Drain spinach at once and refresh with cold water. Take small batches of spinach in your hands and squeeze out as much liquid as possible. Wring out, in batches, in a dish towel to dry well.

Chop spinach fine, in batches, in a food processor fitted with the steel blade. Remove each batch before placing in the next one. Return spinach to food processor bowl and, with motor on, add egg yolks, one at a time, processing until smooth. Transfer mixture to a bowl.

Beat egg whites at high speed until stiff. With a rubber spatula, fold one quarter of the whites into spinach until well combined. Now reverse the process, pouring spinach mixture over remaining whites. Gently fold the two mixtures together, using a motion like a figure eight, until all the whites have disappeared. Be careful not to overfold, or roll will be heavy. Season with salt, pepper, and nutmeg. Transfer batter to the prepared pan, spreading it evenly and smoothing the top.

Bake in center of oven for 12 to 15 minutes, or until top feels firm and springy to the touch. Cover with a damp towel and let cool on a rack.

To make the filling: Peel, quarter, and chop shallots fine in a food processor fitted with the steel blade. Wipe mushrooms with a damp paper towel and trim stem ends if necessary. Quarter mushrooms and chop coarsely, in batches, also in the food processor. Remove each batch to a bowl before placing in the next one.

Heat 2 tablespoons of the butter in a skillet. Sauté shallots over low heat until soft and transparent. Add remaining 2 tablespoons butter and mushrooms. Sauté over high heat, stirring with a wooden spoon, until mushrooms are just coated with butter. Let cool.

Combine farmer cheese and cream cheese thoroughly. Mix in sour cream, mushroom mixture, 6 tablespoons of the Parmesan cheese, and dill. Season with salt and pepper.

To assemble the roulade: Spread out a double fold of wax paper about 2 feet long. Invert cooled roll onto wax paper. Remove pan, then gently peel off wax paper. Trim edges slightly. Spread filling evenly over roll. With the help of the long side of the wax paper, lift edge and roll it up loosely like a jelly roll. Adjust the long shape with wax paper. If roll cracks, don't worry about it. Slide two long, wide spatulas under short ends of roll and carefully lift it from the wax paper to a serving platter. Trim the two short ends slightly. If the roulade is not to be served at once, cover it with foil in order to retain the long shape.

Before serving, sprinkle with remaining 2 tablespoons cheese and heat to lukewarm in a food warmer, a low oven, or over a pan of hot water.

◆Spinach can be blanched, drained, squeezed dry, and refrigerated a day in advance. The filling, except for adding Parmesan cheese, can also be done a day ahead of time.

MUSHROOM CROUSTADES

3 DOZEN
MINI-
CROUSTADES

Small circles of very thin white bread are fitted into minimuffin pans and baked. The toasted cups are then filled with an aromatic, creamy mushroom mixture.

2 tablespoons sweet butter, melted

FILLING:

½ ounce dried Polish or Czechoslovakian mushrooms
⅓ cup boiling water
5 medium shallots
½ pounds firm fresh mushrooms
¼ bunch Italian flat-leaf parsley
3 tablespoons sweet butter

36 very thin slices white bread, about 1½ pounds

1 tablespoon unbleached flour
¾ cup heavy cream
15 sprigs dill, snipped
About ½ teaspoon fresh lemon juice
2 tablespoons freshly grated Parmesan cheese
About ½ teaspoon kosher salt
Black pepper, freshly ground

I suggest you use the following: a 3-inch cookie cutter; three aluminum muffin pans, each with twelve depressions, about 1¾ inches across the top; a food processor; and a large enameled cast-iron skillet.

To make the croustades: Preheat oven to 400°F. Generously butter inside of muffin pans with a pastry brush, using all the melted butter. With a cookie cutter, cut out a 3-inch circle from the center of each bread slice. Fit these carefully into muffin pans and bake in center of oven for about 10 minutes, or until edges are light brown. Remove and let cool on a rack.

To make the filling: Place dried mushrooms in a small bowl and pour over boiling water. Allow to soak for 1 hour. Strain soaking liquid through a sieve lined with a paper towel. Squeeze mushrooms over sieve to extract more liquid, reserve liquid. Wash mushrooms carefully to remove any sand, drain, pat dry with paper towels, and chop medium fine.

Peel, quarter, and chop shallots very fine in a food processor fitted with the steel blade. Wipe fresh mushrooms with a damp paper towel, quarter, then chop fine, in batches, in food processor. Remove each batch to a bowl before placing in the next one. Remove parsley stems; wash leaves, spin dry, and chop fine, also in the food processor if you like.

Heat butter in a large skillet until hot. Add shallots and sauté over low heat until soft and transparent. Add both soaked and fresh mushrooms and sauté over medium heat, stirring with a wooden spoon, till coated with butter. (They will look very wet.) Cook for about 10 minutes, stirring from time to time, until all the moisture has evaporated.

Remove pan from heat, stir in flour, and blend. Add reserved mushroom liquid and cream and cook over high heat, stirring constantly with a wooden spoon, until mixture is thick. Remove from heat and season generously with parsley, dill, lemon juice, Parmesan cheese, salt, and pepper.

To fill the croustades: Preheat oven to 350°F. With a spoon, fill croustades just to the top. (You may have some filling left over.)

Place on a cookie sheet and bake in upper third of oven for about 10 minutes, or until hot. If you like, broil for a minute, but be careful, since the bread burns easily.

◆The croustades can be made in advance and frozen, and the filling can be made several days ahead of time and refrigerated. Simply place cooled croustades in a plastic bag and refrigerate. If you wish to freeze them, wrap them in foil and then place in a plastic bag. Do not defrost frozen croustades before filling, but do bring refrigerated filling back to room temperature before you proceed.

MUSHROOM TARTLETS

5 DOZEN
TARTLETS

I like to prepare one or two dishes way in advance of a party. It makes entertaining so much easier. These miniature tartlets, made with a flaky pastry and a piquant filling, freeze wonderfully.

1 recipe Cream Cheese Dough (page 245)	1½ tablespoons sweet butter, melted
FILLING:	
8 medium shallots	1 egg yolk
1 pound firm fresh mushrooms	About ¾ cup freshly grated
6 tablespoons sweet butter	Parmesan cheese
2 tablespoons unbleached flour	Kosher salt
2 tablespoons milk or heavy cream	White pepper, freshly ground

I suggest you use the following: a food processor; a 3-inch round cookie cutter; five aluminum muffin pans, each with twelve depressions about 1¾ inches at the top; and an enameled cast-iron skillet.

Cut dough into four pieces. Leave one piece at room temperature to soften until malleable, keep the rest refrigerated.

Grease five muffin pans lightly with melted butter, using a pastry brush.

On a floured pastry board, with a floured rolling pin, roll out each piece of dough as thinly as you can. Lift dough and reflour board and pin as necessary. With a cookie cutter, cut out circles and place in prepared muffin pans to form tiny containers. Gather scraps of dough and refrigerate them to be rolled out as you need more dough. Keep finished trays refrigerated.

To make the filling: Peel, quarter, and chop shallots fine in a food processor fitted with the steel blade. Transfer to a bowl.

Wipe mushrooms with a damp paper towel, quarter, and chop coarsely, in batches, in the food processor. Remove each batch before placing the next one in.

Heat 3 tablespoons of the butter in a skillet until hot. Add shallots and sauté over low heat until soft and transparent. Add remaining 3 tablespoons butter and sauté mushrooms over high heat, stirring constantly with a wooden spoon, until dry, about 4 minutes. Stir in flour and cook briefly. Add milk or cream and cook for a minute, stirring. Remove from heat and mix in egg yolk and ½ cup of the Parmesan cheese. Season well and let cool.

To assemble the tartlets: Preheat oven to 450°F. Fill tartlets almost to the top with mushroom filling and sprinkle lightly with remaining Parmesan cheese.

Bake in lower third of oven for 10 minutes, then reduce heat to 350°F, transfer tartlets to center of oven, and bake for another 8 to 10 minutes, or until edges are light brown. Release edges gently with a knife before taking them out.

◆If you like, the filling can be made a day in advance and refrigerated.

SOLE TARTLETS

Follow the recipe for Mushroom Tartlets (opposite) and fill with this delicate fish mixture.

5 DOZEN
TARTLETS

1 pound fresh gray-sole fillets	White pepper, freshly ground
Kosher salt	2 tablespoons dry white wine
6 medium shallots	1 teaspoon dried mustard
3 tablespoons sweet butter	(Coleman's brand)
2 tablespoons milk or heavy	About 1½ tablespoons fresh
cream	lemon juice, strained
1 cup freshly grated Parmesan	Kosher salt
cheese	White pepper, freshly ground
10 sprigs dill, snipped	

I suggest you use the following: a wok with a cover, a metal rack that fits into it, a heatproof dish that fits into the wok, a food processor, and an enameled cast-iron skillet.

To steam the sole: Place sole in a heatproof dish that fits into a wok. Sprinkle lightly with salt, pepper, and wine. Set rack in wok, add 1 quart water, and bring to a boil over high heat. Set dish on rack, cover wok, and steam sole over high heat for 5 minutes. Remove dish and let cool. Drain and flake sole into small pieces.

To make the filling: Peel, quarter, and chop shallots very fine in a food processor fitted with the steel blade. Heat butter in a skillet. Add shallots and sauté over low heat until soft and transparent. Stir in sole and milk or cream. Cook over medium heat for about 1 minute. Remove from heat and combine with about ¾ cup of the Parmesan cheese and dill. Season well and let cool.

To assemble the tartlets: Follow the master recipe.

◆To freeze either tartlets, fill them, cover with plastic wrap and then foil, and place in a plastic bag. Do not thaw before baking, but you will have to allow extra time for baking.

SMOKED SALMON MINIQUICHES

3 DOZEN   The inspiration for this recipe came in Michael Field's cooking class. We were making Quiche Lorraine, which is traditionally made with bacon. Michael, aware of my dietary restrictions, suggested that I experiment with smoked salmon instead.

1 recipe Pâte Brisée (page   1 tablespoon sweet butter,
  243)   melted

FILLING:

¼ pound smoked salmon   Cayenne pepper
½ cup freshly grated   About 1½ teaspoons
  Parmesan cheese   Dijon-type mustard
2 eggs, at room temperature   Kosher salt
½ cup heavy cream
About 1 teaspoon dried
  mustard (Coleman's brand)

I suggest you use a 3-inch round cookie cutter and three aluminum muffin pans, each with twelve depressions, about 1¾ inches across the top.

Cut dough into six pieces. Work with one piece at a time, and keep the rest refrigerated.

Grease three muffin pans with melted butter, using a pastry brush.

Roll out dough, on both sides, between two lightly floured sheets of wax paper until very thin. (Dough will spread more easily if you lift the papers from time to time.) Lift top sheet and put back on dough. Turn dough over and remove what is now the top sheet. With a cookie cutter, cut out circles and place in muffin pans to form tiny containers. Gather scraps of dough and refrigerate them to be rolled out as you need more dough. Keep finished trays refrigerated.

To assemble the miniquiches: Preheat oven to 400°F. Cut salmon into small cubes and divide among pastry shells. Sprinkle each with ½ teaspoon Parmesan cheese.

In a small bowl, beat eggs with a fork. Add cream and seasoning until well blended. (Filling should be well seasoned.) Fill containers with custard, about 2 teaspoonfuls each, and bake in lowest third of oven for 10 minutes. Reduce heat to 375°F and bake in center of oven for about 15 minutes more, or until edges are golden brown and filling is puffy. Release edges gently with a knife before taking them out and serve at once.

◆ If you are not filling the miniquiches the same or the following day, cover with plastic wrap and foil, put in a plastic bag, and freeze. When needed, do not thaw, but fill frozen.

LEEK TART

This tart is very light and delicately seasoned. It can be served either hot or at room temperature.

8 TO 10 SERVINGS

1 10- to 11-inch prebaked pie shell (page 243)
FILLING:

4 medium leeks	⅛ teaspoon freshly grated
3 tablespoons sweet butter	nutmeg
3 eggs, at room temperature	Kosher salt
1 cup half and half or heavy cream	White pepper, freshly ground

I suggest you use a food processor and a thin, flat baking sheet or foil oven liner.

To make the filling: Cut off dangling roots and most of green parts of leeks; discard tough outer leaves. Cut leeks into 2-inch pieces and chop medium fine, in batches, in a food processor fitted with the steel blade. Remove each batch before placing in the next one. Place in a sieve and wash well under cold running water. (Leeks are very sandy.) Drain.

Heat butter in a small saucepan. Add leeks, cover, and braise over low heat for about 30 minutes, or until soft, stirring occasionally with a wooden spoon.

Preheat oven to 375°F. In a medium bowl, whisk eggs and half and half or cream until well blended. Add leeks and season well. Place prebaked pie shell on a thin, flat baking sheet or foil oven liner. Ladle filling into shell. Bake in lowest third of oven for about 20 to 25 minutes, or until top is firm, but still wobbly.

To serve: Place tart on an elevated object, such as a coffee can, and let the rim fall down. Either slide tart to a flat serving platter or place two large, wide spatulas underneath and lift to a serving platter.

NOTE: I like to use a black tin quiche pan; it is a better conductor of heat.
   If you would like to make this filling richer, use heavy cream instead.
   If you would like to make this dish a quiche instead of a tart, sprinkle the filling with Parmesan cheese or a mixture of Parmesan and Gruyère cheese.

SPINACH AND RICOTTA PIE

8 TO 10
SERVINGS

This is my family's favorite. It can be served either hot or at room temperature, as a first course, luncheon dish, picnic, or snack.

1 10- to 11-inch prebaked pie shell (page 243)
FILLING:

1¾ pounds fresh spinach
3 tablespoons olive oil
4 scallions, including green
   parts, chopped fine
1¼ cups freshly grated
   Parmesan cheese

1¼ pounds whole-milk ricotta
4 eggs, at room temperature,
   lightly beaten
Kosher salt
Black pepper, freshly ground

I suggest you use a food processor and a thin, flat baking sheet or foil oven liner.

To make the filling: Discard spinach stems and wilted leaves and wash spinach to remove any sand. Drop into a large pot of boiling water and let water return to the boil. Drain spinach at once and refresh with cold water. Take small batches of spinach in your hands and squeeze out as much liquid as possible. Wring out, in batches, in a dish towel to dry very well. Chop spinach medium fine, in batches, in a food processor fitted with the steel blade. Remove each batch to a bowl before placing in the next one.
   Preheat oven to 375°F. Heat oil in a skillet until hot. Add scallions and sauté over low heat until soft. Add spinach and sauté, stirring, for a few minutes. Transfer to a bowl, let cool a little, and mix in 1 cup of the Parmesan cheese, the ricotta, and eggs. Season well.
   Place prebaked pie shell on a thin, flat baking sheet or oven liner. Spread filling in shell and sprinkle with remaining Parmesan cheese. Bake in lowest third of oven for about 25 minutes, or until top is firm, but still wobbly.

To serve: Place pie on an elevated object, such as a coffee can, and let the rim fall down. Either slide pie to a flat serving platter or place two large, wide spatulas underneath and lift to a platter.

NOTE: I prefer to use a black tin quiche pan; it is a better conductor of heat.

If you like, the pie can be baked earlier in the day and served at room temperature or reheated; either way the bottom will remain crisp.

SORREL (SOURGRASS) TART

Sorrel, also known as sourgrass, is available from May to October. It gives this tart a delicate lemony taste.

8 TO 10 SERVINGS

1 10- to 11-inch prebaked pie shell (page 243)

FILLING:

¾ pound fresh sorrel	3 eggs, at room temperature
2 medium onions	About 2 teaspoons fresh
3 tablespoons sweet butter	lemon juice
1 cup half and half or heavy	Kosher salt
cream	Black pepper, freshly ground

I suggest you use a food processor and a thin, flat baking sheet or a foil oven liner.

To make the filling: Remove stems and center veins from sorrel by folding each leaf in half so that the center becomes the outer edge. Wash leaves well. Drop into a large pot of boiling water. Return water to the boil, drain immediately, and refresh with cold water. Squeeze dry with your hands. Peel, quarter, and chop onions fine, in a food processor fitted with the steel blade.

Heat butter in a skillet until hot. Sauté onions over low heat until soft and transparent. Add sorrel and sauté for a minute. Puree this mixture in a food processor until smooth.

Preheat oven to 375°F. In a medium bowl, with half and half or cream whisk eggs until blended. Add sorrel puree and season well. Place prebaked pie shell on a thin, flat baking sheet or foil oven liner. Ladle filling into shell. Bake in lowest third of oven for about 20 to 25 minutes, or until top feels firm, but still wobbly.

To serve: Place tart on an elevated object, such as a coffee can, and let the rim fall down. Either slide tart to a flat serving platter or place two large, wide spatulas underneath and lift to a serving platter.

NOTE: I prefer to use a black tin quiche pan; it is a better conductor of heat.

This tart has a light filling. If you would like to make it richer, use the heavy cream. To make a quiche instead of a tart, sprinkle the unbaked filling with grated Parmesan or a mixture of grated Parmesan and Swiss or Parmesan and Gruyère.

CHEESE BOEREG

ABOUT
7 DOZEN
TRIANGLES

Whenever I have some time and my children or friends are willing to help, I make large quantities of phyllo tidbits and freeze them. They are marvelous to have on hand. Phyllo is a paper-thin dough, popular in the Middle East, that lends itself to many fillings.

1 pound feta cheese, crumbled	White pepper, freshly ground
5 ounces cream cheese	¼ teaspoon freshly grated
1 egg plus 2 egg yolks	nutmeg
	Kosher salt (optional)
9 tablespoons (1 stick plus 1 tablespoon) sweet butter, melted	1 pound fresh or frozen phyllo dough

I suggest you use two damp dish towels and a pastry brush.

To make the filling: Mix feta and cream cheese with a fork until well blended. Add egg and yolks and combine thoroughly. Season with pepper and nutmeg, adding salt only if necessary (feta cheese is often very salty).

To make the boereg: Preheat oven to 375°F. Clear a large work surface and have ready the melted butter, pastry brush, a knife, damp dish towels, and a foil pan for freezing or refrigerating the boereg.

Remove phyllo sheets from plastic wrapper. Unfold onto one towel and cover with the other. (Phyllo sheets are very fragile and dry out quickly, so they must be kept covered.) Spread one phyllo sheet on a sheet of wax paper. Brush surface lightly with melted butter, using a pastry brush, and cover with another sheet.

Cut sheets into 2-inch strips. Place 1 level teaspoon filling at bottom center of each strip and fold to the opposite side to form into a triangle. Do not fold to the end of the strip, but cut off about 2 inches of the dough before the end is reached. (This way they will be less doughy.) Arrange boereg, seam side down, on a foil pan or baking pan. Brush with melted butter and bake for about 15 minutes, or until crisp and golden. Serve immediately on a folded cloth napkin.

NOTE: If you wish to make half the recipe, use the following proportions:

½ pound feta cheese
3 ounces cream cheese
2 egg yolks

Nutmeg, freshly grated
White pepper, freshly ground

6 tablespoons (¾ stick) sweet butter, melted

◆ If you are not serving the boereg the same day and would like to freeze them, layer them in the foil pan with wax paper to prevent triangles from sticking. Cover with plastic wrap and foil and place in a plastic bag. If you have very little space, freeze them on trays; then, when frozen, wrap in foil and place in a plastic bag. When ready to bake, do not thaw, but allow a few more minutes for baking.

SPINACH BOEREG

FILLING:

1 pound fresh spinach
1 tablespoon sweet butter
1 small onion, grated fine
1 egg yolk
5 ounces feta cheese, crumbled

2 tablespoons freshly grated
    Parmesan cheese
Kosher salt
White pepper, freshly ground

ABOUT
4 DOZEN
MINICIGAR
SHAPES

1 pound fresh or frozen phyllo
    dough

About 6 tablespoons (¾ stick)
    sweet butter, melted

To make the filling: Discard spinach stems and wilted leaves and wash spinach thoroughly to remove sand; drain thoroughly. Gather into small batches and chop coarsely. Heat butter in a large skillet until hot. Add spinach and sauté over high heat, stirring with a wooden spoon, until spinach is almost wilted. Place in a mesh sieve and press with the back of a wooden spoon to extract all liquid. Pat dry with paper towels. Place in a small bowl and combine with onion, egg yolk, feta, and Parmesan. Season well.

To make the boereg: Proceed as in recipe for Cheese Boereg (opposite), but cut dough into 3-inch strips. Place 1 level teaspoon filling at the bottom center of each strip. Roll jelly-roll style until filling is well covered, then fold both sides over and continue rolling tightly, to form a cigar shape. Do not roll to the end of the strip, but cut off about 2 inches of the dough. Follow master recipe for baking and freezing instructions.

CURRIED FISH BOEREG

ABOUT
4 DOZEN
MINISQUARES

FILLING:

1 pound fresh gray-sole fillets
Kosher salt
White pepper, freshly ground
¼ cup dry white wine
3 scallions, white parts only

3 ounces cream cheese
About ¾ teaspoon Madras
 curry powder
About 1 tablespoon fresh
 lemon juice

1 pound fresh or frozen phyllo
 dough

About 6 tablespoons (¾ stick)
 sweet butter, melted

I suggest you use the following: a wok with a cover, a metal rack that fits into it, and a heatproof dish that fits into the wok.

To make the filling: Place fish on a heatproof dish. Season lightly with salt and pepper and sprinkle with wine. Place a metal rack in a wok, add 1 quart water, and bring to a boil over high heat. Set dish on rack, cover wok, and steam fish over high heat for 5 minutes. Remove dish and let fish cool. Drain fillets and place in a bowl. Trim scallions, pat dry with paper towels, and chop fine. Combine fish, scallions, and cream cheese, stirring until texture is medium fine. Season well with curry, lemon juice, salt, and pepper.

To make the boereg: Proceed as in recipe for Spinach Boereg (page 39), but fold dough into squares, cutting off several inches from each end to make it less doughy.

NOTE: You will have extra phyllo sheets left over. I have allowed for that, since some of them may come damaged or dried out.

Pareve

CRUDITÉS WITH ANCHOVY DIP

Because I like crudités to look abundant and colorful, I use only the freshest seasonal vegetables. Some can be served raw, whereas others should be briefly steamed.

VEGETABLES TO BE SERVED RAW:
Carrots, green and red peppers, endives, mushrooms, cucumbers, zucchini, kohlrabi, cherry tomatoes

VEGETABLES TO BE STEAMED:
Cauliflower, broccoli, green beans, snow peas, sugar snap peas, asparagus

DIP:

4 anchovy fillets
½ bunch Italian flat-leaf
  parsley
1 clove garlic, sliced
1 egg yolk, hard-boiled
1 teaspoon caperse
1 tablespoon Dijon-type
  mustard

½ teaspoon dried thyme
1½ tablespoons tarragon wine
  vinegar
½ cup olive oil
Kosher salt
Black pepper, freshly ground
Fresh lemon juice

I suggest you use a stainless-steel collapsible steamer basket and a food processor.

To prepare the raw vegetables: Peel and trim carrots; cut into matchsticks. Remove ribs and seeds of green and red peppers; slice. Separate endives into leaves and trim edges. Wipe mushrooms with a damp paper towel and remove stems (save for soup or sauce). Peel, trim, and seed cucumbers; cut into matchsticks. Wash zucchini, wipe with a paper towel, trim, and cut into matchsticks. Peel, trim, and cut kohlrabi into slices.

To prepare the steamed vegetables: Cut off all but ¼ inch of cauliflower and broccoli stems; separate tops into flowerets. Trim green beans. Pinch off both ends of snow peas and sugar snap peas; pull off string along straighter side. (If they are small and young, there will be no string. If they are larger, there may be a string on both sides, so remove both.) Hold each asparagus stalk in both hands and snap at the point where it breaks off easily (the end is inedible). To test if asparagus requires peeling, cut off a piece and taste; if it is stringy, then peel. Asparagus varies, and usually the medium and thin ones do not require peeling. If it is stringy, peel lower part of stalk lightly with a vegetable peeler. Trim ends to make them all the same length. Rinse.

To steam the vegetables: Place a steamer basket in a pot over just enough water to cover bottom of pot without touching steamer. Bring water to a rolling boil. Arrange a single layer of each vegetable in the steamer; cover pot and steam over high heat for about 2 minutes, or until vegetables are tender but still crisp. Refresh vegetables under cold running water, drain, and wrap in a dish towel till ready to use. If you have peeled the asparagus, do not refresh with cold water, or the stalks may become watery.

To make the dip: Rinse anchovy fillets and pat dry with paper towels. Remove parsley stems; wash leaves and spin dry. Into a food processor fitted with the steel blade, put anchovy fillets, parsley leaves, garlic, egg yolk, capers, mustard, thyme, and vinegar. With the motor running, dribble in oil till mixture is smooth and thick. Add seasonings (the dip should be spicy) and blend again. Transfer to a covered container and refrigerate until needed. Dip will keep for several days.

ARTICHOKES VINAIGRETTE

4 SERVINGS Do not refrigerate artichokes after you steam them; the cold will alter their delicate flavor.

> 4 medium artichokes
> Vinaigrette Dressing (see page 264)

I suggest you use a stainless-steel collapsible steamer basket.

Discard some of the small, bruised outer artichoke leaves. With a serrated knife, cut off about 1 inch of artichoke tops and the stems (1). With a scissors, snip off sharp leaf tips (2). Spread leaves and wash artichokes well.

To steam the artichokes: Place a steamer basket in a pot or wok with just enough water to cover bottom without touching basket. Bring water to a boil. Place artichokes in basket, cover, and steam gently over medium heat for about 20 to 30 minutes. To test if they are ready, pull out the center leaf; if it comes out easily, artichoke is ready.

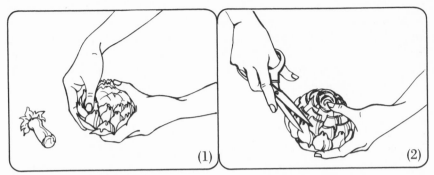

Let artichokes cool a bit and serve on individual plates with vinaigrette dressing on the side. Or, if you like, remove inner chokes and pour dressing inside. Serve at room temperature.

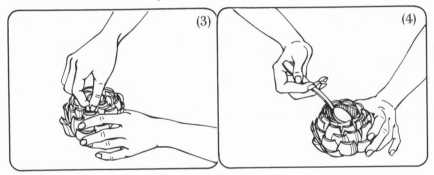

To remove the chokes: Spread artichoke leaves. With fingers, pull out center leaves and inner choke (3). Scrape heart clean with a teaspoon (4).

ASPARAGUS VINAIGRETTE

Generally, I find the medium-to-thin variety of asparagus to be sweeter, less stringy, and more flavorful than the thicker ones. I serve them at room temperature, coated with a vinaigrette dressing. Asparagus is also delicious served warm with Tamara's Mock Hollandaise (page 261) or with brown butter and toasted chopped blanched hazelnuts.

8 MEDIUM
ASPARAGUS
PER PERSON

Medium to thin asparagus
Vinaigrette Dressing (page 264)

I suggest you use a stainless-steel collapsible steamer basket.

Hold each asparagus spear with both hands and snap at point where end breaks off easily; that part is inedible. Trim ends of spears to make them even. To test if asparagus needs peeling, cut off a piece of stalk and taste it. If it is stringy, lightly peel lower part with a vegetable peeler. Asparagus spears vary, but most of the time the medium-to-thin variety does not require any peeling. Rinse.

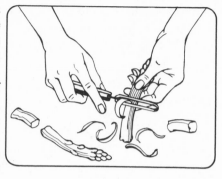

To steam the asparagus: Place a steamer basket in a pot or wok with just enough water to cover bottom without touching basket. Bring water to a boil. Place asparagus in one or two layers in basket. (If you have many, steam in batches.) Cover and steam over high heat for about 3 to 5 minutes, or until *al dente.* Timing will depend on thickness of asparagus. Remove asparagus and wrap in a dish towel until ready to serve.

NOTE: Look for asparagus with closed tips and firm, unwrinkled stalks, preferably of even size. Asparagus varies in taste depending on where it is grown and at what time of the year. Sometimes thick asparagus is also very good.

LEEKS VINAIGRETTE

1½ MEDIUM LEEKS PER PERSON

The leek, a member of the onion family, has been called in France the asparagus of the poor. I like to steam this delicate vegetable and serve it at room temperature, coated with a vinaigrette dressing.

3 medium (even-size) leeks
Vinaigrette Dressing (page 264)

I suggest you use a stainless-steel collapsible steamer basket.

Cut off dangling roots of leeks, but not so deeply as to separate white leaves. Cut off all but ½ inch of green stems and discard tough outer leaves. Make a deep crosslike incision at stem and wash that part well, separating leaves as much as possible to remove any hidden sand.

To steam the leeks: Place a steamer basket in a pot or wok with just enough water to cover bottom without touching basket. Bring water to a boil. Place leeks in basket, cover, and steam over high heat for 10 to 15 minutes, or until just tender but not falling apart. Remove basket, let leeks cool a bit, and cut them lengthwise into quarters. Divide equally and spoon dressing over them or serve dressing on the side.

NOTE: Avoid buying leeks that are wrapped in plastic with the stems cut off. Look for fresh leeks with bright green leaves. Leeks can be steamed earlier in the day, but coat them with dressing just before serving.

CELERY REMOULADE

A late-autumn and winter vegetable with a distinct flavor. (Despite the name, it has nothing to do with celery.) It makes a wonderful first course or accompaniment to cold meats or poultry. Make this dish a day in advance if you like, but serve it at room temperature.

4 TO 6
SERVINGS

3 small to medium celeriacs, about 1¾ pounds without leafy stems
About ⅓ cup Mayonnaise (page 265)
1 to 2 tablespoons olive or safflower oil

About 2 tablespoons tarragon wine vinegar
2 teaspoons Dijon-type mustard
Kosher salt
White pepper, freshly ground

I suggest you use a food processor or a Mouli Julienne with a no. 3 blade.

Drop celeriac in boiling water and boil for 3 minutes. Drain and refresh with cold water.

In the meantime, mix mayonnaise, olive or safflower oil, vinegar, and mustard in a large bowl.

Peel celeriac carefully and remove all the dark embedded spots. (This rough-looking vegetable is a bit tricky to peel.) Cut into quarters to fit horizontally into the feeding tube of a food processor fitted with the grating attachment. Press hard to obtain long, even matchsticks. (Or use a Mouli Julienne, which makes longer and more even matchsticks.) Toss julienned celeriac with dressing and season well.

NOTE: It is important to buy small, young celeriac with bright green stems; otherwise, the inside may be woody and bitter. Toss it with dressing right after shredding, because it discolors if exposed to air.

STIR-FRIED ASPARAGUS

2 OR 3
SERVINGS

Pencil-thin asparagus is ideal for this dish. If it is not available, use the thicker variety. Asparagus can be stir fried a few hours before dinner and served at room temperature.

12 pencil-thin asparagus
1 tablespoon peanut oil
2 tablespoons water
¼ teaspoon sugar

¾ tablespoon black Chinese
  soy sauce
Pinch kosher salt

I suggest you use a wok with a cover.

Hold each asparagus spear with both hands and snap at point where end breaks off easily. Discard that part; trim ends to make them even and rinse.

Heat a wok until hot, then add oil. When oil is hot, add asparagus and water. Cover and cook over high heat for 2 minutes. Add remaining ingredients, reduce heat, stir, and test to determine if vegetables are *al dente*. Remove to a rack to drain.

BRAISED ARTICHOKES

4 SERVINGS

I enjoy any preparation of this marvelous vegetable, but my favorite is this warm, winter version. Serve it in wide soup bowls along with its sauce.

4 medium artichokes
½ bunch Italian flat-leaf
  parsley
3 cloves garlic, minced

Juice of 1½ lemons, strained
3 teaspoons kosher salt
⅓ cup olive oil

I suggest you use a saucepan with lid, just large enough to fit the artichokes.

Discard some of the small bruised outer artichoke leaves. With a serrated knife, cut off about 1 inch from artichoke tops and stems. With a scissors, snip off sharp tips of leaves. Spread leaves and wash well.

Stand artichokes side by side in a saucepan. Add just enough water to cover bottom of pan.

Remove parsley stems. Wash leaves and chop coarsely. Mix well with remaining ingredients. Put a little of the mixture into the center of each artichoke. Bring to a boil and simmer, covered, for 20 to 30 minutes. To test, pull out a leaf; if it comes out easily, artichoke is ready.

RATATOUILLE

>>>

A summer-vegetable medley to make when all the ingredients are flavorful. I serve it either as a first course or as an accompaniment to cold meat or poultry. Make it a day in advance to enable the flavors to blend, and serve it at room temperature.

8 TO 10 SERVINGS

2 eggplants, about 1½ pounds altogether
Kosher salt
5 small zucchini
3 medium onions
4 to 5 cloves garlic
2 green peppers
1 bunch Italian flat-leaf parsley

¾ bunch basil
5 ripe tomatoes
¾ cup olive oil
Black pepper, freshly ground
2 tablespoons tomato paste
Lemon (optional)

I suggest you use a food processor.

Peel eggplants and cut into pieces 2 inches long and 1 inch wide. Soak for 1 hour in a large bowl of ice water to which 2 tablespoons of the salt have been added.

Drain, then squeeze gently in a dish towel to dry.

Wash zucchini, trim ends, and cut into same shape as eggplant. Let drain in a sieve sprinkled lightly with salt for 30 minutes. Pat dry with paper towels.

Peel and quarter onions and coarsely chop them along with garlic in a food processor fitted with the steel blade. Remove each batch before placing the next one in.

Rinse green peppers, remove ribs and seeds, cut vertically into ½-inch strips, and pat dry with paper towels.

Remove bottom half of parsley stems; wash leaves, spin dry, and chop coarsely in food processor. Remove basil stems; wash leaves, spin dry, and chop in food processor. Peel, core, seed, and cut tomatoes into large cubes.

Preheat broiler. Arrange eggplant pieces on a foil-lined broiler pan. Brush with ¼ cup of the olive oil and broil, not too close to heat source, until eggplant is light brown.

Heat remaining olive oil in a large saucepan. Sauté onions and garlic over medium-low heat till soft and transparent. Add zucchini and sauté for a few minutes. Add peppers, then tomatoes, cover saucepan, and cook over medium heat for 15 minutes. Mix in eggplant and cook, uncovered, for another 10 minutes. Mix in parsley, basil, salt, pepper, and tomato paste. Cook for another 5 minutes, or until vegetables are tender but still crisp. Stir gently with a wooden spoon, season with salt, pepper, or fresh lemon juice if you like, and chill. When ratatouille is chilled, season again and serve.

VEGETABLES TEMPURA STYLE

10 TO 12
COCKTAIL
SERVINGS

A long time ago, a friend of mine gave me an exciting present: four private cooking lessons with Millie Chan, a teacher at the China Institute.

I fell in love with the wide range of Oriental seasonings and cooking techniques. Although tempura is Japanese, it became one of my favorite cocktail foods. In tempura, small pieces of raw vegetables are dipped into a light batter, then deep fried until they are crisp on the outside and crunchy on the inside. You can prepare the vegetables, batter, and sauce in advance, but the actual frying must be done just before serving.

1 small eggplant
2 small zucchini
1 medium sweet potato
4 small white onions
¼ pound young green beans
1 small broccoli

1 small cauliflower
12 sprigs Italian flat-leaf
  parsley
¼ bunch watercress
12 small spinach leaves or 6
  large ones

BATTER:

2 cups unbleached flour
2 eggs
1½ tablespoons kosher salt

1 cup dry white wine
1 cup ice water

DIPPING SAUCE:

Scant ¼ cup thin Chinese soy
  sauce
Scant ¼ cup red wine vinegar

2 teaspoons sugar
1 drop chili oil (optional)

1½ to 2 cups peanut oil

I suggest you use a wok or an electric deep fryer and a wire skimmer.

To prepare the vegetables: Peel eggplant. Wash and trim zucchini. Peel sweet potato. Cut these into uniform 1½-inch strips. Peel and quarter onions and separate into two-layer sections. Wash and trim beans. Wash broccoli and cauliflower, remove stem portions (set aside for another use), and cut blossom portions into bite-size florets. Remove bottom half of parsley and watercress stems. Remove entire stems of spinach; if leaves are large, cut them in two. Wash and spin dry parsley, watercress, and spinach. Keep all vegetables wrapped in a towel and refrigerated so that they remain dry and ready for frying.

To make the batter: I have found that whenever I've made the whole batter recipe, it is never crisp enough. Therefore, divide flour, eggs, salt, and wine equally into two bowls. Add ½ cup ice water to each bowl and beat with a whisk until very smooth. Refrigerate batters for about 2 hours. Use one batch at a time.

To prepare the sauce: Put all ingredients in a small saucepan and bring to a boil; set aside. When needed, heat sauce to lukewarm.

To deep fry the vegetables: Heat a wok over high heat. Add oil and heat to 350°F on a frying thermometer. (To test if oil is hot enough without a frying thermometer, dip a chopstick into batter, then dip it into oil: If batter sizzles, oil is hot enough; if it burns, oil is too hot. The temperature must be just right; if too hot, batter will burn; if not hot enough, vegetables will absorb too much oil and taste greasy.)

Dip a few vegetables at a time into batter, carefully place into oil, and deep fry until golden, turning them often with chopsticks. Remove immediately to a cookie sheet lined with several layers of paper towels, changing them frequently as needed.

Serve immediately on a folded cloth napkin with dipping sauce on the side; if you wait, they become soggy, although parsley, watercress, spinach, broccoli, and green beans remain crisp longer than the other vegetables.

NOTE: It is important that the vegetables be young and fresh. You can, of course, experiment with other varieties. It is difficult to calculate how many pieces of vegetables you will need. I generally prepare more vegetables than I expect to use and deep fry them the following day or use them as snacks or for soup.

The frying oil can be reused if you let it cool, then strain and refrigerate it.

POTATO–ZUCCHINI PANCAKES

		ABOUT 2 DOZEN 2½- TO 3-INCH PANCAKES
2 medium zucchini	1½ tablespoons unbleached flour	
2 large Idaho potatoes, about 1½ pounds	¼ teaspoon baking powder	
2 eggs, lightly beaten	1 teaspoon kosher salt	
1 small onion, grated fine	White pepper, freshly ground	

About ¾ cup vegetable shortening (Crisco brand) or
  vegetable oil

I suggest you use a food processor and a large nonstick skillet.

Wash zucchini, pat dry with paper towels, trim stem ends, and grate in a food processor fitted with the grating attachment. Empty zucchini into a sieve, salt lightly, and leave to drain for 15 minutes. Wring out, in batches, in a sturdy dish towel until dry. Place in a medium bowl.

Peel potatoes and grate in the food processor. Empty potato pulp into a sieve and wash well under cold running water till water runs clear. Wring out, in batches, in a dish towel. Add to zucchini and combine with eggs, onion, flour, and baking powder. Season with salt and pepper.

Preheat oven to 300°F. Pour oil into a skillet to a depth of about ¼ inch and heat. When oil is hot, drop in 1 tablespoon batter at a time, flattening it slightly. Fry on both sides until golden. Drain on paper towels, changing them frequently as needed.

Keep pancakes warm on a rack set over a cookie sheet in the preheated oven until all are ready. Serve at once.

TAHINI

6 SERVINGS
AS A
FIRST COURSE

12 SERVINGS
AS A DIP

Tahini is a popular Middle Eastern specialty made with sesame seed paste. It is usually served as a first course with an assortment of salads, such as Baba Ghanoush (opposite), Hummus (opposite), sliced tomatoes, sliced seeded cucumbers, and warm pita (Middle Eastern bread). It can also be served as a dip with a variety of steamed vegetables, such as Crudités (page 41), plus scallions, radishes, cherry tomatoes, seeded strips of cucumber, green pepper, and warm pita.

1 cup sesame seed paste	About ½ cup cold water
1 clove garlic, minced	Kosher salt
Juice of 1½ to 2 lemons, strained	Black pepper, freshly ground

I suggest you use a food processor.

Before opening can of sesame seed paste, shake well in order to combine oil with paste, which tend to separate.

Place sesame seed paste, garlic, and juice of 1½ lemons in a food processor fitted with the steel blade. With the motor on, gradually add water to make a smooth, white, mayonnaiselike mixture. Season with salt, pepper, and more lemon juice. It should be lemony. If it thickens after refrigeration, add a little water and mix well.

NOTE: Sesame seed paste can be found in specialty stores and some supermarkets. Unused paste can be refrigerated for a long time in a covered container.

◆You can make tahini a few days in advance and refrigerate it in a tightly covered container. Serve at room temperature.

BABA GHANOUSH
OR EGGPLANT WITH TAHINI

A harmonious blend of two distinct flavors: smoky eggplant and nutty tahini. It can be served as a first course with tomatoes, cucumbers, green peppers, and warm pita or as a dip with steamed vegetables, such as Crudités (page 41), and pita strips. Make the Baba Ghanoush a day in advance, chill, but serve at room temperature.

6 SERVINGS
AS A
FIRST COURSE

12 SERVINGS
AS A DIP

2 medium eggplants, about 1 pound each	Juice of ¾ to 1 lemon, strained
⅓ cup sesame seed paste	1½ teaspoons kosher salt

I suggest you use a food processor.

Preheat broiler. Rinse eggplants, pat them dry, and cut in half lengthwise. Place, cut side down, on a foil-lined broiler pan. Broil close to heat source for about 20 minutes, or until eggplant skin is charred and inside feels soft. While eggplant is broiling, shake container of sesame seed paste well in order to combine oil with paste.

If eggplants are very seedy, scrape off some of the seeds with a spoon. Drain any liquid that has accumulated. Peel eggplant and puree with lemon juice and sesame seed paste until smooth in a food processor fitted with the steel blade. (Do not let the baked eggplant stand around without adding lemon juice, or it will darken.) Season with salt and more lemon juice; it should be lemony. Refrigerate in a tightly covered container and check seasoning before serving.

NOTE: Sesame seed paste can be found in specialty stores and some supermarkets. Unused paste can be refrigerated for a long time in a covered container.

HUMMUS

Hummus is a Middle Eastern specialty made of chick-peas and sesame seed paste. It is usually served as a first course, part of an assortment of salads along with Tahini (opposite), Baba Ghanoush (above), sliced cucumbers, sliced tomatoes, and warm pita. It can also be served as a dip with a variety of steamed vegetables, such as Crudités (page 41).

6 SERVINGS
AS A
FIRST COURSE

12 SERVINGS
AS A DIP

¾ cup sesame seed paste
1 cup canned chick-peas,
    drained, liquid reserved
Juice of about 1½ lemons,
    strained

1 clove garlic, minced fine
About ½ cup cold water
Kosher salt
Black pepper, freshly ground

I suggest you use a food processor.

Shake can of sesame seed paste very well in order to combine oil with paste, which tend to separate.

Into a food processor fitted with the steel blade place sesame seed paste, chick-peas, ¼ cup of the chick-pea liquid, juice of 1 lemon, and garlic. With motor on, gradually add water through the feeding tube to make a smooth, white, mayonnaiselike mixture. Season with salt, pepper, and more lemon juice if needed. If mixture thickens after refrigeration, add a little water and mix well.

NOTE: Sesame seed paste can be found in specialty stores and some supermarkets. The unused paste can be refrigerated for a long time in a tightly covered container.

◆You can make Hummus a few days in advance and refrigerate it in a tightly covered container. Serve at room temperature.

EGGPLANT CAVIAR

6 SERVINGS
AS A
FIRST COURSE

8 SERVINGS
AS A DIP

Make this piquant dish a day in advance to enable the flavors to blend. Serve it as a first course or as a dip, with seeded cucumbers, green peppers, scallions, and whole wheat crackers.

1 medium eggplant, about 1
    pound
3 tablespoons olive oil
1 small onion, chopped fine
1½ to 2 tablespoons tomato
    paste

About 1 teaspoon fresh lemon
    juice
Kosher salt
Black pepper, freshly ground

I suggest you use a food processor.

Preheat oven to 400°F. Put eggplant in a skillet and bake in oven for about 30 minutes, or until it feels soft and the skin begins to crack.

While eggplant is baking, heat olive oil in a skillet until hot. Sauté onion over low heat until soft and transparent.

Peel eggplant, scrape off some of the seeds with a teaspoon, and pour off any accumulated juices. Puree eggplant until smooth in a food processor fitted with the steel blade. Add eggplant puree and tomato paste to onions in skillet. Increase heat and cook for a few minutes. Let cool, season well with lemon juice, salt, and pepper.

EGGPLANT WITH TOMATOES AND SCALLIONS

This is a simple, tasty dish for those who love eggplant as I do. Make it in advance and serve it with dark, grainy bread.   4 SERVINGS

1 medium eggplant, about 1 pound	1 to 2 tablespoons tarragon wine vinegar
2 scallions, including some of the green parts	2 tablespoons olive oil
1 ripe medium tomato, peeled, seeded, and chopped coarse	Kosher salt
	Black pepper, freshly ground

Preheat oven to 400°F. Put eggplant in a baking dish and bake in oven for about 30 minutes, or until it feels soft and the skin begins to crack. Trim scallions, wipe with a damp paper towel, and chop fine. Peel eggplant, scrape off some of the seeds with a teaspoon, and pour off any accumulated juices. Chop fine and combine with remaining ingredients. Season well, and chill.

HERRING SALAD

This piquant dish has an unusual combination of flavors, semi-smooth texture, and ruby red color. Serve it garnished with snipped dill and with thin slices of black bread. Make it a day ahead of time, but serve it at room temperature.   10 COCKTAIL SERVINGS

2 medium beets	6- or 7-ounce jar Matjes fillet herring in spiced sauce, drained
2 scallions, including green parts	1 tablespoon olive oil
½ medium-tart apple (Granny Smith or greening)	Fresh lemon juice
About 1 tablespoon tarragon wine vinegar	Black pepper, freshly ground
	8 sprigs dill

I suggest you use a food processor.

Preheat oven to 400°F. Trim all but 1 inch from leafy beet tops. Place in an aluminum foil pan and bake in upper third of oven for 1 to 1½ hours, or until tender but still firm; turn beets occasionally as they bake. To test if beets are ready, pierce centers with a thick sewing needle. Let beets cool, then peel and quarter them.

Trim scallions, wipe with a damp paper towel, and quarter. Peel, core, and quarter the half apple. Put beets, scallions, apple, vinegar, herring, and oil into a food processor fitted with the steel blade and puree medium fine.

Transfer salad to a serving bowl. Season with lemon juice, salt, pepper, and 6 of the dill sprigs, which you have snipped to bits with a scissors. (Herring salad should be spicy.) Use remaining dill as a garnish.

GRAVLAX WITH MUSTARD AND DILL SAUCE

12 TO 14 FIRST-COURSE SERVINGS

8 TO 10 MAIN-COURSE SERVINGS

In this Scandinavian delicacy, fresh and center-cut salmon is not cooked, but cured with salt, sugar, and pepper for 3 to 4 days. No cooking or fussing. It is my favorite summer luncheon or dinner dish. I start with a cold soup, such as Perla Meyer's Strawberry Soup (page 76) or Chlodnik (page 75), and serve the Gravlax with a variety of cold salads. You can also serve Gravlax for cocktails on very thin buttered black bread, garnished with dill and capers, or with a thin layer of sauce.

3½ pounds very fresh center-cut salmon, in one piece
¼ cup sugar
¼ cup kosher salt

2 tablespoons freshly ground black or white pepper
15 sprigs dill, about ½ bunch, snipped

MUSTARD AND DILL SAUCE:
6 tablespoons sweet mustard, about 5 ounces
2 tablespoons Dijon-type mustard
¼ cup sugar

2 tablespoons tarragon wine vinegar
⅔ cup olive oil
15 sprigs dill, snipped

I suggest you use a 9-by-9-by-2-inch glass dish.

Have fish man remove center bone of salmon without removing skin and without separating fillets. Rinse salmon and pat dry with paper towels; place in a glass dish. In a small bowl, combine sugar, salt, and pepper. Rub curing mixture inside and outside fillets. Sprinkle dill between fillets. Cover dish with wax paper, then foil. Place a wooden board or plate on top of foil and weigh top down with a heavy stone or heavy pot filled with large cans. (It is important to weigh fish with something heavy.) Refrigerate for 3 to 4 days. Every 12 hours, remove weights and turn fish over, replacing weights each time.

To make the sauce: Whisk sauce ingredients and blend thoroughly. Refrigerate in a tightly covered glass jar. It keeps for a week, but add some freshly snipped dill when ready to serve.

To serve: Place salmon on a cutting board. Open fillets, scraping off and discarding pepper and dill. With a sharp carving knife or a special knife designed for cutting gravlax, cut salmon on the diagonal into thin slices. Serve with sauce on the side.

NOTE: Gravlax can remain in the curing mixture for up to 5 days. Leftovers can be sliced, wrapped well, and frozen.

MARINATED SALMON

This is an adaptation of a popular pickled salmon dish, which I find too vinegary and spongy. In my version, the fish is first steamed, then marinated, giving it a delicate texture and flavor. Serve it with dark bread.

6 TO 8 SERVINGS

3 to 3½ pounds very fresh center-cut salmon, in one piece, bone removed and skin left on

MARINADE:
½ cup olive oil
About ½ cup tarragon wine vinegar
2 bay leaves, crushed

2 medium onions, sliced thin
15 sprigs dill

About 1½ teaspoons kosher salt
White pepper, freshly ground

I suggest you use the following: a wok with a cover, a metal rack that fits into it, a heatproof dish that fits into the wok, and a 9-by-9-by-2-inch heatproof glass (Pyrex) dish to hold the fish in a single layer.

To steam the salmon: Place a metal rack in a wok, add 1 quart water, and bring to a boil over high heat. Place salmon on a heatproof glass dish and set on rack. Cover and steam salmon over high heat for about 10 minutes on each side. (The fish should be undercooked.) Remove dish and pour off any accumulated liquid. Let cool, then chill fish well (it is easier to cut the salmon when cold).

Skin top of fish and cut into 2-inch squares. (They may fall apart.) Arrange in a glass dish. Do the same with the bottom. Scatter onions over salmon. Snip most of dill, leaving a few sprigs for garnish, and scatter over fish. Whisk oil, vinegar, bay leaves, salt, and pepper till well blended. Season generously. Pour over salmon, cover with wax paper and then foil, and refrigerate for 2 to 3 days, turning the fish once a day.

Serve salmon at room temperature on a bed of lettuce, without any juice, but with the onions and dill sprigs.

NOTE: If you find it difficult to turn the fish while steaming, cut into two pieces at skin and steam each piece for 5 minutes on each side.

Because each brand of vinegar varies in strength and taste, start out with less and discover what you prefer.

DEEP-FRIED FISH FILLETS IN A SEAWEED BATTER

10 TO 12
COCKTAIL
SERVINGS

I serve very little with cocktails before dinner, just something to whet the appetite. This fish, which I learned in Millie Chan's cooking class, is one of my favorites. Pieces of sole are dipped into a batter, deep fried, and served immediately with a pepper-and-salt dip.

MARINADE:

1¼ teaspoons kosher salt	¼ teaspoon freshly ground
1 tablespoon dry white wine	white pepper

1¼ to 1½ pounds gray-sole fillets

BATTER:

¾ cups unbleached flour	4½ tablespoons dried seaweed
Generous ⅓ cup cornstarch	(tai tiao) or Japanese
½ teaspoon kosher salt	aonoriko
3 teaspoons baking powder	
1 cup plus 2 tablespoons cold water	

2 cups peanut oil

PEPPER-AND-SALT DIP:

1 teaspoon black peppercorns	2 tablespoons dried Szechuan
¼ cup kosher salt	peppercorns

I suggest you use the following: a wok, a wire skimmer, a blender, and a fine mesh sieve.

Mix marinade ingredients together. Rinse and dry fillets with paper towels and cut into 2-by-2-inch pieces, cutting away center cartilage. Place in a bowl, cover with marinade, and refrigerate for an hour.

To make the batter: Beat flour, cornstarch, salt, baking powder, and water with a whisk until smooth. Just before frying, stir in seaweed; this ensures that you will retain the beautiful speckles.

To deep fry the fish: Heat a wok over high heat. Add oil and heat to 350°F on a frying thermometer. (To test if oil is hot enough without a frying thermometer, dip a chopstick into batter, then dip it into oil: If batter sizzles, oil is hot enough; if it burns, oil is too hot. The temperature must be just right; if too hot, batter will burn; if not hot enough, fish will absorb too much oil and taste greasy.)

Dip a few pieces of fish into batter at a time. Place one at a time in the hot oil. Fry until lightly golden, turning with chopsticks. The pieces should be crisp on the outside and barely cooked on the inside. Remove immediately with a skimmer to a cookie sheet lined with several layers of paper towels, changing them frequently as needed. Serve on a folded cloth napkin with the dip on the side.

To make the dip: Combine all ingredients in a heavy skillet and cook over medium heat, shaking the pan, until salt turns light brown; do not let it burn. The peppercorns will open and release a strong fragrance. Process mixture in a blender until almost fine. Strain through a mesh sieve and discard residue. Pepper-and-Salt Dip will keep indefinitely stored in a tightly covered glass jar.

NOTE: Both Szechuan peppercorns and dried seaweed are available in Oriental stores.

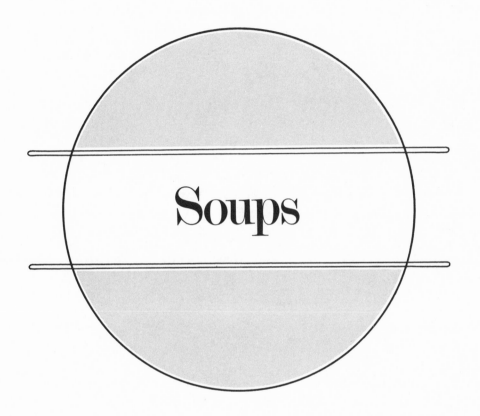

Soups

Meat

GARDEN VEGETABLE SOUP

A hot, nourishing soup eaten with grainy dark bread is a meal   12 SERVINGS
in itself on chilly winter evenings. Be as adventurous as you like
in substituting other vegetables. Make it a day in advance to let
the flavors blend. Incidentally, this soup freezes very well.

½ cup dried chick-peas
½ cup dried baby lima beans
¾ ounce dried imported
    Italian mushrooms
1 cup boiling water
2 onions
4 cloves garlic
3 carrots
9 cups strong Beef Stock,
    strained, with meat cut into
    small cubes (page 255)
1-pound 2-ounce can peeled
    Italian tomatoes, undrained
    and chopped coarse

2 zucchini
¼ pound green beans
1 stalk broccoli
4 firm fresh mushrooms
½ bunch Italian flat-leaf
    parsley
¼ pound sweet peas, shelled
4 sprigs thyme or 2 teaspoons
    dried
Kosher salt
Black pepper, freshly ground

I suggest you use a food processor.

Soak chick-peas and lima beans overnight in separate bowls in enough cold
water to cover them by a few inches. Drain beans and pick them over,
discarding hard ones that did not soften; set aside.

Place dried mushrooms in a small bowl and pour boiling water over them.
Soak for about 1 hour. Strain soaking liquid through a sieve lined with a
paper towel. Squeeze mushrooms over sieve to extract more liquid; reserve
liquid. Wash soaked mushrooms carefully to remove any sand, chop
coarsely, and set aside.

Peel, quarter, and chop onions and garlic coarsely in a food processor
fitted with the steel blade; set aside. Do the same with the carrots.

Put stock with cubed meat, chick-peas and lima beans, canned tomatoes, reserved mushroom liquid, soaked mushrooms, onions, garlic, and carrots into a large pot over high heat. Bring to a boil, reduce heat, and boil gently, covered, for about 1 hour, or until beans are soft.

In the meantime, wash, trim, and cut zucchini into small cubes. Trim green beans and cut into small pieces. Separate broccoli into florets; peel and cube stem. Wipe fresh mushrooms with a damp towel and cube them. Finally, discard bottom half of parsley stems; rinse leaves and chop. Add all these vegetables to the pot, along with the peas, parsley, and thyme. Bring soup back to the boil and continue cooking slowly, covered, for another 30 minutes, or until vegetables are soft. Season.

NOTE: I buy all dried beans in the health food store, not the supermarket. They are fresher and cook more quickly.

◆If you like, you can refrigerate this soup in the same large pot in which it was cooked, but in that case it is essential that you use enameled cast iron to prevent discoloration and change in flavor. Also, cover the pot with wax paper, then with a lid, to seal the flavor in.

BEET BORSCHT

6 TO 8
SERVINGS

There are many versions of beet borscht. This one is well sea-soned, light with a dazzling red color, and can be a meal in itself when served with Meat Boereg (page 8). Make it a day in advance; it tastes better.

8 medium beets	About 1 teaspoon fresh lemon
1 medium onion	juice
3 to 4 cloves garlic	1 teaspoon sour salt (citric
½ bunch Italian flat-leaf	acid)
parsley	About 1 teaspoon brown sugar
7 cups strong Beef Stock,	Kosher salt
strained, with meat cut into	Black pepper, freshly ground
small cubes (see page 255)	
About 1 tablespoon red wine	
vinegar	

I suggest you use a food processor.

Preheat oven to 400°F. Trim all but 1 inch from leafy beet tops. Bake beets in a foil pan for 1 hour, turning occasionally.

Peel, quarter, and chop onion and garlic in a food processor fitted with the steel blade. Remove bottom half of parsley stems; rinse, spin dry, and chop the rest coarsely in the food processor.

In a large saucepan, bring stock, meat, onions, and garlic to a boil. Reduce heat and boil slowly for 30 minutes. Season with some of the vinegar, lemon juice, sour salt, and sugar.

Peel beets and grate coarsely in a food processor fitted with the grating attachment. Add beets and parsley to soup and cook gently, covered, for another 30 minutes, or until beets are tender, but still a little crunchy. Correct the seasoning.

◆ If you like, you can refrigerate this soup in the same saucepan in which it was cooked, but in that case it is essential that you use enameled cast iron to prevent discoloration and change in flavor. Also, cover the pot with wax paper, then with a lid, to seal the flavor in.

CABBAGE BORSCHT

→>>>

A hearty sweet-and-sour winter soup with a brilliant red color. Because it has meat in it, it is an excellent one-dish meal when served with a good black bread. I like to make this soup in large quantities and freeze it to have on hand.

12 TO 14 SERVINGS

4 medium beets
9 cups strong Beef Stock, strained, with meat cut into small cubes (page 255)
2-pound 3-ounce can peeled Italian tomatoes, undrained and chopped
2 leeks
2 onions
4 to 5 cloves garlic
2 carrots
1 bunch Italian flat-leaf parsley

1 very small cabbage, about ¾ pound
About 3 tablespoons cider vinegar
About 2 tablespoons fresh lemon juice, strained
½ teaspoon sour salt (citric acid)
2 to 3 tablespoons dark brown sugar
Kosher salt
Black pepper, freshly ground

I suggest you use a food processor.

Preheat oven to 400°F. Cut off all but 1 inch from leafy beet stems and bake beets in a foil pan for 1 hour, turning occasionally.

Put stock with meat and chopped tomatoes with their juice into a large pot and bring to a boil. Cut off dangling roots of leeks and half of the green parts. Discard tough outer leaves, cut leeks into small pieces, and chop coarsely in a food processor fitted with the steel blade. Wash chopped leeks well under cold running water to remove all sand. Add to stock. Peel and quarter onions, garlic, and carrots, chop coarsely in food processor, and add to soup. Simmer, covered, for about 30 minutes.

Remove half the parsley stems; rinse, spin dry, and chop the rest coarsely in food processor, then add to soup. Discard bruised outer leaves of cabbage; quarter, core, and coarsely shred cabbage in food processor fitted with the slicing attachment. Add to soup along with half the seasoning. Simmer for another 30 minutes. Finally, peel the beets, grate coarsely in food processor fitted with the grating attachment, and add to soup along with the remaining seasoning. Simmer for another 30 minutes. (Vegetables should still have crunch to the bite.)

◆If you like, you can refrigerate this soup in the same pot in which it was cooked, but in that case it is essential to use enameled cast iron to prevent discoloration and change in flavor. Also, cover the pot with wax paper, then with a lid, to seal the flavor in.

CHICKEN SOUP WITH WATERCRESS

5 TO 6
SERVINGS

This well-seasoned chicken soup is simplicity itself.

1½ bunches watercress
5 cups Strong Chicken Stock
 (page 257)
About ½ tablespoon thin
 Chinese soy sauce
About ½ tablespoon black
 Chinese soy sauce
½ teaspoon sugar

1½ tablespoons dry white
 wine
1 tablespoon cornstarch
2 tablespoons cold water
About 1 teaspoon sesame oil
Kosher salt
Black pepper, freshly ground

Remove watercress stems; wash leaves and spin dry; set aside.

Bring stock to a boil over high heat in a saucepan. Add soy sauces, sugar, and wine. Combine cornstarch with water until smooth and stir into soup. Boil for about 2 minutes, season with sesame oil, salt, and pepper. (Soup can be made in advance up to this point, but use an enameled cast-iron saucepan to prevent discoloration and any change in flavor.)

When ready to serve, bring soup to a rolling boil, add watercress leaves, stir, return to the boil, and serve immediately in heated soup bowls. (The watercress leaves, even though limp, should still retain some crunch.)

NOTE: All ingredients can be found in Oriental markets. Sesame oil keeps well in the refrigerator.

If possible, serve this soup with porcelain soup spoons, which are available in most Oriental stores; I have found that metal utensils change the taste.

GARLIC SOUP

-»»

Surprisingly enough, this creamy soup has only the suggestion of garlic flavor.

4 heads garlic (about 50 cloves)
6 cups Strong Chicken Stock (page 257)
3 egg yolks, at room temperature
CROUTONS:
4 slices day-old Italian or French bread
¼ cup olive oil

3 tablespoons olive oil
Kosher salt
White pepper, freshly ground
Dash cayenne pepper

2 cloves garlic, peeled and crushed

Separate heads of garlic without bruising them and drop cloves into boiling water. Bring to the boil again and drain at once in a sieve. Peel very carefully without bruising the cloves, or the soup will have a strong garlicky taste.

In a saucepan, bring the stock with the garlic cloves to a boil. Simmer, covered, for about 30 minutes, or until cloves are soft. Remove garlic with a slotted spoon and discard. (You can make the soup in advance up to this point if the saucepan you use is made of enameled cast iron, which prevents any possible discoloration and change in flavor.)

Just before serving, whisk egg yolks in a small bowl till creamy. Dribble in olive oil and whisk till thick. Bring soup to a boil and drizzle a ladleful of soup into yolk mixture in a slow stream, whisking all the time. Repeat with another ladleful. Return this mixture to the soup, whisking continuously. Make sure soup does not reach the boiling point, or it will curdle. Season with salt, pepper, and cayenne.

Serve in heated bowls, garnished with croutons.

To make the croutons: Remove crust from bread and cut into ½-inch squares. Heat olive oil in a heavy skillet, add garlic, and brown it over medium-high heat. Discard garlic, increase heat, add bread, and brown lightly, constantly stirring with a wooden spoon. Remove croutons with slotted spoon and drain on paper towels.

◆The croutons can be frozen or refrigerated, well wrapped in foil. Reheat in a preheated 250°F oven before serving.

MUSHROOM–BARLEY SOUP

10 TO 12
SERVINGS

Different countries develop characteristic foods that originate because of the availability and excellence of certain ingredients. Poland is known for its marvelously fragrant mushrooms, dill, and barley.

Make this soup a day ahead of time to enable the flavors to blend, and be sure to use only Polish or Czechoslovakian mushrooms; other dried mushrooms are not a good substitute.

¾ ounce dried Polish or
   Czechoslovakian mushrooms
1 cup boiling water
2 medium leeks or onions
½ cup plus 2 tablespoons fine
   pearl barley

9 cups Strong Chicken Stock
   (page 257)
¼ bunch dill
Kosher salt
White pepper, freshly ground

Place dried mushrooms in a small bowl and pour boiling water over them. Let soak for about 1 hour. Strain soaking liquid through a sieve lined with a paper towel, squeezing mushrooms over sieve to extract more liquid; set liquid aside. Wash soaked mushrooms carefully to remove any sand, pat dry with paper towels, and chop coarsely. Cut off dangling roots and most of green stems from leeks and discard tough outer leaves. Dice leeks, put in a sieve, and wash well under cold running water to remove all sand; drain. Wash barley in a sieve under cold running water until water runs clear.

In a saucepan, bring stock, reserved mushroom liquid, chopped mushrooms, leeks, barley, and a few sprigs of dill to a boil. (Reserve remaining dill for garnish.) Reduce heat and boil gently, covered, for about 1 hour, or until barley is soft. Discard dill sprigs and season with salt and pepper.

Serve piping hot, in heated soup bowls, garnished with lots of dill snipped to bits with scissors.

NOTE: If fine barley is unavailable, use ½ cup medium-grain barley instead; the soup will have a coarse texture and a less-delicate flavor.

◆If you like, you can refrigerate this soup in the same saucepan in which it was cooked, but in that case it is essential that you use enameled cast iron to prevent discoloration and change in flavor. Also, cover the pot with wax paper, then with a lid, to seal the flavor in.

FRESH SPINACH SOUP

>>>

If you like texture in your soups, this is a wonderful nonpureed kind. All you need is good chicken stock and fresh blanched spinach. This soup was inspired by an Italian soup that has added rice and Parmesan cheese.

6 TO 8
SERVINGS

1½ pounds fresh spinach
7 cups Strong Chicken Stock (page 257)
About 2 tablespoons farina or couscous

1 clove garlic, minced
Pinch freshly grated nutmeg
Kosher salt
Black pepper, freshly ground

I suggest you use an enameled cast-iron saucepan.

To blanch the spinach: Discard spinach stems and wilted leaves and wash thoroughly to remove any sand. Drop into boiling water and let water return to the boil. Drain spinach at once and refresh with cold water. Take small batches of spinach in your hands and squeeze out as much liquid as possible. Chop very coarsely.

In a saucepan, bring stock, farina or couscous, and garlic to a boil. Reduce heat and boil soup gently for a few minutes. Stir in spinach, return soup to the boil, season, and serve at once in heated soup bowls. (If spinach boils too long, it will lose some of its beautiful green color.)

NOTE: For a thicker soup, add more farina.

◆If you want to make this soup in advance, stir in the spinach and bring to a boil just before serving.

ZUCCHINI SOUP

>>>

Easy to prepare, noncaloric, with a subtle flavor of zucchini, pale green color and velvety texture. It is a delightful summer soup, served either hot or at room temperature. Make it a day ahead of time if you like.

6 TO 8
SERVINGS

6 small zucchini, about 1¾ pounds
5 cups Light Chicken Stock (page 256)
Kosher salt

4 sprigs thyme or 1 teaspoon dried
¾ to 1 tablespoon fresh lemon juice
Black pepper, freshly ground

I suggest you use a blender.

Wash zucchini and pat dry with paper towels. Trim stem ends and slice 5 of the zucchini into thick rounds; reserve the last for garnish. Put sliced zucchini in a sieve, sprinkle lightly with salt, and leave to drain for about 15 minutes. Cut remaining zucchini into cubes, put in another sieve, sprinkle lightly with salt, and let drain.

Bring 4½ cups of the stock, sliced zucchini, and thyme to a boil in a saucepan. Reduce heat and cook slowly, covered, until zucchini is soft. Let cool a bit.

If you have used fresh thyme, remove sprigs and puree soup, in batches, in a blender until very smooth. Return soup to saucepan. Pat cubed zucchini dry and add to soup. Adjust consistency as needed with the remaining ½ cup stock. Season with lemon juice, salt, and pepper.

NOTE: Use only a light chicken stock in order not to overpower the delicate flavor of the vegetable.

◆If you wish to make the soup in advance and then serve it hot, you can refrigerate it in the same saucepan in which it was cooked, but in that case it is essential that you use one made of enameled cast iron to prevent discoloration and change in flavor. Also, cover the pot with wax paper, then with a lid, to seal the flavor in.

CAULIFLOWER SOUP

8 SERVINGS   I serve soups before dinner all year round. This one is light enough to whet the appetite, wonderful for both the purist in taste and the calorie-conscious.

¾ to 1 tablespoon Madras
  curry powder
About 2¾ pounds cauliflower
6½ cups Light Chicken Stock
  (page 256)

Kosher salt
White pepper, freshly ground

I suggest you use a blender.

Preheat oven to 325°F. Wrap curry powder in foil and warm in oven for a few minutes to bring out flavor.

Cut off the green cauliflower leaves and all but ¼ inch of the heavy stem. Separate florets and reserve a few for garnish. Wash and drain the rest of the cauliflower.

Bring 5½ cups of the stock and the cauliflower to a boil over high heat. Reduce heat and cook slowly, covered, for about 20 minutes, or until cauliflower is soft. Let cool a bit.

Puree soup, in batches, in a blender until very smooth. Return soup to saucepan and adjust consistency as needed with the remaining 1 cup stock. Add some of the curry powder. Since the taste of curry takes a while to develop, wait for a few minutes before adding more. Season with salt and pepper.

To prepare the garnish and serve: Make florets very small and trim stems. Steam in a vegetable steamer until tender but firm to the bite. Ladle soup, piping hot, into heated bowls and serve, garnished with blanched florets.

NOTE: When buying cauliflower, look for a creamy-white head with fairly closely packed florets and green leaves at the base.

Use only a light chicken stock in order not to overpower the delicate flavor of the vegetable.

◆ If you like, you can refrigerate this soup in the same saucepan in which it was cooked, but in that case it is essential that you use enameled cast iron to prevent discoloration and change in flavor. Also, cover the pot with wax paper, then with a lid, to seal the flavor in.

CELERY ROOT SOUP

One of my favorite winter soups, with the distinct flavor and pale color of the vegetable.   6 SERVINGS

6 cups Light Chicken Stock
  (page 256)
3 small to medium celeriacs,
  about 1¾ pounds without
  leafy stems

Kosher salt
White pepper, freshly ground

I suggest you use a blender.

Bring 5½ cups of the stock to a boil.

Peel celeriac carefully and remove any embedded dark spots. (This rough-looking vegetable is a bit tricky to peel.) Slice or cube and rinse. Add to stock. Return to the boil, then cook slowly, covered, for about 30 minutes, or until vegetable is soft. Let cool a bit, then puree in a blender, in batches, until very smooth. Return soup to the saucepan and adjust consistency as needed with the remaining ½ cup stock. Season with salt and pepper.

NOTE: It is important to buy young celeriac, with bright green stems, or the inside may be woody and bitter. Drop into stock immediately after slicing; celeriac discolors when exposed to air.

Use only a light chicken stock, so that the distinct vegetable flavor is not overpowered.

◆If you like, you can refrigerate the soup in the same saucepan in which it was cooked, but in that case it is essential that you use one made of enameled cast iron to prevent discoloration and change in flavor. Also, cover the pot with wax paper, then with a lid, to seal the flavor in.

LEEK, ZUCCHINI, AND WATERCRESS SOUP

8 SERVINGS Our family loves soup, and I serve small portions frequently to excite the palate. Soups are ideal for my style of entertaining, since they can be prepared a day ahead of time, leaving me more time to concentrate on last-minute preparations.

This is one of my favorite soups. It is light, creamy, and has a silky texture without the use of cream.

2 medium leeks
4 medium zucchini, about 1¾ pounds
Kosher salt
1 bunch watercress
1 tablespoon olive oil

1 tablespoon unsalted margarine
5½ cups Light Chicken Stock (page 256)
Black pepper, freshly ground

I suggest you use a blender and a mesh sieve.

Cut off dangling roots and most of green stems from leeks; remove tough outer leaves. Dice leeks, place in a sieve, and wash well under cold running water; drain.

Wash zucchini, pat dry with paper towels, trim the ends, and slice into ½-inch rounds. Place in a sieve, sprinkle lightly with salt, and let drain for about 15 minutes.

Remove and discard bottom half of watercress stems. Wash watercress, spin dry, and reserve a few leaves for garnish.

Heat oil and margarine in a saucepan until hot. Add diced leeks and sauté over low heat, stirring from time to time, until leeks are soft and transparent. Add zucchini and sauté for a few more minutes. Add 5 cups of the stock, bring to a boil over high heat, reduce heat, and cook, covered, until zucchini is soft, about 10 minutes. Add watercress, return soup to the boil, and cook, uncovered, for a few minutes, until watercress is wilted. Let cool a bit, then puree soup, in batches, in a blender until very smooth. Now strain soup through a mesh sieve set over a bowl. Push solids with back of a wooden spoon, discarding residue each time. (This technique gives the soup its silky texture and creamy consistency without the use of cream.)

Return soup to saucepan and adjust consistency as needed with the remaining ½ cup stock. Season.

Serve piping hot in heated soup bowls, garnished with reserved watercress leaves.

NOTE: Use a light chicken stock so that the vegetable flavors are not overpowered by the stock.

◆If you like, you can refrigerate this soup in the same saucepan in which it was cooked, but in that case it is essential that you use enameled cast iron to prevent discoloration and change in flavor. Also, cover the pot with wax paper, then with a lid, to seal the flavor in.

LETTUCE AND PEA SOUP

An elegant start for a dinner. The ingredients for this soup are available all year round. It can be made in advance and served at room temperature as well.

6 TO 8 SERVINGS

½ to ¾ tablespoon Madras
  curry powder
2 medium leeks
1 head Boston lettuce
4½ cups Light Chicken Stock
  (page 256)

10-ounce package frozen peas,
  thawed and drained
Kosher salt
Black pepper, freshly ground

I suggest you use a blender and a mesh sieve.

Preheat oven to 325°F. Wrap curry powder in foil and warm in oven for a few minutes to bring out flavor.

Cut off dangling roots and most of green leaves from leeks; remove tough outer leaves. Dice leeks, place in a sieve, and wash well under cold running water to remove all sand; drain. Separate lettuce leaves, wash, and drain well.

Bring stock and leeks to a boil in a saucepan over high heat. Reduce heat and cook slowly, covered, for 10 minutes. Add peas and lettuce leaves. Return soup to the boil and continue cooking slowly, covered, for about 15 minutes. Let cool a bit.

Puree soup, in batches, in a blender until very smooth. Strain it, also in batches, in a sieve set over a bowl. Push solids with back of a wooden spoon, discarding residue each time. (This technique gives the soup its creamy consistency without the addition of cream.) Return soup to saucepan and add some of the curry powder. The taste of curry takes a while to develop, so wait for a few minutes before adding more. If you like a thicker soup, boil it down a bit. Season.

Serve piping hot in heated soup bowls.

NOTE: Use only a light chicken stock, in order not to overpower the delicate flavor of the vegetables.

◆If you like, you can refrigerate this soup in the same saucepan in which it was cooked, but in that case it is essential that you use enameled cast iron to prevent discoloration and change in flavor. Also, cover the pot with wax paper, then with a lid, to seal the flavor in.

Dairy

MINESTRONE

I was anxious to find a nonmeat base for a soup that I could serve with Parmesan cheese and finally found the solution in potato stock. Although one does not taste the potato, the stock enhances the flavor of this light soup. I prefer to make it in advance to allow the flavors to blend.

POTATO STOCK:

5 medium all-purpose potatoes
1 onion, peeled and quartered
1 carrot, cut into large pieces
1 clove garlic, peeled

½ teaspoon kosher salt
5 whole black peppercorns
2 quarts cold water

SOUP:

⅓ cup dried beans (white, baby lima, Great Northern, or any other kind)
1 leek or onion
1 clove garlic
¼ pound green beans
1 stalk broccoli
1 zucchini
½ bunch Italian flat-leaf parsley

1 medium ripe tomato, skinned, seeded, and cubed
1 tablespoon tomato paste
1 tablespoon sweet butter
Black pepper, freshly ground
Parmesan cheese, freshly grated

To make the potato stock: Scrub potato skins thoroughly and slice potatoes. Place all stock ingredients in a large pot. Bring to a boil and cook slowly, covered, till vegetables are soft. Strain stock and discard vegetables. You should have 6 cups potato stock; if not, add more water.

To make the soup: Soak beans separately overnight in enough water to cover by a few inches. Drain and discard beans that remained hard. Cut off dangling roots and a bit of green leaves from leek. Remove tough outer leaves and dice leek or onion. Place in a sieve and wash well under cold running water to remove all sand; drain. Chop garlic fine. Trim green beans and cut into small pieces. Separate broccoli into small florets; peel and cube stem. Trim zucchini and cut into small cubes. Finally, remove half the parsley stems; wash, drain, and chop the rest coarsely.

In a large pot, combine stock with soaked beans. Bring to a boil and cook slowly, covered, for about 30 minutes. Add vegetables, tomato paste, and butter and cook until vegetables are soft, but not mushy. Season. Serve in heated soup bowls sprinkled with Parmesan cheese.

NOTE: Rice or small noodles can be substituted instead of the beans, and of course other vegetables can be added as well.

I suggest buying any dried beans in the health food store rather than the supermarket. They are fresher and cook more quickly.

In the summer use fresh herbs, such as basil, for flavor.

◆The potato stock can be cooked several days ahead of time and refrigerated or frozen. You can refrigerate the soup in the same pot in which you have cooked it, but in that case it is essential that you use enameled cast iron to prevent discoloration and change in flavor. Also, cover the pot with wax paper, then with a lid, to seal the flavor in.

MUSHROOM SOUP

10 SERVINGS   I have only vague memories of Polish delicacies, but I can almost taste the strong flavor and aroma of Polish mushrooms to this day. After much experimentation, I was able to evoke that flavor in a traditional Polish soup by combining Polish dried mushrooms with commercial fresh ones and substituting vegetable bouillon cubes for chicken stock.

Be sure to use only Polish or Czechoslovakian mushrooms; other dried mushrooms do not have the same aroma.

If you like, you can make this soup a day ahead of time.

1 ounce dried Polish or Czechoslovakian mushrooms	4 tablespoons (½ stick) sweet butter
5 cups boiling water	1 cup milk
2 bunches scallions, including green parts	About ½ cup half and half cream or heavy cream
1½ pounds firm fresh mushrooms	Kosher salt
	White pepper, freshly ground
2 vegetable bouillon cubes, 22 grams altogether	12 sprigs dill, snipped

I suggest you use the following: a food processor, a large enameled cast-iron saucepan with lid, and a food mill with a medium blade.

Place dried mushrooms in a small bowl and pour 1 cup of the boiling water over them. Let soak for about 1 hour. Strain soaking liquid through a sieve lined with a paper towel, squeezing mushrooms over sieve to extract more liquid; set liquid aside. Wash soaked mushrooms carefully to remove any sand; set aside. Trim scallions, wipe with a damp paper towel, and chop fine.

Set aside ½ pound of the fresh mushroom caps for garnish. Wipe with a damp paper towel, wrap in a dry paper towel, place in a plastic bag, and refrigerate until needed.

Wipe remaining mushrooms caps and stems clean. Quarter all mushrooms and chop medium fine, in batches, in a food processor fitted with the steel blade. Remove each batch before placing in the next one. Dissolve bouillon cubes in remaining 4 cups boiling water.

Heat butter in a large saucepan until hot. Sauté scallions over low heat until soft. Stir in dried and fresh mushrooms and cook over low heat, stirring with a wooden spoon until mushrooms are well coated with butter. Add reserved strained mushroom liquid, vegetable broth, and milk. Bring to a boil over high heat. Reduce heat and cook slowly, partially covered, for about 10 minutes. Puree soup through a food mill set over a large bowl. Return to saucepan and adjust consistency with half and half or heavy cream. Soup should not be too thin. Season.

Shortly before serving, cut mushroom caps into paper-thin slices. Divide them equally among heated soup bowls and ladle hot soup over them. Garnish with dill.

NOTE: Polish dried mushrooms are available in specialty stores and keep for a very long time. If you cannot find them, use Czechoslovakian ones.

Vegetable bouillon cubes are imported from Switzerland and are available in health food stores and many supermarkets. If you cannot find them, substitute 2 packets MBT broth.

For a rich soup, use heavy cream instead of half and half.

If you like, you can refrigerate this soup in the same saucepan in which it was cooked, but in that case it is essential that you use enameled cast iron to prevent discoloration and change in flavor. Also, cover the pot with a piece of wax paper, then with a lid, to seal the flavor in.

CHLODNIK

In Polish, *chlodnik* means "cooling," which is one of the reasons I like to serve this soup on hot, humid days. It is refreshing, piquant, and requires no cooking. All the ingredients are whisked together and chilled. Serve it in chilled glass bowls.

8 TO 10
SERVINGS

2 cups sour cream
4 to 5 cups buttermilk
About ½ cup sauerkraut juice
15 to 20 sprigs dill, snipped
4 scallions, including green
    parts, chopped fine

1 clove garlic, minced fine
3 to 4 Kirby or regular
    cucumbers
Kosher salt
White pepper, freshly ground

In a large bowl, beat with a whisk sour cream, 4 cups of the buttermilk, and ⅓ cup of the sauerkraut juice until well blended. Stir in most of the dill, the scallions, and the garlic and refrigerate soup overnight.

Several hours before serving, peel cucumbers, trim ends, cut in half lengthwise, remove seeds with a teaspoon, and dice. Place in a sieve, salt lightly, and let drain for 30 minutes.

Pat dry with a paper towel and add to soup. Adjust consistency if needed with remaining buttermilk, and the flavor with remaining sauerkraut juice. Season with salt and pepper. Chill again and serve, garnished with snipped dill.

NOTE: Sauerkraut juice is available in supermarkets.

Kirby cucumbers have less liquid and remain crisper than regular cucumbers.

PERLA MEYER'S STRAWBERRY SOUP

8 TO 10
SERVINGS

I am grateful to Perla Meyer, who taught me this refreshing summer soup many years ago. Make the soup long enough in advance to allow for chilling and serve it in glass bowls so that you can enjoy its deep pink color.

2¼ to 2½ pints fresh
    strawberries
Scant ¾ cup sugar
½ cup cold water
2 teaspoons arrowroot

1 cup freshly squeezed orange
    juice, strained
1 cup good red wine
1 cup sour cream
½ to ¾ cup plain yogurt

I suggest you use a blender.

Rinse, drain, hull, and slice 2 pints of the strawberries. You should have about 4½ cups. Leave the rest for garnish.

Bring strawberries, sugar, and water to a boil over high heat. Dissolve arrowroot in 2 tablespoons cold water and add to berries. Add orange juice and wine. Return to the boil, reduce heat, and cook, uncovered, for several minutes. Let cool a bit.

Puree soup, in batches, adding some sour cream and some yogurt until smooth. The soup should be creamy, but not too thick. Refrigerate. Serve chilled, garnished with sliced strawberries.

NOTE: Arrowroot is a thickening agent and is available in supermarkets.

Strawberries should be flavorful. The amount of sugar you will want to use will vary with the sweetness of the berries, and the amount of yogurt with their juiciness.

If you are not calorie-conscious, you may wish to use sour cream only. I prefer a mixture of sour cream and yogurt, since it is lighter.

Use good quality wine.

Pareve

GAZPACHO

Each summer I wait for the appearance of ripe, flavorful tomatoes to make this delightful uncooked Spanish soup. I serve it chilled and pass chopped vegetables and croutons in individual bowls.

GAZPACHO:

3 pounds ripe, flavorful tomatoes
½ cucumber
4 scallions, including green parts
1 green pepper
1 clove garlic
6 sprigs Italian flat-leaf parsley
1½ to 2 cups tomato juice (depends on juiciness of the tomatoes)

¼ cup olive oil
2 to 3 tablespoons red wine vinegar
About ½ teaspoon cumin powder
Dash Tabasco
Dash Worcestershire sauce
Kosher salt
Black pepper, freshly ground
Fresh lemon juice

VEGETABLE CONDIMENTS:

2 medium ripe tomatoes
2 small cucumbers

2 green peppers
1 medium red onion

CROUTONS:

½ pound day-old whole wheat bread, sliced

2 cloves garlic
¼ cup olive oil

I suggest you use a blender.

To make the soup: Peel, core, seed, and cut tomatoes into large pieces. Peel cucumber, trim end, cut in half lengthwise, remove seeds with a teaspoon, and cut into large pieces. Trim scallions, wipe with a damp paper towel, and cut into large pieces. Seed pepper and cut into large pieces. Peel and quarter garlic. Remove parsley stems and wash leaves.

In a blender, puree, in batches, all soup vegetables plus tomato juice and olive oil until smooth. Pour each batch into a large bowl before pureeing the next one. Stir soup and adjust consistency with tomato juice as needed. Gazpacho should be medium thick.

Season soup well; it should be well seasoned, since the condiments are not. Refrigerate.

To make the condiments: Peel, core, seed, and cut tomatoes into small cubes; place in a bowl. Peel cucumbers, trim ends, cut lengthwise and remove seeds with a teaspoon, and dice. Place in a separate bowl. Seed peppers, cut into same size cubes, and place in a separate bowl. Peel and chop onion coarse and place in a fourth bowl. Cover bowls and refrigerate until needed. All the condiments should be made the day they will be used.

To make the croutons: Trim crusts from bread slices and cut into ½-inch cubes.

Peel and crush garlic with a cleaver or knife blade. Heat olive oil in a skillet until hot. Add garlic and sauté until brown. Discard garlic. Add bread cubes and sauté until light brown, stirring with a wooden spoon. Place croutons on paper towels to drain. Let cool. Wrap in foil, place in a plastic bag, and refrigerate until needed.

NOTE: You can freeze croutons, but be sure to reheat them in order to bring out their flavor.

TOMATO SOUP WITH BASIL

Fresh summer tomatoes and fresh basil are in season together, in time to make this wonderful silky soup. I serve it at room temperature garnished with snipped basil, but it is also very good served hot.

8 SERVINGS

3 cloves garlic
2 medium onions
¼ cup olive oil
8 medium ripe tomatoes, about 4 pounds
1 package MBT Instant Vegetable Broth
1 cup boiling water
½ cup tightly packed basil leaves

1 tablespoon unsalted margarine
2 tablespoons unbleached flour
¼ teaspoon sugar
About 1 teaspoon sherry vinegar
Kosher salt
Black pepper, freshly ground

I suggest you use the following: a food processor, a food mill with a medium blade, and a mesh sieve.

Peel garlic and onions, cut into quarters, and chop fine in a food processor fitted with the steel blade. Heat oil in a large saucepan until hot. Sauté onions and garlic over low heat until soft.

In the meantime, core and cut tomatoes into large pieces. Dissolve MBT in boiling water. Add tomatoes and broth to saucepan. Bring to a boil over high heat, cover, reduce heat, and cook slowly for about 30 minutes, or until tomato skins are separated from flesh.

Puree soup in a food mill. Strain it through a sieve in batches, pushing on solids with a wooden spoon; discard residue. (This technique makes the soup smooth and silky.)

Remove basil stems, rinse leaves, and spin them dry. Cut finely with scissors, leaving a few whole for garnish.

Rinse out the saucepan. Melt margarine, add flour, and stir this roux with a wooden spoon for a few minutes. With a whisk, beat in the tomato soup. Boil, uncovered, for a few minutes, until it is slightly thickened.

Continue to whisk soup again to avoid flour lumps. Remove from heat, add basil, and season with sugar, vinegar, salt, and pepper. At serving time, garnish with reserved basil.

◆If you like, you can refrigerate this soup in the same saucepan in which it was cooked, but in that case it is essential that you use enameled cast iron to prevent discoloration and change in flavor. Also, cover the pot with wax paper, then with a lid, to seal the flavor in.

Poultry

ROAST CHICKEN WITH TARRAGON

The high-heat roasting method makes a moist and crispy chicken, which is also good cold.

3 TO 4 SERVINGS

One 3-pound roasting chicken
½ lemon
2 teaspoons dried tarragon
2 cloves garlic, unpeeled

1½ tablespoons unsalted margarine, melted
Kosher salt
Black pepper, freshly ground

I suggest you use a small roasting pan.

Preheat oven to 450°F. Cut off any excess fat or skin from chicken. Rinse

lightly and pat dry with paper towels. Squeeze lemon into chicken cavity and put in tarragon and garlic. Close cavity by sewing skins together with a thick sewing needle and double thread. Brush chicken with melted margarine and sprinkle lightly with salt and pepper.

Place chicken on its side in a roasting pan and roast in the center of the oven for 15 to 20 minutes. Turn to the other side and roast for 15 to 20 minutes. Finally, turn chicken on its back and roast for the final 15 to 20 minutes, or until golden brown. Total roasting time should be 45 minutes to 1 hour.

To serve, cut thread with scissors and remove. Chicken can be prepared earlier in the day, refrigerated, then brought back to room temperature and roasted.

SPLIT STUFFED ROAST CHICKEN

Chicken prepared this way looks like a butterfly. The skin is crisp and golden; the meat, protected by the stuffing, is moist and delicious.

6 TO 8 SERVINGS

½ pound chicken livers

2 tablespoons brandy (Cognac)

Two 3-pound roasting chickens

¼ pound firm fresh mushrooms

4 cloves garlic

4 medium shallots

6 sprigs Italian flat-leaf parsley

4½ tablespoons unsalted margarine, at room temperature

1 teaspoon dried thyme

¼ cup unseasoned bread crumbs

Kosher salt

Black pepper, freshly ground

1 cup chicken stock, heated

I suggest you use a food processor and a baking dish large enough to hold the chickens in a single layer, or two dishes, each large enough to hold one chicken.

Preheat broiler. Cut chicken livers in half, remove any green spots, which are bitter. Line the broiler pan with foil. Place livers on foil and broil as close to heat source as possible for 1 minute to sear them, or to your taste. Cube livers, place in a bowl, pour brandy (Cognac) over them, and let marinate for 1 hour.

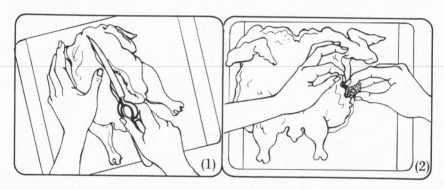

With poultry shears, cut out entire backbone of chickens (1). (Save for stock if you like.) Flatten chickens by pressing them with the heel of your hand. Remove any loose fat. With a small knife or your fingers, loosen skin from breasts, thighs, and some of the drumsticks, being careful not to tear the skin.

Wipe mushrooms with a damp paper towel. Quarter them and mince fine in a food processor fitted with the steel blade. Peel and quarter garlic and shallots and mince in food processor. Remove parsley stems; wash leaves, spin dry, and chop fine.

Cream 4 tablespoons of the margarine in a bowl with a wooden spoon.

Add shallots, garlic, chopped parsley, thyme, bread crumbs, and mush-rooms. Last, add liver cubes and mix well. Adjust seasoning. Push stuffing, a little at a time, under the loosened skin and reshape the bird (2). Pat dry with paper towels. Sprinkle lightly with salt and pepper.

Preheat oven to 375°F. Brush a baking dish or dishes with remaining margarine. Place birds in pan skin side up and roast for about 1 hour. Baste frequently with the heated chicken stock. For extra crispness, broil chickens for 1 to 2 minutes at the end. Skim off surface fat from pan juices and serve degreased juice with chicken.

◆This dish can be completely assembled in advance and refrigerated, then brought back to room temperature and roasted.

BROILED CHICKEN
WITH HONEY AND LEMON

➢➢➢

Simple to make, well seasoned, and delicious. It can also be served at room temperature.

3 TO 4
SERVINGS

One 3- to 3½-pound roasting chicken

MARINADE:

8 sprigs Italian flat-leaf
  parsley
2 cloves garlic, minced
Juice of 1½ lemons, strained

3 to 4 tablespoons thin
  Chinese soy sauce
3 to 4 tablespoons honey

Ask your butcher to cut chicken into eight serving pieces. The joints should be cut cleanly, otherwise the pieces are unattractive and sometimes have protruding splinters. The backbone will have to be removed, as well as the wing tips, gizzard, and neck. (Save those for stock.) You will have two breast halves, two legs, two backs, and two wings. Cut off excess fat and skin. Pat chicken dry with paper towels and place in a glass or ceramic dish.

To make the marinade: Remove parsley stems; wash leaves, spin dry, and chop fine. In a small bowl, combine garlic, parsley, lemon juice, soy sauce, and honey. Cover chicken with marinade and refrigerate for several hours. Bring back to room temperature before broiling.

To serve: Preheat broiler. Line the broiler pan with foil and place chicken parts, skin side down, on it. Broil, not too close to heat source (you don't want honey to burn), for 10 minutes on one side and about 8 to 10 minutes on the other side. The skin will be dark brown and the meat soft and juicy. Watch it.

SPLIT BROILED CHICKEN WITH GREEN PEPPERCORN SAUCE

3 TO 4 SERVINGS

Chicken prepared this way looks like a butterfly; it is simple to make. You can also serve it without the sauce, either hot or at room temperature.

One 3- to 3½-pound roasting chicken
Juice of 1 small lemon, strained
2 tablespoons thin Chinese soy sauce

SAUCE:

3 tablespoons red wine vinegar
¼ cup dry red wine
1 teaspoon green peppercorns, drained, chopped coarse

2 tablespoons unsalted margarine, at room temperature
2 tablespoons Dijon-type mustard
1 tablespoon dried tarragon

½ cup Strong Chicken Stock (page 257)
Kosher salt
Black pepper, freshly ground

With poultry shears, cut away backbone of chicken. Flatten chicken by pressing it with heel of your hand. Remove loose fat and excess skin. Pat dry with paper towels. Coat with lemon juice and soy sauce and let marinate for 1 hour.

Preheat broiler. Line the broiler pan with foil. Place chicken, skin side down, on foil.

Combine margarine, mustard, and tarragon. Brush half of this mixture over chicken and broil close to heat source for 15 minutes. Turn chicken over, coat with remaining mixture, and broil for another 10 to 15 minutes, or until chicken is soft and crispy.

To make the sauce: While the chicken is broiling, boil vinegar and wine in a small saucepan until reduced to about 1½ tablespoons. Add chopped peppercorns and stock and continue boiling for another 5 minutes. Skim off surface fat and season. Serve sauce on the side.

NOTE: Green peppercorns can be found in specialty stores. They usually come in glass jars and can be refrigerated indefinitely.

CHICKEN WITH VINEGAR

3 TO 4 SERVINGS

A favorite. All the ingredients blend into a subtle, flavorful, silky sauce. If you like, you can make this dish earlier in the day and reheat it.

One 3- to 3½-pound roastng
  chicken, cut in eight pieces
1 to 2 tablespoons olive oil
1 tablespoon unsalted
  margarine
Kosher salt
Black pepper, freshly ground
15 cloves garlic, unpeeled
3 tablespoons red wine vinegar
2 medium ripe tomatoes or 4
  plum tomatoes, cut into
  small pieces

1 tablespoon tomato paste
¾ cup Strong Chicken Stock
  (page 257)
¼ cup dry white wine
Bouquet garni: ¼ teaspoon
  dried thyme, 1 bay leaf, and
  4 sprigs Italian flat-leaf
  parsley, tied in a
  cheesecloth
¼ bunch basil

Ask your butcher to cut chicken into eight serving pieces. The joints should be cut cleanly, otherwise the pieces are unattractive and sometimes have protruding splinters. The backbone will have to be removed, as well as the wing tips, gizzard, and neck. (Save those for stock.) You will have two breast halves, two legs, two backs, and two wings. Cut off excess fat or skin. Pat chicken dry with paper towels.

In a saucepan, heat 1 tablespoon of the olive oil with the margarine. Sauté three or four pieces of chicken at a time over medium-high heat until golden on all sides, turning with tongs. Remove finished pieces to a bowl and sprinkle lightly with salt and pepper.

Place dark parts of chicken, skin side down, in a pan and lay breasts, skin side up, on top. (Chicken breasts require less cooking time. If cooked too long, they become dry.) Bury garlic cloves among chicken parts. Cover and simmer for 20 minutes. Sprinkle top with vinegar, increase heat, and boil till vinegar has disappeared. Add tomatoes, tomato paste, stock, wine, and bouquet garni. Cook gently, covered, for about 15 minutes, or until chicken is soft.

Remove chicken parts with tongs to a bowl. Squeeze out liquid from bouquet garni and discard. Strain sauce through a mesh sieve, pushing solids with a wooden spoon to obtain all liquid; discard residue. Return sauce to saucepan, and boil over high heat till thickened. Return chicken parts to sauce.

Remove basil stems; wash leaves, spin dry, and cut coarsely with a scissors. Stir basil leaves into sauce and correct seasoning. Serve with rice.

CHICKEN WITH TART APPLES AND CIDER

This is an adaptation of a dish from Normandy, where apples are in abundance and where the apple brandy Calvados is made. The original recipe is made with cream, butter, and egg yolks.

3 TO 4
SERVINGS

Mine is a simplified, almost noncaloric, version that can be made earlier in the day and reheated.

One 3- to 3½-pound frying chicken, cut in eight pieces
2 leeks
3 tablespoons olive oil
3 tablespoons unsalted margarine
Kosher salt
Black pepper, freshly ground
¼ cup Calvados or good applejack, heated

Bouquet garni: 1 bay leaf, 10 black peppercorns, ½ teaspoon dried thyme, 5 sprigs Italian flat-leaf parsley, tied in a cheesecloth
¾ cup medium-dry hard apple cider or apple juice
½ pound firm fresh mushrooms
3 large tart apples (Granny Smith or greening)
1 tablespoon brown sugar

I suggest you use an enameled cast-iron saucepan with lid.

Ask your butcher to cut chicken into eight serving pieces. The joints should be cut cleanly, otherwise the pieces are unattractive and sometimes have protruding splinters. The backbone will have to be removed, as well as the wing tips, gizzard, and neck. (Save those for stock.) You will have two breast halves, two legs, two backs, and two wings. Cut off excess fat or skin. Pat chicken dry with paper towels.

Cut off dangling roots and green leaves from leeks. Remove tough outer leaves and discard; chop the rest coarsely. Place in a sieve and wash well under cold running water to remove all sand; drain.

Heat 2 tablespoons of the olive oil and 1 tablespoon of the margarine in a skillet. Sauté three to four chicken pieces at a time over medium-high heat until golden on all sides. Turn with tongs. Transfer chicken pieces to a saucepan as they are finished and sprinkle lightly with salt and pepper. Pour heated Calvados or applejack over chicken and ignite. When flames have subsided, remove chicken breasts and reserve. (They require less cooking time.)

Add rest of chicken, the leeks, bouquet garni, and apple cider or juice to the saucepan. Bring to a boil, cover with wax paper and a lid, and cook gently for 15 minutes. Turn chicken pieces over, add the reserved breasts, skin side down, and simmer for another 10 minutes.

Meanwhile, wipe mushrooms clean with a damp paper towel and slice thin. Place 1 tablespoon of the margarine in the same skillet and heat until hot. Add sliced mushrooms and sauté over high heat, stirring with a wooden spoon until just coated with margarine. Transfer to a bowl and sprinkle lightly with salt and pepper.

Peel, core, and quarter apples. Cut each quarter into three wedges and pat dry with paper towels.

Heat remaining 1 tablespoon margarine and remaining 1 tablespoon olive oil in the skillet. Sauté apples and sugar over high heat, stirring with a wooden spoon, for about 5 minutes, or until apples are lightly brown and still firm.

Skim surface fat from sauce. Remove bouquet garni and discard. Stir in mushrooms and apples and season with salt and pepper. Serve with rice.

NOTE: Medium-hard cider is fermented apple cider and is available in liquor stores. I prefer to cook chicken with cider, which gives it a tangy flavor; chicken cooked with apple juice has a milder taste.

LEMON CHICKEN

→≫

A delicate Chinese dish I learned in Millie Chan's cooking class. The chicken is crispy on the outside, moist and tender on the inside.

2 TO 3 SERVINGS

2 medium chicken breasts, skinned, boned, and split to make four pieces

MARINADE:

1 tablespoon thin Chinese soy sauce

1 teaspoon sesame oil
1 teaspoon kosher salt

SAUCE:

1 cup Strong Chicken Stock (page 257) or ½ ounce kosher consommé cube dissolved in 1 cup boiling water

1½ teaspoons cornstarch
3 tablespoons white vinegar

¼ cup fresh lemon juice, about 1 lemon, strained
¼ cup sugar
2 scallions, including green parts
Kosher salt

GARNISH:

1 to 2 lemons

BATTER:

½ cup unbleached flour
¼ cup cornstarch
2 teaspoons baking powder
¼ teaspoon sugar

¾ cup cold water
1 tablespoon vegetable oil, heated

2 cups peanut oil

I suggest you use a wok and a wire skimmer.

To prepare the chicken: Cut each piece of chicken in half, so that you have eight pieces. Combine marinade ingredients. Cover chicken with marinade and let stand for 30 minutes or longer.

To make the sauce: In a small saucepan, combine stock or consommé, cornstarch, vinegar, lemon juice, and sugar. Keep near the stove.

Trim scallions and wipe with a damp paper towel. Cut into very thin strips. Keep near the sauce. (They will wilt if added too soon.)

To prepare the garnish: Cut lemon with a serrated knife into very thin rounds. Trim off all the rind, leaving only the smallest layer of pith to prevent the rounds from falling apart.

To make the batter: Whisk flour, cornstarch, baking powder, sugar, and water until smooth. Reserve hot oil till last minute before deep frying.

To deep fry the chicken: Preheat oven to 325°F. Have a cookie sheet, a rack, and paper towels ready.

Heat a wok over high heat. Add peanut oil and heat to 350°F on a frying thermometer. (To test if oil is hot enough without a frying thermometer, dip a chopstick into batter, then dip it into oil: If batter sizzles, oil is hot enough; if it burns, oil is too hot. The temperature must be just right; if too hot, batter will burn; if not hot enough, batter will absorb too much oil and taste greasy.)

Stir heated oil into batter. Dip three pieces of chicken into batter. Let some batter drip back into bowl and place chicken carefully in oil in wok. Deep fry over medium heat for about 3 minutes, or until golden and crisp. Turn frequently with chopsticks to get an even color. Remove finished pieces with a skimmer to a cookie sheet lined with several layers of paper towels, changing them frequently as needed. Place drained chicken on a rack set over a cookie sheet in oven while you are frying the next batch.

To serve: Boil sauce until it thickens to a thin glaze, add scallions, and season to taste with salt.

Cut each piece of chicken into three pieces without cutting through completely. Arrange on a heated platter. Decorate with lemon rounds. Pour sauce into a sauceboat and spoon it over chicken at the table. This is not the traditional way to serve lemon chicken, but I prefer it because it keeps the batter crisp.

NOTE: There is enough batter for three whole breasts.

CHICKEN BREASTS
WITH LEMON AND RAISINS

4 TO 6
SERVINGS

My family and I rarely tire of chicken because it can be prepared in so many different ways. Fortunately, kosher poultry is very good.

This family favorite has a sweet-and-sour taste. I serve it with rice and allow 1 to 1½ chicken breasts per person.

This dish can also be prepared earlier in the day and reheated.

SAUCE:

¾ cup seedless golden raisins
½ cup brandy (Cognac)
8 chicken wings
2 tablespoons unsalted
  margarine
1 tablespoon olive oil
Kosher salt

White pepper, freshly ground
5 medium white onions
Grated rind of 2 lemons
Juice of 3 large ripe lemons,
  about 5 ounces, strained
1½ cups Strong Chicken
  Stock (page 257)

3 tablespoons unbleached flour
1½ tablespoons unsalted
  margarine
1½ tablespoons olive oil
4 medium chicken breasts,
  skinned, boned, and split in
  half to make eight pieces

Kosher salt
White pepper, freshly ground

I suggest you use the following: a food processor and an enameled cast-iron saucepan with lid, large enough to fit the chicken breasts in a single layer.

To make the sauce: Place raisins in a small bowl, cover with brandy (Cognac), and let stand for about 1 hour.

Pat wings dry with paper towels. Heat margarine and olive oil in a small saucepan until hot. Sauté three to four wings at a time until golden. Remove finished pieces with tongs and sprinkle with salt and pepper.

Slice onions into very thin rounds in a food processor fitted with the slicing attachment, pressing hard on the feed tube. Sauté sliced onions in the same saucepan over low heat until transparent. Add wings, raisins with brandy (Cognac), lemon rind, lemon juice, and stock. Bring to a boil, cover pan with a sheet of wax paper and then a lid, and boil gently for about 1 hour, or until wings are soft.

Remove wings (which were used only for their flavor and can be saved to be eaten at a later time if you wish). Skim surface fat from sauce. Season with salt and pepper. (If you like, make sauce a day in advance.)

To make the chicken: Spread flour on a sheet of wax paper. Heat margarine and olive oil in skillet until hot. Pat chicken breasts dry with paper towels. Dip three or four pieces into flour at a time, shake off excess, and sauté over low to medium heat, turning with tongs, until outside of chicken is just seared and still pale and inside is pink. Transfer finished pieces to saucepan and sprinkle lightly with salt and pepper; repeat with second batch.

Pour sauce over chicken and cook for a few minutes, covered, until inside of chicken loses its pale pink color and turns white. To make it heat through quickly, turn pieces with tongs. Be careful not to overcook chicken, or it will become tough and dry. Adjust seasoning again.

◆If you wish to prepare this dish earlier in the day, pour sauce over chicken, set aside, and then cook through just before serving.

CHICKEN BREASTS IN CURRY SAUCE

10 TO 12
SERVINGS

A dish for a large buffet dinner, one that looks complicated, but is in fact quite simple. The inspiration for it came from two sources: an old friend of mine and Michael Field. The entire dish, except for the condiments, should be prepared a day ahead of time to enable the flavors to blend and then carefully reheated at serving time. Serve with condiments, rice, and Indian bread.

About 2 tablespoons Madras
  curry powder
⅓ cup unbleached flour
About 5 tablespoons unsalted
  margarine
About 5 tablespoons olive oil
8 medium to large chicken
  breasts, skinned, boned, and
  split in half to make sixteen
  pieces
Juice of 1 lemon, strained
Kosher salt
Black pepper, freshly ground
2 medium onions
4 stalks celery

Three 7½-ounce cans
  caponata eggplant appetizer
  (Progresso brand)
¾ cup chutney
1 to 1½ cups Strong Chicken
  Stock (page 257)
½ cup dry white wine
About 2 tablespoons tomato
  paste
½ teaspoon turmeric
6 cardamom pods, freshly
  ground
4 medium tart apples (Granny
  Smith or greening)

CONDIMENTS:
¾ cup dried currants
⅓ cup port
¾ cup seedless golden raisins
⅓ cup brandy (Cognac)
2 ripe avocados, sliced
Juice of ½ lemon, strained
1 cup chutney

1 cup shredded or sliced
  unsweetened coconut
1 cup sliced, slivered, or
  coarsely chopped blanched
  almonds, toasted
5 scallions, including green
  parts, chopped coarse

I suggest you use a food processor and an enameled cast-iron saucepan with lid.

To make the chicken: Preheat oven to 325°F. Wrap curry powder in foil and warm in oven for a few minutes to bring out flavor.

Spread flour on a sheet of wax paper. Heat 3 tablespoons of the margarine and 3 tablespoons of the olive oil in a skillet until hot. Pat chicken breasts dry with paper towels. Dip three or four pieces into flour at a time, shake off excess, and sauté over low to medium heat, turning with tongs, until outside of chicken is just seared and still pale and inside is pink.

Transfer finished pieces to a dish. When all pieces are sautéed, cut them into large, more-or-less uniform pieces, about 1½ inches. Place in a large saucepan and season with lemon juice, salt, and pepper.

Peel, quarter, and chop onions fine in a food processor fitted with the steel blade. Peel celery, cut into pieces and chop in the same manner. Add another tablespoon each margarine and olive oil to skillet and sauté onions and celery over low heat until transparent. Stir in curry powder, caponata, chutney, 1 cup of the stock, wine, tomato paste, turmeric, and cardamom. Bring to a boil and cook gently for a few minutes, stirring from time to time. Pour this sauce over chicken.

Peel, quarter, core, and slice apples thin. Add remaining 1 tablespoon margarine and 1 tablespoon olive oil to skillet and sauté apples over medium heat, stirring with a wooden spoon for about 5 minutes, or until they are soft, but still retain their shape. Add to the chicken and mix well. Adjust seasoning and consistency of sauce with remaining ½ cup stock. Let the taste of the curry develop before you add extra curry powder. Let chicken cool, then refrigerate in the same saucepan you cooked it in, with a sheet of wax paper beneath the lid to keep the flavor in.

To prepare the condiments: Place currants in a small bowl with the port and place raisins in a small bowl with the brandy. Let soak for about 3 hours. Both currants and raisins need time to absorb the wine and liquor. Slice avocados shortly before serving and sprinkle with lemon juice to prevent discoloration. Serve each condiment in a separate bowl.

To serve: Preheat oven to 400°F. Bring chicken back to room temperature. Cook in oven until inside of chicken loses its pale pink color and turns white. To help it heat through quickly, stir from time to time. It may take about 20 to 30 minutes. If you are doubling this recipe, heat it in two separate saucepans. Be careful not to overcook chicken, or it will become tough and dry. Adjust seasoning again.

NOTE: It is important to use medium to large chicken breasts and to cut them into large pieces, or they may dry out while cooking.

Caponata is available in most supermarkets. Cardamom seeds are available in specialty stores, and so is coconut. Health food stores also carry these ingredients. You can grind cardamom seeds in a Mouli grater and then discard the dry outer skin. You can also add other condiments, such as chopped seeded green peppers, chopped peeled and seeded cucumbers, cubed fresh pineapple, or caramelized bananas.

For a large buffet you can serve this dish in the same saucepan, chafing dish, or casserole.

CHICKEN BREASTS IN TOMATO–MUSHROOM SAUCE

8 TO 10 SERVINGS

I find myself making this piquant dish frequently. Chicken breasts are sautéed briefly, then combined with an aromatic, well-seasoned sauce. I allow 1 to 1½ chicken breasts per person. The entire dish can be assembled earlier in the day and reheated.

1 ounce dried Italian mushrooms
1 cup boiling water
3 tablespoons unbleached flour
3½ tablespoons olive oil
3½ tablespoons unsalted margarine
7 medium chicken breasts, skinned, boned, and split in half to make fourteen pieces
8 shallots
3 cloves garlic
½ bunch Italian flat-leaf parsley

½ cup extra-dry vermouth or dry white wine
1 cup Brown Veal Stock (page 255)
1-pound 12-ounce can peeled Italian tomatoes, drained, and chopped coarse
About ¼ teaspoon Worcestershire sauce
⅛ teaspoon Tabasco
Kosher salt
Black pepper, freshly ground

I suggest you use a food processor and a 12-by-4-inch enameled cast-iron saucepan with lid to fit the chicken breasts in a single layer.

Place dried mushrooms in a small bowl and pour boiling water over them. Let soak for about 1 hour. Strain soaking liquid through a sieve lined with a paper towel, squeezing mushrooms over sieve to extract more liquid; set liquid aside. Wash soaked mushrooms carefully to remove any sand. Pat dry with paper towels and chop coarsely; set aside.

Spread flour on a sheet of wax paper. Heat 3 tablespoons of the olive oil and 3 tablespoons of the margarine in a skillet until hot. Pat chicken pieces dry with paper towels. Dip three or four pieces into flour at a time, shake off excess, and sauté over low to medium heat, turning with tongs, until outside of chicken is just seared and still pale and inside is pink. Transfer finished pieces to a large saucepan and sprinkle lightly with salt and pepper.

To make the sauce: Peel, quarter, and finely chop shallots and garlic in a food processor fitted with the steel blade. Remove bottom half of parsley stems; wash leaves, spin dry, and chop fine in food processor.

Heat remaining ½ tablespoon olive oil and ½ tablespoon margarine in the same skillet and sauté shallots and garlic over low heat until soft and transparent. Add vermouth or wine and boil down over high heat until 1 tablespoon liquid remains. Add reserved mushroom liquid, chopped mushrooms, stock, and tomatoes to sauce along with parsley and seasoning. Boil gently for about 5 minutes and season well; sauce should be spicy.

Pour sauce over chicken and cook for a few minutes, covered, until inside of chicken loses its pale pink color and turns white. To help it heat through quickly, turn pieces with tongs. Be careful not to overcook chicken, or it will become tough and dry. Adjust seasoning again.

NOTE: You can pound chicken breasts between two lightly oiled sheets of wax paper to make them resemble veal scaloppini. In that case, do not make the dish in advance, or it will become too dry.

◆If you wish to prepare this dish earlier in the day, pour sauce over chicken and then cook through just before serving.

ROLLED STUFFED CHICKEN BREASTS

My favorite way to cook chicken breasts. They are filled with an aromatic mushroom filling, looking like little packages, and served in a natural sauce.

6 TO 8 SERVINGS

If you develop a good relationship with your butcher, he will pound them for you; if not, you can do it yourself. I generally allow 1 to 1½ packages per person. This dish is good served with Plain Boiled Rice (page 160) and Stir-Fried Snow Peas (page 149).

FILLING:

1 ounce dried Italian
  mushrooms or dried morels
  or a mixture of both
1 cup boiling water
10 medium shallots
1 tablespoon unsalted
  margarine
½ pound firm fresh
  mushrooms

1 bunch Italian flat-leaf
  parsley
1 bunch chives
¼ cup olive oil
About ¼ cup fresh lemon
  juice, strained
About 1 tablespoon kosher
  salt
Black pepper, freshly ground

CHICKEN AND SAUCE:

5 large chicken breasts, boned,
  skinned, pounded, and split
  in half to make ten pieces
3 tablespoons unbleached flour
About 3 tablespoons olive oil
About 3 tablespoons unsalted
  margarine
Kosher salt

Black pepper, freshly ground
¼ cup extra-dry vermouth or
  dry white wine
1½ cups Brown Veal Stock
  (page 255), reduced to 1 cup
About 1 to 2 tablespoons
  fresh lemon juice, strained
1 teaspoon dried tarragon

I suggest you use the following: a food processor; an enameled cast-iron saucepan with lid, large enough to fit the chicken pieces in a single layer; and cotton string.

To make the filling: Place dried mushrooms or morels in a small bowl and pour boiling water over them. Let soak for about 1 hour. Strain soaking liquid through a sieve lined with a paper towel, squeezing mushrooms over sieve to extract more liquid; set liquid aside. Wash soaked mushrooms carefully to remove sand (especially morels). Pat dry with paper towels, chop coarsely, and place in a large bowl.

Peel, quarter, and chop shallots fine in a food processor fitted with the steel blade. Heat margarine in a skillet until hot. Sauté shallots over medium heat for 2 minutes only (they will still be raw). Add shallots to chopped mushrooms. Wipe fresh mushrooms with a damp paper towel, trim stem ends, quarter, and chop coarsely, in batches, in food processor. Remove each batch before chopping next one. Add to shallots. Remove parsley stems; wash leaves, spin dry, and chop fine in food processor. Rinse chives, dry with paper towels, and snip with scissors into small bits. Add parsley and chives to other vegetables. Add oil and season with lemon juice, salt, and pepper; the filling should be well seasoned.

To make and stuff the chicken breasts: If your butcher will not do this for you, pound chicken breasts between two lightly oiled sheets of wax paper with a smooth meat pounder in order to flatten them. The pieces should be about ⅛ inch thick and will almost double in width. If some of the breast meat separates, remove it, shred it, and leave for the sauce.

Place chicken breasts on a sheet of wax paper. Spread 1 tablespoon filling (or more, depending on the size of the breast) along the longer side of each breast and fold over halfway. Fold the shorter side in toward the center, then continue rolling the longer side to make a little package (1). Tie with

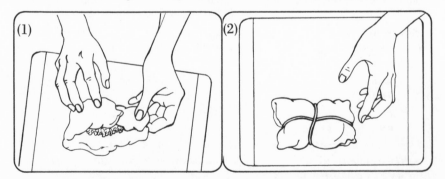

strings like a parcel (2). Repeat until all the breasts are rolled. Place the little parcels on paper towels to keep dry. If you have some filling left over, save it for the sauce.

Spread flour on a sheet of wax paper. Heat half the oil and half the margarine in a skillet until hot. Dip three or four chicken parcels at a time into flour, shake off excess, and sauté over low to medium heat, turning with tongs, until chicken loses its pink color and turns white. Transfer finished parcels to saucepan. Add remaining margarine and oil to skillet and sauté the rest. Sprinkle finished chicken lightly with salt and pepper and leave to cool completely.

To make the sauce: Using the same skillet, and without adding extra shortening, sauté leftover shredded chicken bits, if any. Add any remaining filling, the reserved strained mushroom liquid, vermouth or wine, stock, lemon juice, and tarragon. Boil sauce for a few minutes and correct seasoning.

Cut strings tying chicken and discard them. Pour sauce over chicken, shake pan, and cook for a few minutes until inside of chicken loses its pink color and turns white. Adjust seasoning again. To help chicken heat through quickly, turn the pieces with tongs. Be very careful not to overcook the chicken, or it will become tough and dry.

◆If you wish to prepare this dish earlier in the day, pour sauce over stringless parcels and cook through just before serving.

STEAMED CHICKEN SALAD

⇢⟫⟫

I have adopted an Oriental recipe in which the chicken is first marinated, then steamed, and finally coated with a strong vinaigrette. The natural flavor of the chicken is thus preserved, and it remains moist and firm. I serve it on a bed of alfalfa sprouts, watercress, arugula and surround the salad with other vegetables, such as steamed green beans, steamed asparagus, cucumbers, and so on.

8 TO 10
SERVINGS

8 medium chicken breasts, boned, skinned, and split to make sixteen pieces	¼ to ½ bunch fresh basil
	¼ to ½ bunch Italian flat-leaf parsley
¼ cup olive oil	About ½ cup strong Vinaigrette Dressing (page 264)
¼ cup fresh lemon juice, strained	
White pepper, freshly ground	Kosher salt

I suggest you use the following: a wok with a cover, a metal rack that fits into it, and a Pyrex or heatproof ceramic dish that fits into the wok.

Cut chicken into 1-by-1-inch pieces and place, preferably in a single layer, in a glass dish. Mix together olive oil, lemon juice, and 1 teaspoon of the pepper. Pour over chicken, cover with plastic wrap, and refrigerate for about 8 hours or overnight.

To steam the chicken: Place a metal rack in a wok, add 1 quart water, and bring to a boil over high heat. Drain chicken pieces of their marinade and place as many as will fit in a single layer on a heatproof dish; set on rack. Steam chicken, covered, over high heat for about 5 to 6 minutes, or until it just loses its pale pink color. Remove with tongs to a bowl and proceed with the next batch, adding more boiling water to wok as needed. If too much liquid accumulates in dish during steaming, pour off.

Let chicken cool and pour off accumulated juices. Cut chicken pieces, if you like, into smaller, more uniform pieces. (It is easier to do this after chicken has been steamed.)

Remove basil and parsley stems. Wash leaves, spin dry, chop coarsely. Toss chicken with some of the Vinaigrette Dressing and chopped herbs. Season with salt and pepper.

Serve salad at room temperature with extra dressing on the side. If you like, you can substitute scallions or chives for the basil.

◆This salad can be made a day ahead of time.

BROILED OR ROASTED ROCK CORNISH HENS

2 SERVINGS   Quick, easy, well seasoned, and elegant. They resemble large butterflies.

Two ¾- to 1-pound Rock Cornish hens
MARINADE:

Juice of ½ lemon, about 2 tablespoons, strained	2 medium shallots, minced
2 tablespoons vegetable oil	½-inch piece fresh gingerroot, peeled and minced
1 tablespoon honey	
1½ tablespoons black Chinese soy sauce	

With poultry shears or sturdy scissors, cut away backbone from each hen. Press down to flatten, and place in a glass or ceramic dish.

Mix marinade ingredients and pour over hens. Let stand for a couple of hours, turning from time to time. The flavor of the hens is delicate, so do not let them marinate too long.

Preheat broiler. Line the broiler pan with foil and place hens, skin side down, on it. Broil in the center of the oven for about 10 minutes. Turn over and broil for about 8 to 10 minutes longer. Watch hens carefully; the skin should be slightly charred and crisp and the meat soft.

To roast: Preheat oven to 450°F. Roast hens for about 15 minutes on each side.

NOTE: If fresh Rock Cornish hens are unavailable, use frozen ones, but make sure to rinse them well, since they tend to be salty. Select small hens. Those over 1 pound are too large for single servings.

ROAST DUCK

The only kosher ducks I know of are the Long Island variety. They have a thick layer of fat underneath the skin and are difficult to cook so that they have a crisp, fatless skin yet are not overcooked. I have adopted a Chinese method of roasting duck; the duck is boiled briefly, patted dry, and then blown dry before being roasted at high heat. The boiling opens the duck's pores, and the heat from the blower keeps them open so that the fat pours out. Try the duck with any of the following sauces, or simply brushed with honey.

2 TO 3 SERVINGS

One 3½- to 4-pound duck
2 to 3 tablespoons black
   Chinese soy sauce (depends
   on the saltiness of the duck;
   frozen ones tend to be more
   salty)

2 cloves garlic, minced
Black pepper, freshly ground

I suggest you use an electric hair blower and a roasting pan with a rack.

Preheat oven to 450°F. Remove loose fat from inside duck's cavity. With scissors, cut off excess skin, especially around the neck and cavity. Boil water in a large pot, enough to cover duck. Drop duck into boiling water, return to the boil, and continue boiling, covered, for 5 minutes. Remove duck, drain, and pat dry with a dish towel. Leave duck on towel and blow dry the skin with the hair blower for about 8 minutes, wiping the skin with the towel as you blow it. Prick skin with a fork, especially around groin and under wings. Coat skin with soy sauce, garlic, and pepper and place on a rack.

   Roast, breast side up, in center of oven for 25 minutes. Pour off fat. Turn duck over and roast, breast side down, for 25 minutes. Pour off fat again. Turn over again and roast for another 15 minutes. Keep pouring off fat. The total roasting time is 1 hour and 5 minutes. Cut away backbone with poultry shears and carve duck into quarters or eighths.

   I serve this duck with any of the following sauces, or just brushed with honey and broiled for a few minutes (far away from the heat to prevent honey from burning).

You can carve the roast duck 1 hour before serving it. When ready to serve, broil for a few minutes to crisp up the skin.

VINEGAR AND RAISIN SAUCE:

¼ cup seedless dark raisins
1 tablespoon brandy (Cognac)
½ tablespoon olive oil
½ tablespoon unsalted margarine
3 medium shallots, minced
1 clove garlic, minced
3 tablespoons red wine vinegar

½ cup dark Brown Veal Stock (page 255)
1 tablespoon currant jelly
½ teaspoon Dijon-type mustard
Kosher salt
Black pepper, freshly ground

To make Vinegar and Raisin Sauce: Soak raisins in brandy (Cognac) for 30 minutes. Heat olive oil and margarine in a small saucepan and sauté shallots and garlic over low heat until soft and transparent. Add vinegar and boil over high heat until liquid is reduced by half. Add stock, currant jelly, mustard, and raisins. Boil for 5 minutes and season well. (The sauce should be tart.)

TOMATO–OLIVE SAUCE:

10 pearl onions, 1 inch in diameter and uniform in size
¼ bunch Italian flat-leaf parsley
7 green olives
1 teaspoon capers
2 tablespoons olive oil
1 tablespoon unsalted margarine
2 medium shallots, minced
2 cloves garlic, minced

⅓ cup dry red wine
½ cup Brown Veal Stock (page 255)
8-ounce can peeled Italian tomatoes, drained and chopped fine
About ½ teaspoon Dijon-type mustard
About ½ teaspoon fresh lemon juice
Black pepper, freshly ground

To make Tomato–Olive Sauce: Peel onions. Remove bottom half of parsley stems; wash leaves, spin dry, and chop fine. Pit olives and cut into slivers. Rinse capers and chop fine. Heat 1 tablespoon of the olive oil and the margarine in a small saucepan and sauté onions until light brown. Add remaining 1 tablespoon olive oil along with shallots and garlic and sauté till soft. Add wine and boil over high heat till 1 tablespoon remains. Add stock, tomatoes, parsley, olives, capers, mustard, and lemon juice. Simmer, covered, for about 25 minutes. Season well with pepper. (The sauce should be spicy.)

GREEN PEPPERCORN SAUCE:

2 medium shallots, minced

2 cloves garlic, minced

3 tablespoons red wine vinegar

½ teaspoon cornstarch

½ cup Brown Veal Stock
  (page 255)

About 1 teaspoon Dijon-type
  mustard

1 teaspoon green peppercorns,
  chopped coarse

Kosher salt

To make Green Peppercorn Sauce: In a small saucepan, combine shallots, garlic, and vinegar. Boil over high heat until shallots are dry. Dissolve cornstarch in stock and stir into sauce along with mustard and peppercorns. Boil for a few minutes. Season well.

NOTE: Avoid ducks that weigh over 5 pounds; they tend to be tough. If buying frozen ducks, check if skin is salty; if so, rinse thoroughly.

All the sauces can be made in advance.

Green peppercorns can be found in specialty stores. They usually come in glass jars and can be refrigerated indefinitely.

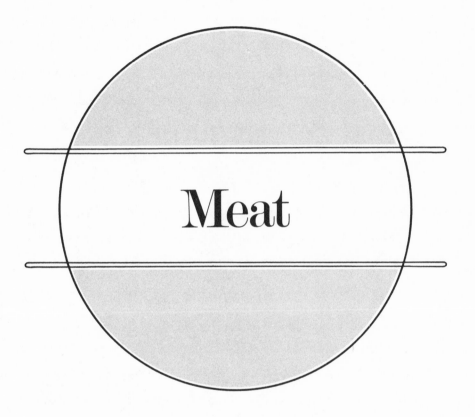

Meat

BARBECUED STEAK WITH BASIL

A summer favorite of mine when basil is plentiful and barbecu-   4 SERVINGS
ing is convenient.

BASIL MARINADE:

1 large bunch basil
Juice of 1 large ripe lemon,
    about ¼ cup, strained
2 cloves garlic, quartered

1 teaspoon kosher salt
3 tablespoons olive oil
Black pepper, freshly ground

2½ pounds deveined center-cut minute steak, trimmed of
    fat and gristle

I suggest you use a food processor and a ceramic or glass dish.

Remove basil stems; wash leaves and spin dry. (You should have about
1¼ cups tightly packed basil leaves.) Place basil, lemon juice, garlic, salt,
and olive oil into a food processor fitted with the steel blade and puree until
smooth.

Place steaks in a ceramic or glass dish and coat with marinade.

Cover with plastic wrap and refrigerate for several hours, turning meat
occasionally.

Bring to room temperature before barbecuing.

Grill meat on both sides, basting it from time to time until it is cooked
to your taste. Cut steaks into thin slices, across the grain. Sprinkle with
freshly ground pepper and serve at once.

NOTE: You can also use this marinade with chicken, but use less, since it
is very strong.

STEAK IN DILL SAUCE

This is an easy-to-make delicacy with a wonderful dill-flavored   4 SERVINGS
sauce, an adaptation of a Swedish dish.

2 pounds center-cut minute steak, deveined and trimmed of all fat	Kosher salt
8 medium shallots	Black pepper, freshly ground
½ pound firm fresh mushrooms	½ cup kosher cream sherry (Madeira)
About 4 tablespoons (½ stick) unsalted margarine	½ cup Brown Veal Stock (page 255)
About ¼ cup olive oil	About 1½ tablespoons fresh lemon juice, strained
	10 sprigs dill, snipped

I suggest you use a food processor and an enameled cast-iron skillet.

Freeze meat for 30 minutes to make it easier to cut. In the meantime, peel, quarter, and chop shallots fine in a food processor fitted with the steel blade; set aside. Wipe mushrooms with a damp paper towel and slice them into paper-thin slices; set aside.

Cut meat into ½-inch-wide julienne strips and pat dry with paper towels. (Meat should be dry in order to brown evenly.)

Heat half of the margarine and half of the olive oil in a skillet until hot. Sauté about six pieces of meat at a time over high heat, turning with tongs. It should be light brown on the outside, rare on the inside. Transfer finished pieces to a dish and continue sautéeing the rest. You may need to add extra olive oil and margarine. Sprinkle lightly with salt and pepper.

To make the sauce: In the same skillet, heat another tablespoon each of margarine and olive oil. Sauté shallots over low heat until soft; remove to a dish. Heat remaining margarine and olive oil, add mushrooms, and sauté over high heat until just coated with shortening; remove to a dish.

Return sautéed shallots to skillet, add sherry (Madeira), and boil over high heat until liquid is reduced a bit. Add stock, lemon juice, and dill. Boil sauce for a few minutes. Return meat, with its accumulated juices, and the mushrooms to the pan and return to the boil again. Serve at once. The sauce should be well seasoned, and the steak should be medium rare, or to your taste.

NOTE: To make this dish a couple of hours in advance, combine the sautéed meat with the sauce, but don't bring it to a boil until just before serving.

BEEF IN RED WINE
WITH SHALLOTS AND MUSHROOMS

6 SERVINGS This is a hearty, well-seasoned winter dish that, served with rice or wide noodles, makes a convenient buffet dinner. You must make it a day ahead of time to bring out its special flavor.

3 pounds center-cut lean
   chuck, trimmed of fat and
   gristle and cut into 2-inch
   cubes (not smaller)
3 tablespoons unbleached flour
¼ cup olive oil
4 tablespoons (½ stick)
   unsalted margarine
Kosher salt
Black pepper, freshly ground
1 cup Brown Veal Stock (page
   255) or ½ ounce kosher
   bouillon cube dissolved in 1
   cup boiling water

1 tablespoon tomato paste
About 1 cup dry red wine
Bouquet garni: 1 bay leaf, 8
   sprigs Italian flat-leaf
   parsley with stems, 10 black
   peppercorns, 1 teaspoon
   dried thyme, tied in a
   cheesecloth
20 medium shallots or small
   white onions
1 pound firm fresh mushrooms
½ bunch Italian flat-leaf
   parsley

I suggest you use a heavy skillet and a 4-quart enameled cast-iron saucepan with lid.

Preheat oven to 325°F. Pat meat dry with paper towels. Spread flour on a sheet of wax paper. Heat half the olive oil and half the margarine in a skillet until hot. Dip three or four pieces of meat into flour at a time, shake off excess, and brown over medium-high heat, turning with tongs, until crusty brown. Do this patiently, sautéeing only a few pieces at a time, or meat may exude too much moisture and therefore will not brown evenly. Transfer finished pieces to a large saucepan and proceed with the next batch. Sprinkle lightly with salt and pepper.

Mix stock or bouillon with tomato paste and add to meat. Pour in wine (liquid should come almost to top of meat, but not cover it). If there is not enough liquid, add more stock and wine. Bury bouquet garni under meat. Bring to a boil, cover pot with heavy foil, then a lid. Cook in center of oven for 1 hour.

In the meantime, peel shallots or onions by dropping them into boiling water, returning water to the boil, then draining and peeling them.

Wipe skillet with paper towels to remove burned particles. Heat 1 tablespoon olive oil and 1 tablespoon margarine until hot and sauté shallots or onions over medium heat, stirring with a wooden spoon for a few minutes, until lightly brown; set aside.

Wipe mushrooms with a damp paper towel. If they are large, quarter them; if not, leave whole. In the same skillet, heat remaining tablespoon each olive oil and margarine and sauté mushrooms over high heat until coated with shortening. Remove from heat, sprinkle lightly with salt and pepper, and set aside. Remove bottom half of parsley stems; wash leaves, spin dry, and chop coarsely.

After meat has cooked for 1 hour, stir in shallots or onions with their accumulated juice and cook for approximately 1 hour more. The meat should be soft, but not falling apart.

Stir in mushrooms with accumulated juice and parsley. Remove bouquet garni and discard. Season and let cool. If there is too much sauce (sometimes meat shrinks a lot), place a sieve over a saucepan and pour contents through sieve. Reduce sauce over high heat and return meat to sauce.

NOTE: It is important to buy the right quality of meat. Explain to your butcher that you will be cooking the meat for at least 2 hours and would like the right cut for this.

◆You can refrigerate the meat in the saucepan in which it was cooked, leaving the foil beneath the lid. Remove from refrigerator, skim off the top layer of fat, and reheat gently.

BRAISED VEAL

6 TO 8
SERVINGS

Natural, light juices are served with this flavorful meat.

4 cloves garlic	2 tablespoons olive oil
¼ bunch Italian flat-leaf parsley	Kosher salt
	Black pepper, freshly ground
3 pounds center-cut boned shoulder of veal in one piece, rolled and tied	1 teaspoon dried tarragon
	1 cup dry white wine
	3 small ripe tomatoes, skinned, seeded, and chopped coarse
1 tablespoon unsalted margarine	

I suggest you use an enameled cast-iron oval pan with lid, preferably no larger than the size of the meat.

Peel garlic and cut into slivers; set aside. Remove bottom half of parsley stems; wash leaves, spin dry, and chop coarsely; set aside.

Pat veal dry with paper towels. Heat margarine and olive oil in a large pan until hot. Brown meat on all sides over medium heat, turning with tongs, for about 10 minutes. Remove from heat and sprinkle lightly with salt and pepper.

Make small incisions in top of meat with a sharp-pointed knife and insert garlic slivers. Sprinkle with tarragon and add wine, tomatoes, and parsley.

Bring to a boil, then reduce heat to barest simmer. Cover pan, leaving a very small opening. Braise veal for 1½ to 1¾ hours, turning with tongs from time to time.

To serve: Place meat on a carving board. Cut off strings and carve meat into very thin slices. Some of the meat may fall apart when sliced hot; that is unavoidable; just put it back together. Also, the center slices may look pink, but the color will change right away, and it does not mean that the meat is undercooked.

Arrange overlapping slices of veal on a heated platter, cover with foil, and keep warm while you are finishing the sauce.

Lightly skim fat from sauce if necessary, add juices from the board, season, and bring to a boil. Coat meat with the sauce.

NOTE: If you cannot get your heat low enough, place an asbestos pad over the flame and put saucepan on top of it.

◆If you wish to make this dish earlier in the day, let meat cool, then slice it. Skim off surface fat and season sauce, then return sliced meat to it. Reheat gently at serving time, without letting meat cook longer than just necessary to make it very hot, or else it will be overcooked and dry.

BRAISED VEAL WITH CURRY

——⟫⟫⟫—————————————————————

Veal is one of my favorite meats, but top-quality kosher veal is not always available, and the hind quarters of calves cannot be used. These limitations make the preparation of veal dishes rather tricky.

6 TO 8 SERVINGS

I found this recipe, however, to be very successful. This slow oven braising method without any added liquids keeps the veal moist, soft, and produces a clear, natural, aromatic sauce. It is an elegant dish, which can be prepared in advance and served with Plain Boiled Rice (page 160).

1 pound medium to large
  shallots
3 tablespoons unsalted
  margarine
2 teaspoons dried tarragon
3 pounds center-cut boned
  shoulder of veal in one
  piece, rolled and tied
1¾ teaspoons Madras curry
  powder
SEALING PASTE:
¼ cup flour

1 tablespoon olive oil
Kosher salt
Black pepper, freshly ground
Bouquet garni: 1 teaspoon
  dried thyme, 1 bay leaf, 6
  sprigs Italian flat-leaf
  parsley with stems, tied in a
  cheesecloth

About ⅓ cup water

I suggest you use an enameled cast-iron oval pan with lid, prefera-bly no larger than the size of the meat, and a 2-inch-wide strip of cloth long enough to seal the lid to the pan.

To make it easier to peel shallots, drop them into a saucepan of boiling water, return water to the boil, drain, and peel.

Melt 2 tablespoons of the margarine in a small saucepan and add shallots and half the tarragon. Cover pan and braise shallots over low heat for 10 minutes.

Preheat oven to 325°F. Pat veal dry with paper towels and place it on a sheet of wax paper. Rub curry powder over whole roast.

Heat remaining tablespoon margarine and the olive oil in the braising pan until hot. Brown meat all over, over medium heat, turning with tongs, for about 10 minutes. When meat is brown, sprinkle lightly with salt and pepper. Add bouquet garni to pan along with remaining tarragon and the shallots with their juices. (No extra liquid is added.) Cover pan.

Make a paste of the flour and water. Dip a long, 2-inch-wide strip of cloth into this paste and place it along the edges of the pan and lid to seal them together. If the pan has handles, seal those as well. Braise veal in center of oven for 1¼ hours.

To serve: Break seal. Place meat on a carving board, cut off strings, and carve into very thin slices. Some of the meat may fall apart, especially when it is sliced hot. Furthermore, the center slices will look pink, but the color will change right away, and it does not mean that the meat is undercooked.

Arrange overlapping slices of veal on a heated platter, cover with foil, and keep warm while you are finishing the sauce.

Lightly skim surface fat from sauce, add juices from the board, season, and bring to a boil. Pour some sauce over the meat and serve the rest in a sauceboat.

◆If you wish to make this dish earlier in the day, let meat cool, then slice it, degrease and season sauce, and return the sliced meat to sauce. Gently reheat at serving time without letting the meat cook for more than just necessary to make it very hot, or it will be overcooked and dry.

VEAL STEW WITH SAFFRON

6 SERVINGS   I love to serve stews on cold, wintry days, especially one like this, in which tomatoes, onions, and saffron blend into an aromatic sauce. I serve this dish with rice, but wide noodles are a good accompaniment as well. Even though this is a stew, I recommend buying the best quality meat. Make it a day ahead of time to allow the flavors to blend.

4 medium onions

2 to 3 cloves garlic

½ bunch Italian flat-leaf
  parsley

3 pounds boned shoulder of
  veal, cut into 2-inch cubes,
  all gristle and fat removed

4 tablespoons (½ stick)
  unsalted margarine

¼ cup olive oil

3 tablespoons unbleached flour

Kosher salt

Black pepper, freshly ground

¼ ounce kosher consommé
  cube, dissolved in ½ cup
  boiling water

¼ cup dry white wine

1-pound 12-ounce can peeled
  Italian tomatoes, undrained,
  chopped coarse

1½ teaspoons dried rosemary

½ teaspoon saffron threads

*I suggest you use a food processor and a 4-quart enameled cast-iron
saucepan with lid.*

Preheat oven to 375°F. Peel, quarter, and chop onions and garlic fine in
a food processor fitted with the steel blade. Do it in batches, removing each
one before placing in the next.

Remove bottom half of parsley stems; wash leaves, spin dry, and chop
coarsely in food processor.

Pat meat dry with paper towels.

Heat 3 tablespoons of the margarine and 3 tablespoons of the olive oil
in a skillet until hot. Spread flour on a sheet of wax paper and dip about
four pieces of meat into flour at a time, shake off excess, and sauté over
medium-high heat, turning with tongs, until light brown. Transfer finished
pieces to saucepan, sprinkling lightly with salt and pepper.

Wipe the skillet, because it may have some burned particles in it. Heat
remaining 1 tablespoon margarine and 1 tablespoon olive oil and sauté
onions and garlic for a few minutes. Add onions, garlic, consommé, wine,
tomatoes, parsley, rosemary, and saffron to meat. Bring to a boil, cover, and
cook in center of oven for about 1½ hours, or until meat is soft, but not
falling apart. Season with salt and pepper. Sometimes veal shrinks a lot and
exudes too much liquid. If there is too much sauce, boil it down. When
completely cold, place a sheet of wax paper beneath lid and refrigerate
overnight.

At serving time, skim off top layer of fat and reheat gently. (It is easier
to degrease sauce after it has been refrigerated.)

◆This stew freezes very well; defrost it in the refrigerator.

MARINATED VEAL SPARERIBS

These sweet-and-sour spareribs are an adaptation of a Chinese
dish. They are very tasty either hot or at room temperature.
There is not much meat on these bones, but they are delicious.

4 TO 6
SERVINGS

7 pounds veal spareribs, trimmed of fat

MARINADE:

¼ cup dark Chinese soy sauce   3 cloves garlic, minced
¼ cup thin Chinese soy sauce   2 tablespoons honey
Juice of 1½ lemons, strained   2 tablespoons Hoisin sauce
¼ cup olive oil

I suggest you use a glass or ceramic dish and a roasting pan large enough to fit the ribs in a single layer.

Place ribs in a glass or ceramic dish. Whisk marinade ingredients together and pour over meat. Cover with plastic wrap and marinate for several hours or overnight, turning meat occasionally.

Preheat oven to 350°F. Place ribs, meaty side down, in a roasting pan and pour over the marinade. Roast for 1½ hours. Turn ribs over and roast for about 1 more hour, or until meat is soft and brown. If ribs appear fatty, and if you like a nice crust on them, place them under the broiler for a few minutes (but not too close to the heat source, or they will burn).

NOTE: Occasionally the veal shrinks a good deal, in which case there will be too much sauce; just pour it off.

BROILED CALVES' LIVER

4 SERVINGS   To make this dish more elaborate, garnish it with thinly sliced sautéed onions.

2 teaspoons Dijon-type mustard
1 tablespoon unsalted margarine, at room temperature
Vegetable oil

2 tablespoons unbleached flour
4 calves'-liver steaks, about 1 inch thick
Kosher salt
Black pepper, freshly ground

Combine mustard and margarine.

Preheat broiler. Line the broiler pan with foil and brush it with a little oil.

Spread flour on a sheet of wax paper. Dry liver with paper towels and dip into flour. Shake off excess, place liver on foil, and spread with mustard mixture. Sprinkle lightly with salt and pepper.

Broil on one side only, as close to heat source as possible, for about 7 minutes or to your taste.

NOTE: If you would like to broil the liver on both sides, double proportions of mustard and margarine and broil for a shorter time on each side.

BROILED LAMB CHOPS

Look for tender, young lamb, which is at its best in spring,   3 SERVINGS
summer, and early fall. Older lamb tends to be darker and
fattier, with a discernible aroma.

8 first-cut baby rib lamb
  chops, cut double to 1½- to
  2-inch thickness, trimmed
  of fat and bone cut down
  and scraped clean

Juice of 1 large lemon,
  strained
2 cloves garlic, minced
Kosher salt

COATING:

2½ tablespoons black mustard
  seeds or 1 teaspoon dried
  tarragon or rosemary

Generous 2½ tablespoons
  Dijon-type mustard

Place chops in a glass or ceramic dish. Season with lemon juice, garlic, and
salt. Marinate for 4 to 5 hours. If you are refrigerating the lamb chops,
bring them back to room temperature before broiling.

Preheat broiler. Combine mustard seeds or dried herbs with mustard.
Place chops on a broiler pan or rack set over a pan. Brush with half the
coating and broil close to heat source for about 7 minutes. Turn with tongs,
brush with remaining coating, and broil for about 5 minutes more, or to
your taste.

NOTE: Mustard seeds are available in specialty stores; they keep indefinitely in a glass jar.

ROAST RACK OF LAMB

Develop a relationship with your butcher and depend on him to   6 SERVINGS
give you young, unfatty lamb. Spring lamb is generally sweeter
and more flavorful.

2 racks of lamb, 6 to 7 chops per rack, trimmed of all but a thin
  layer of fat, the bones shortened and scraped clean

MARINADE:

¼ cup olive oil
Juice of 2 lemons, strained
2 tablespoons Dijon-type
  mustard

4 cloves garlic, minced
2 tablespoons dried tarragon
Kosher salt
Black pepper, freshly ground

*I suggest you use a glass or ceramic dish and a roasting pan with
an adjustable metal rack.*

Put lamb in a glass or ceramic dish. Mix olive oil, lemon juice, mustard, garlic, and tarragon in a small bowl. Coat lamb with marinade and refrigerate for at least 4 hours. An hour before roasting, take meat out of refrigerator.

Preheat oven to 500°F. Sprinkle lamb lightly with salt and pepper.

Adjust rack to a V shape inside the roasting pan. Place lamb on rack, meaty side close to the sides of the rack and bones up. If you do not have such a rack, stand the lamb racks up on their base and interlace the tops of the bones to form an arch.

For medium-rare meat, roast for 20 minutes. Remove from oven and wait for 5 minutes before carving. (Letting meat rest permits juices to flow back to meat tissues.)

NOTE: This kind of meat is so expensive that it is safer to cook it rare than to risk overcooking it. Or you can use a meat thermometer for accuracy.

MEAT LOAF

3 TO 4 SERVINGS   The addition of a raw potato makes this meat loaf light and moist.

1 tablespoon vegetable oil	Fresh thyme or basil
¾ pound lean chuck, ground,	(optional)
and ¾ pound lean veal,	1 tablespoon tomato paste
ground, then ground	1 tablespoon ketchup
together twice	About 1 tablespoon black
1 onion	Chinese soy sauce
1 clove garlic	Kosher salt
1 medium potato	Black pepper, freshly ground
1 egg	
¼ bunch Italian flat-leaf	
parsley	

I suggest you use a food processor and a 6-by-9-inch baking pan.

Preheat oven to 375°F. Line a baking pan with foil and brush with vegetable oil.

Place meat in a large bowl.

Peel and quarter onion, garlic, and potato. Place, along with egg, in a food processor fitted with the steel blade and puree until smooth. Add to meat.

Remove bottom half of parsley stems; wash leaves, spin dry, and chop coarsely in food processor. Add to meat. If you are using thyme or basil, wash and chop coarsely and add to meat. Add tomato paste, ketchup, and soy sauce. Mix meat with your hands until thoroughly combined. Season with salt and pepper.

Place meat in the foil-lined pan and shape into a loaf. Tuck foil in along sides. Bake in center of oven for 55 minutes. To get a nice brown top and to absorb some of the accumulated liquid, broil meat loaf close to heat source for 5 minutes.

Let meat rest for a few minutes before slicing it.

NOTE: Ask your butcher to grind the meat separately, mix it together, and grind it again; it makes a fluffier meat loaf. If you like, you can use only veal or only beef, but be sure to adjust the seasonings.

CURRIED MEAT PIE

An interesting way to serve ground meat. A convenient Sabbath luncheon dish that can be eaten either warm or at room temperature.   8 SERVINGS

DOUGH:

⅔ cup vegetable shortening (Crisco brand)

2 cups unbleached flour

⅛ teaspoon salt

About ¼ cup ice water

FILLING:

1 medium potato

1 medium onion

6 tablespoons corn or peanut oil

¾ pound lean chuck, ground, and ¾ pound lean veal, ground, then ground together twice

2 tablespoons black Chinese soy sauce

1½ teaspoons sugar

About 1½ teaspoons kosher salt

2 teaspoons Madras curry powder

1 tablespoon vegetable shortening (Crisco brand)

1 egg, lightly beaten

I suggest you use the following: a pastry blender, a wok, and a 10-inch round Pyrex or ceramic dish.

To make the dough: Place vegetable shortening, flour, and salt in a large mixing bowl. Combine with pastry blender until mixture resembles coarse crumbs. Gradually sprinkle on ice water until you can gather dough into a ball. Turn dough out onto a pastry board and knead with the heel of your hand into a smooth ball. Divide into two balls, flatten them a bit, and refrigerate until filling is ready.

To make the filling: Boil potato in its skin until soft. Peel and mash with a fork until smooth. Peel and chop onion fine.

Heat a wok over high heat until hot. Add 4 tablespoons of the oil. When oil is hot, stir fry meat until it changes color and separates. Mix in soy sauce, sugar, and salt. When well combined, transfer to a large bowl. Heat wok again and add remaining 2 tablespoons oil. When oil is hot, stir fry onion over medium heat until soft and transparent. Stir in curry powder, increase heat, and add mashed potato and meat. Combine thoroughly and season well. Transfer to a bowl and let cool completely.

To make the pie: Preheat oven to 400°F. Grease a heatproof glass pie pan lightly with vegetable shortening. Roll out each ball of dough into a very thin round on a lightly floured board. Drape one round over rolling pin and unroll over the prepared dish. Fit into dish. (If dough cracks, you can patch it with a little extra dough and water.) Spread cooled filling over dough. Cover meat with second round. With a scissors, cut off overlapping dough to make an even circle. Seal edges with a fork, tuck in or cut off excess dough, and brush top lightly with beaten egg. With the tip of a knife, make a few holes to release steam. Bake in center of oven for about 30 minutes, or until top is lightly golden.

MOUSSAKA

6 SERVINGS   Moussaka is a Greek dish that is usually made with milk, butter, and ground lamb. This kosher version has no milk, butter, or cheese, of course. It is equally delicious served hot or at room temperature. You can assemble this dish in the morning and refrigerate it, then bake before serving.

3 medium eggplants, about 1 pound each
Kosher salt
2 medium onions
½ bunch Italian flat-leaf parsley
½ bunch basil
5 tablespoons vegetable oil
1¼ pounds lean chuck, ground, and 1¼ pounds lean veal, ground, then ground together twice

2 tablespoons tomato paste
2 to 3 tablespoons black Chinese soy sauce
Black pepper, freshly ground
⅓ cup olive oil
3½ cups very thick, well-seasoned Fresh Tomato Sauce (page 263)

I suggest you use the following: a food processor, a wok, and a 9-by-14-by-2-inch ovenproof dish.

Peel eggplants and slice into ½-inch-thick rounds. Soak for about 1 hour in a very large or two medium bowls of ice water to which 5 tablespoons salt have been added. Drain, then squeeze gently in a dish towel to dry.

While eggplants are soaking, peel, quarter, and chop onions fine in a food processor fitted with the steel blade; set aside.

Remove bottom half of parsley stems; wash leaves and spin dry. Remove basil stems and do the same. Chop both coarsely in food processor; set aside.

Heat a wok and add 2 tablespoons of the oil. When oil is hot, sauté chopped onions until soft and transparent. Add remaining 3 tablespoons oil. When oil is hot, add meat and sauté over high heat, stirring all the time, until meat changes color and separates. Stir in tomato paste, soy sauce, parsley, and basil. Remove to a bowl and season with salt and pepper.

Preheat broiler. Line the broiler pan with foil. Arrange eggplant rounds on broiler pan. Brush each slice lightly with olive oil and broil close to heat source, on one side only, until light brown.

To assemble moussaka: Preheat oven to 375°F. Coat an ovenproof dish with tomato sauce. Make a layer of eggplant and a layer of meat sauce. Repeat until all ingredients are finished.

Heat in upper part of oven for about 25 minutes, or until bubbles appear. Place directly under broiler for 5 minutes to absorb some liquid.

NOTE: I prefer sautéeing chopped meat in a wok because it heats very quickly and sears the meat. If your tomato sauce is not thick enough, boil it down to a very thick consistency.

RIGATONI WITH TOMATO–MEAT SAUCE

A hearty, satisfying main-course pasta to be followed by salad and fruit. Since the sauce takes a while to cook, I make it in large quantities and freeze whatever I don't immediately need. This recipe is enough for 2 pounds of pasta.

10 TO 12
SERVINGS

½ ounce dried imported
  Italian mushrooms
1 cup boiling water
2 onions
4 cloves garlic
1 carrot
1 bunch Italian flat-leaf
  parsley
½ bunch fresh basil
⅓ cup olive oil

¾ pound lean chuck, ground,
  and ¾ pound lean veal,
  ground, then ground
  together twice
1½ cups dry red wine
19-ounce can peeled Italian
  tomatoes, undrained
1 tablespoon tomato paste
Kosher salt
Black pepper, freshly ground

2 pounds dried imported rigatoni or any other ridged pasta

I suggest you use a food processor and an enameled cast-iron saucepan with lid.

Place dried mushrooms in a small bowl and pour boiling water over them. Let soak for 30 minutes. Strain soaking liquid through a sieve lined with a paper towel, squeezing mushrooms over sieve to extract more liquid; set liquid aside. Wash mushrooms carefully to remove sand and chop coarsely; set aside.

Peel and quarter onions, garlic, and carrot. Chop in a food processor fitted with the steel blade. Remove bottom half of parsley stems; wash the rest, spin dry, and chop coarsely in food processor. Remove basil stems and do the same.

Heat olive oil in the saucepan until hot. Sauté onions, garlic, and carrots over low heat until soft. Increase heat to high, add meat, and sauté, stirring, until meat looses its red color. Add wine and cook over high heat until dry. Add reserved mushroom liquid and do the same. Stir in parsley, chopped mushrooms, basil, tomatoes, and tomato paste. Bring to a boil and cook at the barest simmer, uncovered, for about 4 hours, stirring from time to time.

(If you cannot cook this sauce in one stretch, shut it off, but resume cooking the same day.) Season with salt and pepper.

To cook the pasta: Bring 5 quarts water to a rolling boil in a large covered pot. Add 2 tablespoons of the salt and all the pasta at once, stirring with a wooden spoon. Boil briskly for about 8 minutes, or until *al dente*. Test frequently, since it is impossible to gauge the cooking time precisely. Drain well, shaking vigorously in a sieve. Place in a heated serving bowl and toss with the hot sauce. Season to taste.

NOTE: If you cannot get your heat low enough, place an asbestos pad over the flame and put saucepan on top of it.

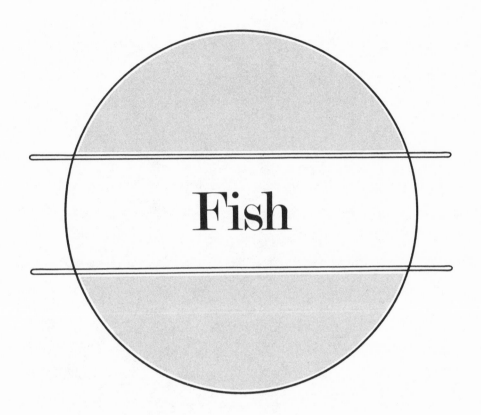

Fish

Dairy

SALMON SCALLOPS WITH SORREL SAUCE

The well-seasoned sauce adds a wonderful flavor to this subtle, elegant dish. It is easy to prepare, but make sure that the salmon is of the finest, freshest quality.

4 SERVINGS
AS A LIGHT
MEAL

If you wish to make this dish when sorrel is not in season, you may use watercress leaves instead.

2 large very fresh center-cut
  salmon steaks, about 1½
  inches thick

Kosher salt
White pepper, freshly ground
½ tablespoon sweet butter

SAUCE:

6 ounces sorrel or sour grass
3 tablespoons sweet butter
4 medium shallots, minced
  very fine
3 tablespoons dry white wine
  or dry vermouth

1 cup heavy cream
Fresh lemon juice
Kosher salt
White pepper, freshly ground

I suggest you use a small enameled cast-iron saucepan and a large nonstick skillet.

Have fish man remove center bones and skin from fish and cut it into four pieces. Pat dry with paper towels. Place pieces between two oiled sheets of wax paper and flatten them slightly with a smooth meat pounder or with

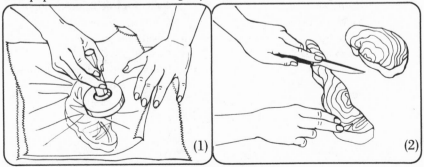

(1)　　　　(2)

the flat side of a cleaver (1). With tweezers, pull out tiny bones. Cut off some of the ends and gently reshape the sides to form a scallop shape (2). Season fish lightly with salt and pepper.

To make the sauce: Remove the stem all the way to the center from each sorrel leaf. You can do this easily by folding each leaf in half so that the center becomes the outer edge. Wash and spin dry the leaves. If they are large, tear them into small pieces; set aside.

In a small saucepan, heat butter and sauté shallots over low heat until soft and transparent. Add wine or vermouth and boil over high heat until shallots are almost dry. Add cream and boil slowly, uncovered, until sauce is thick enough to coat a spoon heavily. Add sorrel or watercress leaves and season with lemon juice, salt, and pepper. The sauce should be tart and well seasoned.

Keep sauce warm while you cook fish. Or, if you like, make the sauce, without adding the sorrel, a couple of hours ahead of time. Keep it covered and, when ready, reheat, add sorrel and seasonings.

To sauté the fish: Heat a large skillet until hot and grease it lightly. Sauté scalloped fish for about 30 seconds on each side, or until fish changes color, but is still a bit rare inside. The hot sauce will continue cooking it. Serve immediately on heated plates coated with the sauce.

NOTE: If you prefer, ask your fish man to make you four fillets of equal thickness, each weighing about 6 ounces. He can even pound them for you.

BROILED BLUEFISH FILLETS
WITH BASIL AND PARSLEY

4 SERVINGS   An easy, last-minute, wonderful dish. The topping on the fish is piquant and complements both the flavor and texture of bluefish.

¼ bunch basil
¼ bunch Italian flat-leaf
  parsley
1 clove garlic
1 teaspoon Dijon-type
  mustard
4 tablespoons (½ stick) sweet
  butter, melted
3 tablespoons unseasoned
  bread crumbs

2 tablespoons freshly grated
  Parmesan cheese
4 medium or 2 large bluefish
  fillets, cut in half
Vegetable oil
Kosher salt
Black pepper, freshly ground
Lemon wedges

I suggest you use a food processor.

Preheat broiler. Remove basil and parsley stems; wash leaves and spin dry. Place leaves and garlic in a food processor fitted with the steel blade and puree until smooth. Remove to a bowl and combine with mustard, butter, bread crumbs, and Parmesan cheese.

Line the broiler pan with foil and brush lightly with vegetable oil. Pat fillets dry with paper towels and place on foil. Season lightly with salt and pepper and spread top with coating.

Broil on one side only for about 5 minutes, or to your taste.

Serve with lemon wedges.

ROLLED FILLETS OF GRAY SOLE WITH TOMATO–CREAM SAUCE

→>>

An easy yet elegant winter delight, at a time when not many varieties of fish are available. The dish can be assembled in advance. Serve it with buttered rice and Endive, Arugula, and Alfalfa Sprout Salad (page 171).

5 TO 6 SERVINGS

FILLING:

5 medium shallots
4 tablespoons (½ stick) sweet butter
6 ounces firm fresh mushrooms

6 sprigs dill, snipped
Kosher salt
Black pepper, freshly ground

1½ tablespoons sweet butter
6 medium fresh fillets of gray (lemon) sole, about 2 pounds

Kosher salt
White pepper, freshly ground
Juice of ½ lemon, strained
½ cup Fish Stock (page 258)

SAUCE:

5 medium shallots
½ cup dry white wine
2 medium ripe tomatoes, peeled, cored, seeded, and chopped coarsely

1 cup Fish Stock (page 258)
1 cup heavy cream
Kosher salt
White pepper, freshly ground

I suggest you use the following: a food processor, an enameled cast-iron skillet, wooden toothpicks, a 9-by-14-by-2-inch ovenproof dish, and an enameled cast-iron sauce pan.

To make the filling: Peel, quarter, and chop shallots very fine in a food processor fitted with the steel blade. In a skillet, heat 2 tablespoons of the butter until hot and sauté shallots over low heat until soft and transparent, mixing with a wooden spoon. Wipe mushrooms with a damp paper towel, quarter, and chop coarsely in food processor. Add remaining 2 tablespoons butter to shallots in skillet, add mushrooms, and sauté over high heat, mixing constantly with a wooden spoon until mushrooms are just coated with butter. Remove from heat, add dill, and season with salt and pepper.

Preheat oven to 350°F. Grease an ovenproof dish with ½ tablespoon of the butter.

Pat fillets dry with paper towels. Place, darker side up, on a sheet of wax paper and season lightly with salt and pepper.

Place about 2 tablespoons filling within ½ inch of the thin tail-end of one of the fillets and roll to end. Secure with toothpicks. Repeat with each fillet. Place fillets in the prepared dish, not too close to one another. (This makes it easier to lift them out when done.) Sprinkle with lemon juice, pour on stock, and dot with remaining butter, cut into small pieces. Cover dish with buttered wax paper and bake for about 20 minutes, or until fish is opaque. Do not overbake, since fillets will continue cooking when covered with the hot sauce.

To make the sauce: Peel, quarter, and chop shallots fine in food processor fitted with the steel blade. In a saucepan, boil shallots and wine over high heat until shallots are dry. Add tomatoes, stock, and cream and boil gently until sauce is reduced to half. It should be thick, since it will thin out when the fish juices are added. Sauce can be made in advance up to this point and covered, to be reheated.

To finish, pour sauce into a measuring cup and add just enough fish juices to thin it out. Season. Remove toothpicks from fillets and coat with sauce. Serve immediately.

◆If you like, the filling can be made a day in advance and refrigerated. If you wish to prepare the entire dish in advance, place the fillets in dish without the lemon juice, stock, and butter and refrigerate until ready.

GRAY SOLE STUFFED WITH SOLE MOUSSE

3 TO 4
SERVINGS

This dish is a tour de force, but not hard to make if you have a Kitchen Aid mixer with a colander-sieve attachment (page xxvi) for the mousse. Serve the fish whole, skinned, coated lightly with some of the sauce, and garnished with watercress leaves. Braised Shredded Leeks (page 143) or Sautéed Cucumbers (page 141) complement it very well.

The entire dish can be assembled in advance.

MOUSSE:

¾ pound fillets of gray
  (lemon) sole
1 egg white, lightly beaten
½ tablespoon sweet butter
2 medium shallots, minced
  very fine
1 cup heavy cream, very well
  chilled

⅛ teaspoon nutmeg, freshly
  ground
About 1½ teaspoons kosher
  salt
White pepper, freshly ground

One 2-pound gray (lemon)
  sole, inside bone removed,
  head and tail left on
Juice of ¼ lemon
Kosher salt

White pepper, freshly ground
3 sprigs tarragon or ½
  teaspoon dried
½ tablespoon sweet butter
Vegetable oil

SAUCE:

3 medium shallots, minced
  very fine
2 tablespoons tarragon wine
  vinegar
½ cup dry white wine

¾ cup heavy cream
3 tablespoons sweet butter, at
  room temperature
Kosher salt
White pepper, freshly ground

*I suggest you use the following: a food processor, a Kitchen Aid
mixer with a flat spatula and colander-sieve attachment, a jelly roll
pan, heavy foil, and an enameled cast-iron saucepan.*

To make the mousse: Cube fillets and puree until smooth in a food processor fitted with the steel blade. To further lighten fish and rid it of bone and
gristle, pass it through the colander-sieve attachment of a Kitchen Aid;
discard residue. Attach flat spatula to mixer and dribble in egg white
at lowest speed. Place mixer bowl with fish puree in freezer for 15
minutes.

  In the meantime, heat butter in a small skillet until hot and sauté shallots
over low heat until soft and transparent. Remove bowl from freezer and
dribble in cream at lowest speed with the same flat spatula. Do it very slowly
and patiently to enable fish puree to absorb cream. Add shallots and season
with nutmeg, salt, and pepper.

To prepare the fish: Preheat oven to 375°F. Scale, rinse, and pat fish dry
with paper towels. Sprinkle inside and out with lemon juice, salt, and
pepper. Place tarragon in cavity. Grease a jelly roll pan with vegetable oil
and lay fish in. Stuff fish cavity with mousse and reshape the body. Grease
head and wrap tail with a small piece of oiled foil. Cover pan tightly with
well-oiled sheet of heavy foil. Bake in center of oven for about 20 minutes.
Test with the tip of a knife to see if fish is ready; the flesh should be opaque.

With a sharp knife, carefully remove top skin and backbone. (Some
of the bottom skin will also come off
when you remove the backbone.)
Slide two large, wide spatulas under
fish and lift to a heated platter. Decorate fish, coat lightly with sauce,
and serve the rest in a sauceboat.

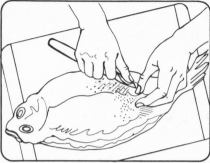

To make the sauce: In a saucepan,
boil shallots, vinegar, and wine until
almost dry. Add cream and boil slowly, uncovered, until sauce is thick
enough to coat a spoon heavily. Whisk in butter, 1 tablespoonful at a time, until smooth. Season. Sauce can be made in advance, covered, and reheated.

NOTE: If you do not have a colander-sieve attachment, strain the fish puree
through a fine mesh sieve in batches, pushing on the solids with a wooden
spoon.

BAKED STUFFED STRIPED BASS

**4 TO 5
SERVINGS**

STUFFING:

¼ cup pine nuts
1 medium onion
½ pound firm fresh
  mushrooms
¼ bunch Italian flat-leaf
  parsley

4 tablespoons (½ stick) sweet
  butter
¼ cup fresh unseasoned bread
  crumbs
Kosher salt
Black pepper, freshly ground

One 4½-pound striped bass, inside bone removed, head and tail
  left on

Vegetable oil
1 lemon
Kosher salt

Black pepper, freshly ground
¼ cup dry white wine
1 tablespoon sweet butter

Lime and watercress for garnish

*I suggest you use the following: a food processor, an enameled
cast-iron skillet, a shallow baking pan large enough to fit the fish,
and heavy foil.*

To make the stuffing: Preheat oven to 350°F. Roast pine nuts in oven for
10 minutes, or until light brown (they burn easily).

Peel, quarter, and chop onion fine in a food processor fitted with the steel blade. Wipe mushrooms with a damp paper towel, quarter, and chop coarsely in food processor. Remove parsley stems; wash leaves, spin dry, and chop fine in the same manner.

Heat 2 tablespoons of the butter in a skillet until hot and sauté onion over low heat until soft and transparent. Increase heat, add remaining 2 tablespoons butter, and sauté mushrooms, mixing with a wooden spoon, until they are coated with butter.

Add pine nuts and bread crumbs. Remove from heat, mix in parsley, and season well with salt and pepper. Let cool.

To bake the fish: Preheat oven to 400°F. Rinse fish and pat dry with paper towels. Cut a sheet of heavy foil 18 inches wide and long enough to enclose fish. Grease foil lightly with vegetable oil and place it in pan. Set fish in center of foil and grease its head and tail. Wrap tail with a heavily oiled sheet of foil. (The tail dries out quickly and sticks to the foil.) Squeeze lemon juice over inside and outside of fish and sprinkle generously with salt and pepper inside and outside as well.

Spoon stuffing into cavity of fish and reshape body with your hands. Bring up edges of foil, pour wine over fish, and dot with small pieces of butter. Seal edges of foil tightly and bake in center of oven for about 25 minutes. Test with the point of a knife; the flesh should be opaque.

To serve: Unwrap foil and fold edges down. With a small knife, carefully remove skin. Pour off liquid. Flip fish onto a heated platter and remove rest of skin. Wipe up juices that have accumulated on platter with paper towels. Decorate with thin slices of lime and watercress leaves and serve at once.

NOTE: If the fish does not fit into your pan, place it on the diagonal and do not worry if the head and tail stick out.

BLUEFISH EN PAPILLOTE WITH TOMATO–BASIL BEURRE BLANC SAUCE

Bluefish has a long season, from April to December. Cooked by this closed-casing steaming method, it remains moist, its natural flavor enhanced by a creamy sauce.

3 TO 4 SERVINGS AS A LIGHT MEAL

One 3-pound bluefish	Kosher salt
3 tablespoons vegetable oil	White pepper, freshly ground
Juice of ½ lemon, strained	2 basil leaves
SAUCE:	
4 medium shallots	¼ cup dry white wine
1 medium ripe tomato	3 tablespoons tarragon wine
12 basil leaves	vinegar
8 tablespoons (1 stick) sweet	Kosher salt
butter, at room temperature	White pepper, freshly ground

I suggest you use the following: a jelly roll pan, heavy foil, and a small enameled cast-iron saucepan.

Have the fish man dress and fillet fish without removing skin. Halve each fillet; you will have four pieces. Pat dry with paper towels. Cut two sheets of heavy foil, about 18 by 18 inches each, and brush each one with ½ tablespoon of the vegetable oil.

Place two pieces of fish (1 whole fillet) in center of each sheet. Sprinkle with lemon juice and season generously with salt and pepper. Add 1 basil leaf to each package. Fold foil over, doubling edges to seal securely. Pour remaining 2 tablespoons oil into a jelly roll pan. Place papillotes, side by side, in pan.

Preheat oven to 475°F. Before baking fish, partially prepare sauce.

To make the sauce: Peel and mince shallots very fine. Peel, core, seed, and coarsely chop tomato. Wash basil leaves, spin dry, and snip thinly with scissors. Cut butter into 8 tablespoons. Place shallots, wine, and vinegar in a small saucepan. Have a whisk ready.

Place fish in center of oven. Bake for about 8 minutes; the fish should look opaque on the outside and still a bit gray on the inside. (It should be a bit undercooked.)

While fish is baking, boil shallots with wine and vinegar over medium-high heat until liquid is reduced to about 1 tablespoon. Remove saucepan from heat and beat in 2 tablespoons of the butter vigorously with the whisk until well blended. Return pan to low heat and continue vigorously whisking in remaining butter, 1 tablespoonful at a time, until it is all used and the sauce is creamy. Add chopped tomato and basil. Season with salt and pepper. Keep sauce over a low flame or in a warm-water bath until fish is ready.

To serve: Open the papillotes and put fish on heated plates without the accumulated juices. Coat with sauce. Or, if you like, serve the papillotes on a platter and open them at the table. In that case, serve the sauce separately.

NOTE: This sauce is tricky to make, but with the following precautions you cannot fail: Cut butter into tablespoons and be sure it is at room temperature. Have your heat so low that you can stick your finger into the sauce without burning it. You must whisk without stopping and add the butter 1 tablespoon at a time. If sauce starts to thin out, add 1 tablespoon hot water.

If you want to serve steamed bluefish without the sauce, you may wish to add vegetables, such as finely shredded zucchini, sliced tomatoes, and more basil to the papillotes. The beurre blanc sauce can also be flavored without the use of basil.

WHOLE RED SNAPPER STEAMED IN FOIL
WITH BEURRE BLANC–CAVIAR SAUCE

→»»

A favorite of mine.   4 SERVINGS

One 4-pound red snapper,   White pepper, freshly ground
  inside bone removed, head   4 sprigs Italian flat-leaf
  and tail left on   parsley
Vegetable oil   ¼ cup dry white wine
½ lemon
Kosher salt   Boiling water
SAUCE:
3 medium shallots, minced   ¾ cup heavy cream
  very fine   3 tablespoons sweet butter, at
3 tablespoons tarragon wine   room temperature
  vinegar   2 ounces natural salmon
½ cup Fish Stock (page 258),   caviar
  concentrated and well   Kosher salt
  seasoned   White pepper, freshly ground

*I suggest you use the following: heavy foil, a 1½-inch-deep pan
large enough to fit the fish, and a small enameled cast-iron saucepan.*

Preheat oven to 375°F. Rinse fish and pat dry with paper towels. Cut an
18-inch-wide sheet of heavy foil long enough to enclose fish and oil it lightly
with vegetable oil. Place fish in center of foil and lightly oil head and tail.
In addition, wrap tail with a heavily oiled sheet of foil. (The tail dries out
quickly and sticks to the foil.)

Squeeze lemon juice over inside and outside of fish and sprinkle lightly
with salt and pepper in the same manner. Wash parsley, chop coarsely, and
place in fish cavity.

Bring up edges of foil on both sides, pour wine over fish, and seal edges
tightly. Place foil-enclosed fish in the pan. Pour in about ½ inch of boiling
water. Steam in center of oven for 25 to 30 minutes. Loosen foil and test
with the tip of a knife to see if fish is ready; it should be opaque but a bit
undercooked. The steaming time should be about 6 minutes per pound.
Pour off pan water. Open foil, fold edges down, and pour off liquid. With
a small knife, remove skin carefully. Flip fish over onto a heated platter
and remove the rest of the skin. Wipe up juices that have accumulated on
the platter with paper towels. Coat fish very lightly with the sauce and serve
the rest in a sauceboat.

To make the sauce: In a small saucepan, boil shallots and vinegar over high heat until shallots are almost dry. Add stock and heavy cream and boil slowly, uncovered, until sauce is thick enough to coat a spoon heavily, about 10 minutes.

Whisk in butter, 1 tablespoonful at a time. The sauce can be made in advance up to this point, covered, and then reheated. Just before serving, heat sauce, add caviar, bring to a boil, correct seasoning, and serve at once. Do not let caviar boil, or it will harden and discolor.

NOTE: If the fish does not fit into your pan, place it on the diagonal and do not worry if the tail and head stick out.

STRIPED BASS STEAKS
WITH TOMATOES AND OLIVES

-≫≫

My favorite dish, because of its piquant flavor, firm texture, and   8 SERVINGS
the versatility of being able to serve it either hot or at room
temperature.

8 small striped bass or halibut
  steaks, about 6 ounces each
  and 1¼ inches thick, skin
  removed

SAUCE:

6 medium shallots
2 cloves garlic
½ bunch Italian flat-leaf
  parsley
About 1½ pounds ripe plum
  tomatoes or canned Italian
  tomatoes, drained
30 imported black olives
  (Gaeta)
⅓ cup olive oil

2 teaspoons kosher salt
Juice of 1 lemon, strained

⅔ cup dry vermouth or dry
  white wine
About 1 tablespoon tomato
  paste
½ teaspoon dried thyme
Generous ¼ teaspoon saffron
  threads
Kosher salt
Black pepper, freshly ground

*I suggest you use a 9-by-14-by-2-inch ovenproof dish or one large
enough to hold fish in a single layer without crowding and a food
processor.*

Pat steaks dry with paper towels. Place in an ovenproof dish and sprinkle
with salt and lemon juice. Let stand, refrigerated, for about 2 hours.

To make the sauce: Peel, quarter, and chop shallots and garlic fine in a
food processor fitted with the steel blade. Remove bottom half of parsley
stems; wash the rest, spin dry, and chop fine in food processor. Skin, core,
seed, and chop tomatoes fine. If you are using canned tomatoes, squeeze
out seeds, and chop fine. Pit olives and cut into thin slivers.

Heat olive oil in a skillet and sauté shallots and garlic over low heat until soft and transparent.

Add vermouth or wine, chopped tomatoes, olives, tomato paste, thyme, and saffron. Simmer, covered, for about 10 minutes. Add parsley and season with salt and pepper. You can make this sauce in advance.

Preheat oven to 450°F. Spoon sauce over fish, cover dish tightly with heavy foil, and bake in center of oven for about 20 minutes, or until fish is opaque.

NOTE: Gaeta olives come from the Campania region of Italy. They are used mostly in cooking and have a dark purple color.

MARINATED FILLETS OF MACKEREL

8 SERVINGS A summer luncheon dish in which mackerel fillets are seasoned with lime juice, sautéed briefly, and then marinated for at least 24 hours. If you do not like the oiliness of mackerel, substitute bluefish.

8 small to medium mackerel or bluefish fillets, skin left on

½ cup fresh lime or lemon juice, strained

MARINADE:

3 medium leeks

2 medium onions

6 cloves garlic

2 green peppers

½ cup olive oil

2 bay leaves, crushed

½ teaspoon dried thyme

1¼ cups cold water

½ cup tarragon wine vinegar

Kosher salt

10 whole black peppercorns

⅓ cup olive oil

¼ cup unbleached flour

Kosher salt

Black pepper, freshly ground

2 limes, sliced thin

¼ bunch Italian flat-leaf parsley, chopped

2 green peppers, cut into strips

I suggest you use a 1- to 2-inch-deep glass or ceramic platter large enough to fit the fillets in a single layer.

Pat fillets dry with paper towels. Place in a glass or ceramic dish and sprinkle evenly with lime or lemon juice. Let stand for 20 minutes only; if left longer, the citric acid will cook the fillets. Dry with paper towels.

To make the marinade: Cut off dangling roots and green leaves from leeks. Remove tough outer leaves and discard. Slice the rest into thin rounds.

Place in a sieve and wash well under cold running water to remove all sand; drain. Peel and slice onions and garlic very thin.

Cut peppers in half horizontally. Seed and slice into very thin strips.

Heat olive oil in a saucepan until hot and sauté leeks, onions, garlic, and peppers over medium heat, stirring with a wooden spoon, until wilted. Add remaining ingredients, bring to a boil, and simmer, covered, for about 10 minutes, or until vegetables are slightly soft.

To sauté the fillets: Heat ¼ cup of the olive oil in a medium skillet. Spread flour on a sheet of wax paper. Dip two or three fillets in flour at a time, shake off excess, and sauté fillets on both sides until just seared and pale. Lift with a large, wide spatula to a platter, add remaining oil to skillet, and sauté the rest. Sprinkle finished fillets lightly with salt and pepper. Pour very hot marinade over fish and spread vegetables evenly. Let cool. Cover platter with heavy foil and refrigerate for at least 24 hours.

Serve fish at room temperature, decorated with limes, parsley, and peppers.

NOTE: The marinade must be very hot when poured over the fish.

BAKED RED SNAPPER
WITH POTATOES AND ONIONS

>>>

This dish is easy to prepare, yet it can be a meal in itself,   2 SERVINGS
followed by a salad and a rich dessert.

One 1½-pound red snapper or   ½ cup olive oil
  bluefish, inside bone   1 medium onion, sliced very
  removed, head and tail left   thin
  on   2 medium baking potatoes,
Juice of ½ lemon, strained   sliced very thin
Kosher salt   1 clove garlic, minced fine
Black pepper, freshly ground   ¼ cup dry white wine
½ bunch Italian flat-leaf   1 ripe tomato, sliced thin
  parsley

I suggest you use a 9-by-14-by-2-inch ovenproof dish.

Preheat oven to 450°F. Rinse fish and pat dry with paper towels. Sprinkle inside and outside with lemon juice, salt, and pepper.

Remove bottom half of parsley stems; wash the rest, spin dry, and chop coarsely.

Heat 2 tablespoons of the olive oil in a skillet until hot and sauté onion over low heat until soft and transparent. Remove onion to an ovenproof dish. Add 3 more tablespoons of the olive oil to the skillet, add potatoes, and sauté for about 10 minutes, stirring occasionally with a wooden spoon.

Add potatoes to onion in dish, spreading evenly, and sprinkle generously with salt and pepper.

Place fish on top of potatoes and onions. Mix parsley and garlic and place half the mixture inside fish and the rest on top. Dribble remaining olive oil and wine over fish and top with sliced tomatoes.

Bake in upper third of oven for about 20 minutes, or until fish is opaque. Baste occasionally and loosen any of the browned potatoes that may be sticking to the pan, turning to allow the rest to brown as well.

NOTE: You can slice onion and potatoes in a food processor fitted with the slicing attachment. Make sure, however, that they come out very thin, or they will take longer to cook than the fish.

WHOLE SALMON TROUT STEAMED IN FOIL WITH CREAMY VINAIGRETTE SAUCE

4 SERVINGS   The classic Western method of poaching fish is in a court bouillon; I prefer this simple method of steaming, where the fish cooks in its own juices and retains its natural flavor and moistness. Serve at room temperature with sauce on the side. Refrigeration may alter the subtle flavor of the fish.

One 4-pound salmon trout or striped bass, inside bone removed, head and tail left on	Kosher salt
	White pepper, freshly ground
	4 sprigs Italian flat-leaf parsley
Vegetable oil	¼ cup dry white wine
½ lemon	

Boiling water	
SAUCE:	
2 medium shallots	About 1 tablespoon tarragon wine vinegar
6 sprigs Italian flat-leaf parsley	⅓ cup olive oil
3 medium ripe tomatoes	Kosher salt
1 tablespoon Dijon-type mustard	Black pepper, freshly ground

I suggest you use the following: heavy foil about 18 inches wide, a large pan about 1½ inches deep, and a food processor.

Preheat oven to 375°F. Rinse fish and pat dry with paper towels. Cut a sheet of heavy foil long enough to enclose fish and grease lightly with vegetable oil. Place fish in center of foil, grease its head and tail lightly, and wrap tail with a heavily greased piece of foil. (The tail dries out quickly and sticks to the foil.)

Squeeze lemon juice over the inside and outside of the fish and sprinkle lightly with salt and pepper. Wash parsley, chop coarsely, and place inside cavity of fish.

Bring up edges of foil on both sides, pour wine over fish, and seal edges tightly. Place foil-enclosed fish in the pan and pour in about ½ inch of boiling water. Steam in center of oven for about 25 to 30 minutes. Loosen foil and test with the tip of a knife to see if fish is ready. It should be only slightly opaque (that is, slightly undercooked), because fish will continue to cook while it cools. The steaming time should be about 6 minutes per pound. Reseal edges of foil, pour off pan water, and let cool. When outside of foil feels cool, open top, fold back edges, and pour off the liquid. With a small knife, carefully remove skin. Flip fish over onto a platter and remove skin on the other side. Wipe off juices that accumulate on the platter with paper towels. Decorate with parsley sprigs or watercress leaves and serve with sauce on the side.

To make the sauce: Peel and chop shallots very fine. Remove parsley stems; wash leaves, spin dry, and chop fine. Peel, core, and seed tomatoes and cut into cubes. Place shallots, mustard, and vinegar in a food processor fitted with the steel blade. With the motor on, dribble in the olive oil through the feeding tube. Sauce will become pale and slightly thick. Transfer to a serving bowl, combine with chopped parsley and tomatoes, and correct seasoning.

NOTE: If the fish does not fit into your pan, place it on the diagonal and do not worry if the head and tail stick out.

BOUILLABAISE

This is a different version of the famous specialty of the south of France. In the traditional dish, many fresh local fish are boiled with herbs and a lot of garlic. In my adaptation, a well-seasoned fish broth is combined with a thick tomato sauce, to which large pieces of halibut or striped bass are added at the last minute. It is one of my favorites, which I like to serve as a main course, piping hot, in heated soup bowls with rice. Follow this meal with a salad and a wonderful dessert, such as Chocolate Roll (page 189), Dacquise (page 201), or Tarte Tatin (page 200).

6 TO 8 SERVINGS

Although the preparation requires several steps, each one can be done in advance.

FISH STOCK:

About 4 pounds fresh fish heads and trimmings or the equivalent of whiting or other bony fish

1 onion

1 carrot

2 leeks, green parts only (reserve white parts for broth)

1 tomato

1 slice orange rind

1 bay leaf

1 teaspoon dried thyme

1½ cups dry white wine

5 cups cold water

2¼ cups thick Fresh Tomato Sauce (page 263)

FISH BROTH:

2 leeks, reserved from stock

1 small onion, chopped fine

4 cloves garlic, minced

½ bunch Italian flat-leaf parsley

½ teaspoon saffron threads

Kosher salt

Black pepper, freshly ground

Few drops Tabasco

FISH:

3¾ to 4 pounds center-cut halibut or striped bass, bones and skin removed, in one piece

RICE:

1½ cups long-grain rice (Uncle Ben's converted brand)

About 1½ teaspoons kosher salt

1¾ cups cold water

I suggest you use an approximately 5-quart enameled cast-iron saucepan and a small enameled cast-iron saucepan.

To make the stock: Rinse fish and place in a large saucepan. Peel and quarter onion and carrot. Cut leek leaves into quarters and wash well. Cut tomato in half and squeeze out seeds. Add all vegetables to fish along with remaining ingredients. Bring to a boil over high heat. Skim off some of the froth as it rises to the surface. Cook slowly, uncovered, for 30 minutes. Press solids with a spoon to extract additional flavor. Boil for another 10 minutes. Let cool a bit.

Strain stock, in batches, through a mesh sieve lined with a double layer of cheesecloth. Press on solids to extract all liquid; discard residue. Wash pot and pour back stock. If necessary, degrease a bit. Or, if you like, you can make the stock a day ahead of time, refrigerate it in the same saucepan, then remove the layer of fat that may have accumulated on top. (Place a sheet of wax paper beneath the lid to keep the flavor in.)

Reduce tomato sauce to a very thick concentrated puree by cooking over medium heat, stirring from time to time.

To make the broth: Cut off dangling roots from reserved leeks and finely cube white parts. Place in a sieve and rinse well under cold running water to remove all sand; drain well. Remove bottom half of parsley stems. Wash the rest, spin dry, and chop coarsely. Combine stock with reduced tomato sauce, chopped onion, minced garlic, leeks, parsley, and saffron. Bring to a boil and cook slowly, uncovered, for about 15 minutes. Season with salt, pepper, and Tabasco. It should be spicy.

To make the rice: Follow instructions for Plain Boiled Rice (page 160).

To complete the final assembly: Cut fish into approximately 2-inch squares and season lightly with salt and pepper. If you are serving the stew right away, drop fish chunks into boiling broth, return to the boil, and cook for about 1 minute, or just until fish changes color. (Fish should be under-cooked.) Correct seasoning and ladle broth with fish into heated rice-filled bowls.

   If you are not serving the stew right away, let broth cool, season fish, and coat with a ladle or two of broth. At serving time, follow instructions for final assembly.

Vegetables

STIR-FRIED MUSHROOMS

I love all varieties of mushrooms, but especially the combination of Shiitake and commercial mushrooms.   4 SERVINGS

½ pound Shiitake mushrooms,
  stems removed
½ pound firm fresh
  mushrooms
¼ bunch Italian flat-leaf
  parsley

1 clove garlic, minced
2 to 3 tablespoons olive oil
Kosher salt
Black pepper, freshly ground

I suggest you use a wok.

Wipe mushrooms with a damp paper towel and quarter them. Remove parsley stems; wash, spin dry, and chop leaves fine.

Heat a wok until hot, then add oil. When oil is hot, add mushrooms and garlic and stir rapidly over high heat until mushrooms are hot and well coated with oil. Add parsley, season with salt and pepper, and serve at once.

NOTE: If you like, you can make this dish with only one kind of mushroom. You can also prepare it with butter, then season it with fresh lemon juice and snipped dill.

SAUTÉED CUCUMBERS

The pale color and mild taste of sautéed cucumbers is an excel-   6 SERVINGS
lent accompaniment to poached, broiled, or steamed fish.

5 medium cucumbers
1 teaspoon kosher salt
2 tablespoons sweet butter

5 sprigs dill, snipped
White pepper, freshly ground

Peel cucumbers, trim ends, cut in half lengthwise, and remove seeds with a teaspoon. Cut into ¼-inch half-rounds and place in a sieve. Sprinkle with salt and let drain for 30 minutes. Pat dry with paper towels.

Heat butter in a skillet until hot. Add cucumbers and sauté over medium-high heat for several minutes, or until hot but still crisp. Stir in dill and season with pepper.

◆Cucumbers can be sliced and drained early in the day, wrapped in a dish towel, and refrigerated until ready to use.

RICHARD OLNEY'S ONION PUDDING

4 TO 6
SERVINGS

It looks like a tart and is light, with a touch of sweetness. I like to serve it either hot or at room temperature with fish or on picnics.

1 pound yellow onions	½ cup milk
3 tablespoons sweet butter	2 tablespoons unbleached flour
2 eggs	About ½ teaspoon kosher salt

I suggest you use a food processor and a 9-by-2-inch round oven-proof dish.

Preheat oven to 450°F. Peel onions and slice very thin in a food processor fitted with the slicing attachment.

Heat 2 tablespoons of the butter in a skillet until hot. Add onions and sauté over low heat, mixing with a wooden spoon until they are soft, pale, and transparent (it will take about 10 minutes); let cool.

Butter an ovenproof dish with the remaining 1 tablespoon butter. Whisk eggs, milk, and flour until smooth. Combine with onions and season with salt. Pour into the prepared dish and bake for 15 to 20 minutes, or until puffy and golden. Wait for 5 minutes before serving, since the flavor of onions is more distinct when they have cooled a bit.

GRATIN OF POTATOES

4 TO 5
SERVINGS

A tasty accompaniment to broiled fish.

2 pounds baking potatoes	Black pepper, freshly ground
2½ tablespoons sweet butter, melted	¾ cup beer
Kosher salt	⅓ cup heavy cream

I suggest you use a food processor and an 9-by-2-inch round oven-proof dish.

Preheat oven to 450°F. Peel potatoes and slice very thin in a food processor fitted with the slicing attachment. Place potato slices in a sieve and rinse under cold running water until the water runs clear. Drain and pat dry in a dish towel.

Grease an ovenproof dish with some of the melted butter and arrange sliced potatoes in dish, sprinkling each layer lightly with salt and pepper. Pour on beer and melted butter.

Bake in center of oven for 10 minutes. Lower heat to 375°F and bake for another 30 minutes. Pour on cream and bake for another 10 to 15 minutes, or until top is brown and potatoes are just cooked.

BRAISED SHREDDED LEEKS

Thanks to the food processor, shredding leeks takes only a minute.

2 TO 3
SERVINGS

2 medium leeks	Kosher salt
About 1½ tablespoons butter	White pepper, freshly ground

I suggest you use a food processor.

Cut off dangling roots and green leaves from leeks. Remove tough outer leaves and discard. Cut leeks into pieces to fit sideways into the feed tube of a food processor. Use the shredding attachment to shred leeks into thin julienne strips. Place shredded leeks in a mesh sieve and wash very well under cold running water to remove all sand; drain well.

Heat butter in a saucepan until hot. Add leeks and braise, covered, over low heat for about 5 to 10 minutes, or until soft. Season well with salt and pepper.

NOTE: Avoid buying leeks that are wrapped in plastic with stems cut off. Look for fresh leeks with bright green leaves.

Pareve

BAKED POTATOES

2 SERVINGS   I am a potato-skin freak, who bakes a potato just for the crisp skin.

2 medium baking potatoes   Kosher salt
1 teaspoon unsalted margarine
    or sweet butter

Preheat oven to 450°F. Scrub potatoes with a soft vegetable brush and dry with paper towels. Rub margarine or butter over skins and sprinkle lightly with salt. Bake in a baking pan, turning once, for about 1 hour, or until potato is soft to the touch when squeezed. Serve at once.

I serve them uncut, but you can split them and serve with extra margarine, butter, or sour cream. Never wrap potatoes in foil; it prevents the skin from becoming crisp.

CORN ON THE COB

One of summer's great delights. Buy freshly picked corn straight from the farm and cook it as quickly as possible.

Corn   Kosher salt
Unsalted margarine or sweet   Pepper, freshly ground
    butter

Remove corn husks.

Bring a large pot of water to a boil. Drop in corn, cover pot, and return water to a rolling boil. Remove from heat and leave for only a minute. Take out corn with tongs and place in a cloth-lined dish. A cloth napkin keeps the corn dry and warm. Serve immediately with margarine or butter, salt, and pepper.

NOTE: When buying corn, look for small kernels; they are sweeter and less starchy.

BROILED POTATO ROUNDS

Quick, easy, greaseless potato chips.   2 SERVINGS

2 medium baking potatoes or   Kosher salt
  the equivalent in new red   Black pepper, freshly ground
  potatoes

Preheat broiler. Line the broiler pan with foil. Peel or scrub potatoes and
slice into very thin rounds (I prefer them unpeeled). Dry well in a dish
towel, place on foil, sprinkle lightly with salt and pepper, and broil very
close to heat source for about 3 minutes on each side, or until brown and
soft. Serve at once.

BAKED CHERRY TOMATOES

A last-minute quickie. Wonderful with broiled chops, poultry,   2 SERVINGS
steak, or liver.

12 medium to large cherry   2 tablespoons olive oil
  tomatoes   Kosher salt
4 sprigs Italian flat-leaf   Black pepper, freshly ground
  parsley or 4 sprigs dill

Preheat oven to 450°F. Discard tomato stems. Rinse and pat tomatoes dry.
  Remove parsley stems; wash leaves, spin dry, and chop coarsely. Or snip
dill with a scissors into small bits.
  Place cherry tomatoes in a small pan or skillet, sprinkle with olive oil,
and season lightly with salt and pepper.
  Bake for about 10 minutes, or until tomato skin begins to crack.
  Serve at once, garnished with parsley or dill.

BRAISED GRATED CARROTS

For years I have been looking for a pareve, natural alternative   4 SERVINGS
to cream. While browsing through an Indian cookbook, I
thought of experimenting with coconut cream.

1 pound medium carrots, about 6	About 1 tablespoon fresh lemon juice
¼ cup coconut cream	About 1 teaspoon sugar
3 tablespoons boiling water	About ½ teaspoon kosher salt
2 tablespoons unsalted margarine	White pepper, freshly ground

I suggest you use a food processor and a small enameled cast-iron saucepan with lid.

Peel, trim, and coarsely grate carrots in a food processor fitted with the grating attachment. Combine coconut cream with boiling water and mix until smooth. Heat margarine in a saucepan and add carrots, coconut cream and water mixture, and remaining ingredients. Mix well, bring to a boil over high heat, cover, and simmer for about 30 minutes, stirring from time to time, until carrots are soft and still crunchy. Season with salt and pepper.

NOTE: Avoid buying large carrots, since they may be tough and less sweet.

Coconut cream can be found in Indian specialty stores. It comes in a glass jar and keeps indefinitely under refrigeration. It hardens when cold, so bring it back to room temperature before measuring; if still hard, chop off the amount needed.

◆This dish can be made in advance, and then gently reheated.

BRAISED CHESTNUTS

8 SERVINGS   My favorite winter vegetable and a delightful accompaniment to any roast. Although chestnuts are time-consuming to peel, it is well worth the effort.

2½ pounds fresh chestnuts	2 tablespoons unsalted margarine
1 cup chicken stock or ½-ounce kosher consommé cube dissolved in 1 cup boiling water	Kosher salt
	Black pepper, freshly ground

I suggest you use a small enameled cast-iron saucepan with lid.

Place chestnuts in a saucepan with enough water to cover. Boil, uncovered, for 10 to 15 minutes. Remove from heat, but do not drain. One by one, peel off outer shell and inner skin. If chestnuts become difficult to peel once water has cooled, reheat and resume peeling.

Preheat oven to 325°F. Place peeled chestnuts along with remaining ingredients in a small saucepan, bring to a boil, and cover. Bake in oven for about 45 minutes, or until soft but still whole. Season.

NOTE: Chestnuts should be heavy, hard, and shiny, with no hollow feel. You can peel them several days before and keep them refrigerated.

◆This vegetable can be made earlier in the day, then reheated gently.

SHREDDED ZUCCHINI

A versatile vegetable with a crisp texture and a two-tone green color. If you are serving it with fish, sauté it in butter and sprinkle with Parmesan cheese.   6 SERVINGS

5 medium firm, unblemished zucchini	1 tablespoon unsalted margarine
2 teaspoons kosher salt	Black pepper, freshly ground
1 to 2 tablespoons olive oil	

I suggest you use a food processor.

Scrub zucchini with a vegetable brush and pat dry with paper towels. Trim ends and cut into pieces to fit into the feed tube of a food processor. Shred zucchini with the coarse shredding attachment. Empty zucchini into a sieve, sprinkle lightly with salt, mix, and let drain for 30 minutes. Wring out batches of zucchini in a dish towel.

In a skillet, heat olive oil and margarine until hot. Sauté zucchini over high heat, stirring with a wooden spoon, until zucchini is very hot but still crisp, a few minutes only. Season.

◆Zucchini can be shredded earlier in the day, wrapped in a dish towel, and refrigerated until ready to be sautéed.

BROCCOLI PUREE

1 bunch broccoli, about 1¾ pounds	1 tablespoon olive oil 4 SERVINGS
1 tablespoon unsalted margarine	Kosher salt
	Black pepper, freshly ground

I suggest you use a stainless-steel collapsible steamer basket and a food processor.

Cut off broccoli stems, peel, and cut into small pieces. Separate top into florets; rinse.

Place a steamer basket in a pot or wok with just enough water to cover bottom without touching basket. Bring water to a boil over high heat. Place broccoli in steamer, cover pot, and cook for about 2 minutes, or until *al dente.* Remove basket and let vegetable cool.

Coarsely chop steamed broccoli, in batches, in a food processor fitted with the steel blade. Remove each batch before placing in the next.

In a skillet, heat margarine and olive oil until hot. Sauté broccoli over high heat until very hot. Season with salt and pepper.

NOTE: You can make Green Bean Puree the same way by substituting 1 pound green beans. This is a good way to cook beans that are not absolutely young and snappy.

◆If you want to prepare this earlier in the day, you may steam and puree it in advance, then sauté just before serving.

STIR-FRIED SPINACH

2 TO 3 SERVINGS	1 pound fresh spinach	½ teaspoon sugar
	2 tablespoons peanut oil	1 tablespoon dry white wine
	1 clove garlic, crushed	About ¾ teaspoon kosher salt

I suggest you use a wok.

Remove spinach stems and wilted leaves and wash spinach thoroughly to remove any sand. Spin dry. If leaves are large, cut in half.

Heat a wok over high heat until hot, add oil, and heat again. Stir fry garlic for a minute; remove and discard. Add spinach and stir fry quickly until leaves are just coated with oil. Season with sugar, wine, and salt. Remove immediately with a slotted spoon to a serving platter.

NOTE: To crush garlic, bang it with a cleaver or a knife.

STIR-FRIED WATERCRESS

2 SMALL SERVINGS   Quick and delicious. A pleasant accompaniment to broiled or roasted chicken or meat.

1 bunch watercress	About 1 teaspoon black
1½ tablespoons peanut oil	Chinese soy sauce
⅓ teaspoon sugar	⅓ teaspoon kosher salt

I suggest you use a wok.

Remove bottom half of watercress stems. Wash the rest and spin dry.

Heat a wok over high heat until hot. Add oil and heat again until hot. Add watercress and stir fry very quickly until watercress is just coated with oil. Season with sugar, soy sauce, and salt. Watercress will accumulate a bit of liquid.

Dish out immediately with a slotted spoon.

STIR-FRIED SNOW PEAS

I have become fascinated with the cooking techniques and the emphasis on aesthetic presentation of food in Oriental cuisine and try to make my menus eclectic by including at least one such dish. These edible pods, once seen only in Chinese markets, have become widely available. They have a dazzling green color, crisp texture, delicate taste, and are an excellent accompaniment to any dish.

4 TO 6
SERVINGS

1 pound small young snow peas	About 1½ teaspoons kosher salt
2 tablespoons peanut oil	1½ to 2 tablespoons black Chinese soy sauce
½ teaspoon sugar	

I suggest you use a wok.

Pinch off both ends of snow peas and pull off string running along the straighter side. (If peas are very young, there may be no string. If they are more mature, there may be strings on both sides; remove them both.) Wash and drain.

Heat a wok until hot, add oil, and heat again. Add snow peas, stirring all the time until well coated with oil. Add sugar, salt, and soy sauce and cook for a minute. Remove peas with a slotted spoon to a serving dish.

NOTE: If snow peas are large, they will be less tender. In that case, steam them for about a minute before following the recipe. If you are serving the peas with a dairy meal, sauté them in butter rather than oil and omit the soy sauce.

Pasta and Grains

Dairy

CAPELLINI WITH PESTO

➤➤➤

Each season I wait for the basil to appear in the market so that I can make pesto. I like to serve it with capellini, a very thin pasta, sometimes called angel's hair. On hot summer days I serve the pasta at room temperature followed by Chlodnik (page 75), Gravlax with Mustard and Dill Sauce (page 54), salad, cheese, and fruit.

8 TO 10
FIRST-COURSE
SERVINGS

4 TO 6
MAIN-COURSE
SERVINGS

1½ cups tightly packed basil
    leaves, about 1 large bunch
2 cloves garlic, peeled and
    quartered
2 tablespoons pignolias (pine
    nuts) or walnuts
Kosher salt

½ cup olive oil
¾ to 1 cup freshly grated
    Parmesan cheese
1 pound fresh or dried
    imported capellini
Black pepper, freshly ground

I suggest you use a food processor.

To make the sauce: Remove basil stems; wash leaves and spin dry. Place in a food processor fitted with the steel blade and add garlic, pignolias, and 1 teaspoon of the salt. With the motor on, dribble in the oil. Scrape down sides of bowl with a spatula and puree until very smooth. Transfer pesto to a bowl and combine with ¾ cup of the Parmesan cheese.

To cook the pasta: Bring 5 quarts water to a rolling boil in a large covered pot. Add 2 tablespoons of the salt and all the pasta at once, stirring with a wooden spoon. Boil briskly for about 3 to 4 minutes for fresh pasta, longer if dried, or until *al dente.* Test frequently, since pasta is very thin and cooks rapidly. Drain well, shaking vigorously in a sieve.

    Toss with sauce. (If you do not mind, the best way of tossing this pasta is with your hands.) Adjust seasoning with salt and pepper and serve with remaining Parmesan cheese.

NOTE: Pesto made with pignolias has a brighter green color than that made with walnuts.

◆If you wish to make pesto several days ahead of time, puree the basil with the olive oil and nuts, but omit the garlic, salt, pepper, and Parmesan cheese. Add those when ready to serve. Similarly, if you want to prolong basil's short season, you can freeze the pureed basil, oil, and nuts in covered containers and add the remaining ingredients at serving time.

I often make this entire dish a day in advance and serve it at room temperature. After refrigeration, the strands of pasta stick to one another and have to be tossed with the hands to separate them; adjust the seasoning again.

CAPELLINI WITH
RAW TOMATO–BASIL SAUCE

8 TO 10
FIRST-COURSE
SERVINGS

4 TO 6
MAIN-COURSE
SERVINGS

A delightfully easy-to-make summer dish that doesn't require any cooking. I serve it at room temperature, but it is equally good hot. You can omit the Parmesan cheese and have it pareve.

5 medium ripe tomatoes
Kosher salt
1¼ cups tightly packed basil
  leaves
2 cloves garlic
⅓ cup olive oil

About ½ cup freshly grated
  Parmesan cheese
Black pepper, freshly ground
1 pound fresh or dried
  imported capellini

I suggest you use a food processor.

To make the sauce: Skin, core, seed, and chop tomatoes coarsely. Place them in a bowl and mix with 1 tablespoon of the salt. Let stand for about 1 hour.

Remove basil stems; wash leaves and spin dry. Place basil and garlic in a food processor fitted with the steel blade. With the motor on, dribble in olive oil and blend until smooth.

Combine basil puree with tomatoes and cheese. Season with salt and pepper.

To cook the pasta: Bring 5 quarts water to a rolling boil in a large covered pot. Add 2 tablespoons of the salt and all the pasta at once, stirring with a wooden spoon. Boil briskly for about 3 to 4 minutes for fresh pasta, longer if dried, or until pasta is *al dente.* Test frequently, since this pasta cooks very rapidly. Drain well, shaking vigorously in a sieve. Place in a bowl and toss well with sauce. Season with salt and pepper.

NOTE: If you wish to serve this pasta hot, heat the sauce and the serving bowl. Have extra Parmesan cheese on hand.

SPINACH FETTUCCINE WITH
SOUR CREAM, PARSLEY, AND DILL SAUCE

Serve either hot or at room temperature.

6
FIRST-COURSE
SERVINGS

2 cloves garlic	10 sprigs dill, snipped
3 scallions, including green parts	1 cup sour cream
	Kosher salt
¼ bunch Italian flat-leaf parsley	Black pepper, freshly ground
	1 pound fresh or dried
1 tablespoon sweet butter	imported spinach fettuccine

I suggest you use a small enameled cast-iron saucepan.

To make the sauce: Peel and chop garlic very fine. Trim scallions, wipe with a damp paper towel, and chop very fine. Remove parsley stems; wash leaves, spin dry, and chop fine.

Heat butter in a small saucepan and sauté garlic over low heat for a few minutes. Stir in scallions, parsley, dill, and sour cream. Remove from heat and season with salt and pepper.

When pasta is ready, reheat sauce, but do not let it boil for more than a minute.

To cook the pasta   Bring 5 quarts water to a rolling boil in a large covered pot. Add 2 tablespoons of the salt and all the pasta at once, stirring with a wooden spoon. Boil briskly for about 3 to 4 minutes for fresh pasta, longer if dried, or until pasta is *al dente.* Test frequently, since it is impossible to gauge the cooking time precisely. Drain well, shaking vigorously in a sieve. Toss thoroughly in a bowl with the sauce. Season with salt and pepper.

LINGUINE WITH ANCHOVY CREAM
AND ZUCCHINI SAUCE

Anchovies give this sauce a piquant flavor, and the zucchini gives it a beautiful color.

6 SERVINGS

2 medium zucchini	White pepper, freshly ground
1 cup heavy cream	1 pound fresh or dried
2 to 3 anchovy fillets	imported linguine
2 tablespoons sweet butter	Parmesan cheese, freshly
Kosher salt	ground

I suggest you use a food processor and an enameled cast-iron saucepan.

To make the sauce: Wash zucchini and pat dry with paper towels. Trim ends and slice into thin strips with the coarse grating attachment of a food processor. Wring the juliennes in a towel to dry.

Boil cream uncovered in a saucepan over medium heat until it is reduced to slightly more than half. Stir from time to time.

Rinse anchovy fillets, pat dry with paper towel, and mince very fine. Stir into sauce along with butter and zucchini. Season with salt and pepper.

To cook the pasta: Bring 5 quarts water to a rolling boil in a large covered pot. Add 2 tablespoons of the salt and all the pasta at once. Stir with a wooden spoon and boil briskly for about 2 to 3 minutes for fresh pasta, longer if dried, or until pasta is *al dente.* Test frequently. Drain well, shaking vigorously in a sieve. Place in a heated serving bowl and coat with the hot sauce. Season with salt and pepper. Serve with Parmesan cheese.

PENNE WITH EGGPLANT, TOMATOES, ANCHOVIES, AND OLIVES

6 SERVINGS   Summer ingredients blend into a well-flavored sauce. This pasta can be served either hot or at room temperature.

1 medium eggplant, about 1 pound	About 15 black olives (Gaeta)
	About ⅓ cup olive oil
Kosher salt	1 pound dried imported penne
1 large onion	or other tubular pasta
4 cloves garlic	About ½ cup freshly grated
4 anchovy fillets	Parmesan cheese
4 medium ripe tomatoes	Black pepper, freshly ground
¾ to 1 cup tightly packed basil leaves	

I suggest you use a food processor.

To make the sauce: Peel eggplant and cut into ¼-inch cubes. Soak for about 1 hour in a large bowl of ice water to which 2 tablespoons of salt have been added. Drain, then squeeze gently in a dish towel to dry; set aside.

Peel onion and garlic, cut into quarters, and chop fine in a food processor fitted with the steel blade.

Rinse anchovy fillets, pat dry with a paper towel, and chop fine; set aside.

Peel, core, seed, and chop tomatoes coarsely. Remove basil stems; wash leaves, spin dry, and chop coarsely in the food processor. Pit olives and cut into slivers.

In a medium skillet, heat 4 tablespoons of the olive oil until hot. Sauté eggplant over high heat for about 5 minutes; transfer to a bowl. Add remaining olive oil and sauté onion and garlic over low heat until soft and transparent. (If too dry, add more olive oil.) Add anchovies, tomatoes, and eggplant and cook sauce slowly for about 10 minutes. Add basil and olives and keep warm.

To cook the pasta: Bring 5 quarts water to a rolling boil in a large covered pot. Add 2 tablespoons of the salt and all the pasta at once, stirring with a wooden spoon. Boil briskly for about 7 minutes, or until *al dente.* Test frequently. Drain well, shaking vigorously in a sieve. Place pasta in a heated bowl and toss well with the sauce and Parmesan cheese. Season with salt and pepper.

NOTE: Gaeta olives are indigenous to the Campania region of Italy. They are mostly used in cooking and have a dark purple color.

TAMARA'S RISOTTO

The classic risotto is made with Italian Arborio rice, is cooked slowly in chicken broth, white wine, and saffron, and is combined with butter and Parmesan cheese. This unconventional method, taught to me by a dear friend, is incredibly easy and a wonderful addition to a kosher cuisine.

4
FIRST-COURSE
SERVINGS

1 cup long-grain rice (Uncle Ben's converted brand)
1¼ cups cold water
½ cup dry white wine
About ½ teaspoon kosher salt
White pepper, freshly ground

2 tablespoons sweet butter
About ½ cup heavy cream
½ cup freshly grated Parmesan cheese
Water

I suggest you use an enameled cast-iron saucepan with lid.

In a saucepan, combine rice, water, and wine. Bring to a boil and cook briskly over high heat until all the liquid is absorbed and little holes appear on top of the rice. Cover and simmer over the lowest heat for 3 to 5 minutes, depending on how soft you like the rice. Stir with a fork and add salt, pepper, butter, cream, ¼ cup of the Parmesan cheese, and some water if necessary. Rice should be moist and well seasoned. Serve immediately in individual heated plates with remaining Parmesan cheese and a pepper mill on the side.

NOTE: For variety, add steamed seasonal vegetables: sautéed sliced mushrooms, steamed asparagus tips, cooked green peas, or steamed fish.

PENNE WITH MUSHROOM SAUCE

6 SERVINGS   I love the flavor and aroma of fresh wild mushrooms, but they are not easily available in the United States. To approximate that flavor, I have combined dried imported Italian mushrooms with fresh cultivated ones. This pasta can also be served at room temperature.

¾ ounce dried Italian mushrooms
¾ cup boiling water
3 scallions, including green parts, or 1 small onion
3 cloves garlic
4 tablespoons (½ stick) unsalted margarine

5 tablespoons olive oil
1 pound firm fresh mushrooms
½ bunch Italian flat-leaf parsley
½ bunch fresh basil (optional)

1 pound dried imported penne or other tubular pasta

Kosher salt
Black pepper, freshly ground

I suggest you use a food processor and a large enameled cast-iron skillet with lid.

To make the sauce: Place dried mushrooms in a small bowl and pour boiling water over them. Let soak for about 1 hour. Strain soaking liquid through a sieve lined with a paper towel, squeezing mushrooms over sieve to extract more liquid; set liquid aside. Wash mushrooms carefully to remove sand, pat dry with paper towels, and chop coarsely; set aside.

Trim scallions, dry with a damp paper towel, and cut into small pieces; or peel and quarter onion. Peel and quarter garlic. Place scallions or onion along with garlic in a food processor fitted with the steel blade and chop fine.

Heat 1 tablespoon of the margarine and 1 tablespoon of the olive oil in a large skillet until hot. Sauté scallions and garlic over low heat for a few minutes.

In the meantime, wipe fresh mushrooms with a damp paper towel and quarter them if they are too large to fit into the feed tube of your food processor. Shred mushrooms in food processor fitted with the coarse grating attachment. Add reserved mushroom liquid to skillet and boil over high heat until liquid is reduced to 1 tablespoon. Add remaining 3 tablespoons margarine and 4 tablespoons olive oil, soaked dried mushrooms, and shredded fresh ones. Mix well and cook, covered, over low heat for 15 minutes, stirring once in a while.

Remove parsley and basil stems. Wash leaves, spin dry, and chop fine. Add to sauce and season well.

To cook the pasta: Bring 5 quarts water to a rolling boil in a large covered pot. Add 2 tablespoons of the salt and all the pasta at once, stirring with a wooden spoon. Boil briskly for about 7 minutes, or until pasta is *al dente.* Test frequently, since it is impossible to gauge the cooking time precisely. Drain well, shaking vigorously in a sieve. Toss with the hot sauce.

SPAGHETTINI WITH BASIL, PARSLEY, AND TUNA SAUCE

The sauce for this pasta does not require any cooking; all the ingredients are simply blended together, a summer meal-in-itself.

8
FIRST-COURSE SERVINGS

6
MAIN-COURSE SERVINGS

3 to 4 tablespoons pine nuts	⅓ cup olive oil
1½ cups tightly packed basil leaves	10 ounces Italian light tuna (Genova or Pastene brand), drained and separated into large pieces
1 cup tightly packed Italian flat-leaf parsley	
2 cloves garlic	Kosher salt
6 anchovy fillets	Black pepper, freshly ground
Juice of about ½ lemon, strained	1 pound fresh or dried imported spaghettini

I suggest you use a food processor.

To make the sauce: Preheat oven to 350°F. Roast pine nuts in oven for about 10 minutes, or until golden. (Roasting brings out their flavor.)

Remove basil and parsley stems. Wash leaves and spin dry. Peel and quarter garlic. Soak anchovies in cold water for 5 minutes, drain, and pat dry with paper towels.

Place basil, parsley, garlic, and anchovies in a food processor fitted with the steel blade. With the motor on, pour in most of lemon juice and oil.

Puree until smooth. Transfer sauce to a large serving bowl and combine with tuna and pine nuts.

To cook the pasta: Bring 5 quarts water to a boil in a large pot. Add 2 tablespoons of the salt and all the pasta at once, stirring with a wooden spoon. Boil briskly for about 7 minutes, or until pasta is *al dente*. Test frequently, since it is impossible to gauge the cooking time precisely. Drain well, shaking vigorously in a sieve. Mix with sauce and season with salt and pepper and extra lemon juice if needed.

NOTE: If imported tuna is unavailable, use a domestic brand.

PLAIN BOILED RICE

4 TO 6
SERVINGS

I am grateful to a Japanese lady who used to baby-sit for my children for teaching me this foolproof method of boiling rice, in which each grain remains separate and firm to the bite. You can make it more elaborate by adding sliced sautéed mushrooms, chopped parsley, or powdered saffron; you can also cook it without any shortening.

1 cup long-grain rice (Uncle Ben's converted brand)

1 tablespoon unsalted margarine or sweet butter

1 cup cold water

About 1 teaspoon kosher salt

I suggest you use a small enameled cast-iron saucepan with lid.

Place all ingredients in a saucepan with a tight-fitting lid. Cover and cook over lowest heat for about 45 minutes, or until water is absorbed and rice is cooked to your taste. If undercooked, add 1 to 2 tablespoons boiling water and cook for another few minutes. Fluff rice with a fork while hot.

◆This rice can be cooked in advance and then gently reheated.

CHINESE-STYLE BOILED RICE

6 SERVINGS

This unseasoned boiled rice is served with Chinese dishes only. It is cooked until soft, so that it can be picked up with chopsticks.

1½ cups extra-long-grain rice (enriched Carolina brand)

2 cups cold water

Place rice in a sieve and rinse under cold running water until water runs clear. Drain well and place in a small saucepan with a tight-fitting lid. Add water and bring to a boil, uncovered, over high heat. Boil for 1 to 2 minutes, or until zigzag lines appear in rice. Cover and cook over the lowest heat for 20 minutes. Remove from heat and leave cover on for another 10 minutes. Fluff rice with a fork or chopsticks.

◆This rice can be cooked earlier in the day and then gently reheated.

BULGUR

‑⫸⫸

A Middle Eastern specialty. I like it with meat or poultry, but not fish. 2 SERVINGS

½ cup water	About ½ teaspoon kosher salt
½ tablespoon unsalted margarine	½ cup fine- or medium-grain bulgur

I suggest you use a small enameled cast-iron saucepan with lid.

Bring water, margarine, and salt to a boil in a small saucepan. Add bulgur, cover, and simmer for about 15 minutes, or until water is absorbed; the texture should be crunchy. If you prefer it softer, add 1 to 2 tablespoons boiling water and simmer for a few more minutes. Stir with a fork to fluff grains while still hot.

◆You can make bulgur in advance and then gently reheat it.

COUSCOUS

‑⫸⫸

Couscous is a fine semolina made from wheat grain. 2 SERVINGS

½ cup water	About ½ teaspoon kosher salt
½ tablespoon unsalted margarine	½ cup couscous

I suggest you use a small enameled cast-iron saucepan with lid.

Bring water, margarine, and salt to a boil in a small saucepan. Add couscous, cover, and simmer for about 10 minutes, or until all water is absorbed. Stir with a fork to fluff grains. Season to taste.

◆Couscous can be cooked in advance and then gently reheated.

STIR-FRIED RICE

2 TO 3
SERVINGS

A wonderful rice variation; a good accompaniment to roasted or broiled meat or fowl.

1½ cups extra-long-grain rice (enriched Carolina brand)
⅔ cup cold water
2 tablespoons peanut oil
2 scallions, including green parts, chopped fine

¼ pound raw shelled sweet peas or the equivalent in frozen
About 1 tablespoon black Chinese soy sauce
About ½ teaspoon kosher salt

I suggest you use a wok.

Rinse rice in a sieve under cold running water until water runs clear. Combine rice and water in a saucepan and bring to a boil over high heat. Boil for 1 to 2 minutes, or until zigzag lines appear in rice. Cover and steam over lowest heat for 15 minutes. Do not uncover for another 10 minutes. Fluff grains with a fork.

Heat a wok over high heat until hot. Add oil and heat. Lower heat a bit and stir fry rice along with scallions and peas. (If you are using frozen peas, first defrost them, drain, and pat dry with paper towels.) Season with soy sauce and salt.

◆If you are not serving the rice right away, transfer to a saucepan and reheat gently later.

BAKED WILD RICE WITH WHITE RICE

6 SERVINGS

A delightful accompaniment to any roast poultry or beef.

½ cup long-grain wild rice
½ cup natural long-grain rice (Uncle Ben's converted brand)
1 small onion, chopped fine
1 tablespoon thin Chinese soy sauce

2 cups boiling water
1 package MBT Instant Vegetable Broth
¼ bunch Italian flat-leaf parsley, chopped fine
½ cup Macadamia nuts, chopped coarse
Kosher salt

I suggest you use a 1- to 1½-quart enameled cast-iron saucepan with lid.

Preheat oven to 350°F. Combine both rices, onion, and soy sauce in a saucepan. In boiling water, dissolve vegetable granules. Pour over rice, cover, and place in center of oven for 30 minutes.

Uncover, stir in parsley and nuts, and continue cooking in oven for another 15 minutes, or until soft. Fluff rice grains with a fork and correct seasoning.

◆Rice can be prepared earlier in the day and then gently reheated.

KASHA

A nutritious staple in Russian and Eastern European cuisine. For variety, add sliced sautéed mushrooms, sautéed chopped onions, cooked bow-tie noodles, chopped parsley, or snipped dill. I like it with meat or poultry, but not fish.

4 TO 6
SERVINGS

1 egg	1 tablespoon unsalted
About ¾ tablespoon kosher	margarine
salt	2 to 3 tablespoons vegetable
1 cup kasha (medium-grain	oil
buckwheat groats)	Generous 1 cup boiling water

I suggest you use a small enameled cast-iron saucepan.

In a small bowl, beat egg with a fork and add salt and kasha. Heat margarine and oil in a small saucepan. Add kasha and stir with a wooden spoon until groats are well coated with shortening. Add boiling water, cover, and simmer over very low heat for about 15 minutes, or until all the water is absorbed and the grains are soft. If grains are not soft, add 1 to 2 tablespoons boiling water and simmer for another few minutes. Stir with a fork at once in order to fluff the grains. Correct seasoning. If you are adding other vegetables or herbs, do it after kasha is fluffed.

NOTE: I prefer medium-grain kasha; it is more delicate.

◆Kasha can be made in advance and gently reheated.

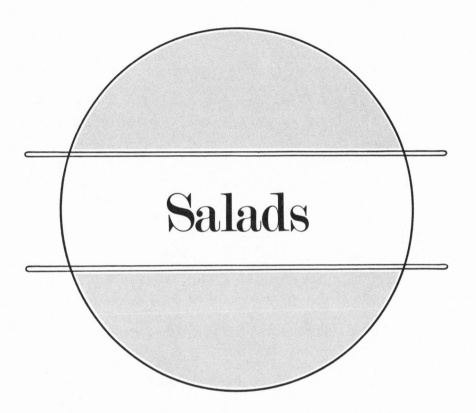

Salads

Pareve

BEAN SPROUT SALAD

Crunchy and pale with an unusual combination of flavors. I find it to be a good accompaniment to cold meats or poultry.

2 TO 3
SERVINGS

1 pound fresh bean sprouts
1 clove garlic
1-inch piece fresh gingerroot
2 scallions, including green parts
2 tablespoons corn or peanut oil

1 teaspoon kosher salt
½ teaspoon sugar
White pepper, freshly ground
1 teaspoon dry white wine
1 teaspoon sesame oil

I suggest you use a wok.

Snip off yellow heads and brown tips of bean sprouts. (It is a tedious job, but the salad looks so much prettier without them.) Place bean sprouts in a sieve and wash. Pour boiling water over them and drain very well.

Peel and crush garlic by smashing it with the blade of a knife or cleaver. Peel gingerroot and chop very fine. Trim scallions, pat dry with paper towel, and shred so they are same size as bean sprouts.

Heat a wok over high heat until hot; add oil. When oil is hot, add garlic and stir fry over medium-high heat. Remove and discard garlic. Add gingerroot, scallions, bean sprouts, salt, sugar, pepper, and wine to wok. Mix over high heat until sprouts are well coated. Remove with a slotted spoon to a bowl and season with sesame oil. Let cool, then chill.

NOTE: Look for chalky white, not gray, bean sprouts.
Sesame oil is available in Oriental stores; keep it refrigerated.

BEET SALAD

Fresh beets seem to be an underrated vegetable in the United States, but they are quite popular in Europe. They are full of vitamins and minerals. Their flavor and color are enhanced by

4 TO 6
SERVINGS

baking, rather than boiling. You can serve them in many different shapes: julienned, cubed, thinly sliced. You can also serve
them alone, with olive oil and lemon juice, or vinaigrette dressing, or combine them with endives and watercress.

8 small to medium beets	Fresh lemon juice, strained, or
About 2 tablespoons olive oil	Vinaigrette Dressing (page
Kosher salt	264) to taste
Black pepper, freshly ground	

I suggest you use a food processor.

Preheat oven to 400°F. Trim all but 1 inch from leafy beet tops. Place in
baking pan and bake in upper part of oven for 1 to 1½ hours, or until
tender but still firm, turning them occasionally. To test if beets are ready,
pierce centers with a thick sewing needle. Let cool, peel, and cut into any
shape you like in a food processor. Toss with olive oil. Just before serving
(or they will discolor), toss with salt, pepper, and lemon juice, or Vinaigrette
Dressing.

NOTE: Avoid buying large beets or those without leafy green tops; they
may be woody and colorless.

◆If you like, you can bake the beets a day ahead of time, but serve them
at room temperature.

BROCCOLI SALAD

4 SERVINGS   Bright green and crunchy.

1 bunch fresh broccoli, about	Black pepper, freshly ground
1¾ pounds	White wine vinegar or fresh
2 tablespoons olive oil	lemon juice to taste
Kosher salt	

I suggest you use a collapsible stainless-steel steamer basket.

Cut off all but ¼ inch from broccoli stems. Peel and cut it into 1-inch-long
julienne strips. Separate top into florets. Rinse.
     Place a steamer basket in a pot or wok and add enough water to reach
just below it. Arrange broccoli in basket and steam over high heat for about
3 minutes, or until *al dente.* Place in a bowl and toss while still warm with
olive oil, salt, and pepper. Just before serving, season with vinegar or lemon
juice. (Vinegar and lemon discolor this green vegetable.)

NOTE: When buying broccoli, look for young, green, unopened buds and thin, nonwoody stems.

◆If you like, you can steam the broccoli a day ahead of time, but serve it at room temperature.

CAULIFLOWER SALAD

I prefer to steam cauliflower and serve it plain to preserve its natural flavor.   4 SERVINGS

1 medium head cauliflower, about 1¾ pounds
2 tablespoons olive oil
Kosher salt

White pepper, freshly ground
White wine vinegar or fresh lemon juice to taste

I suggest you use a collapsible stainless-steel steamer basket.

Cut off all but ¼ inch from heavy stem. Separate top into florets; rinse. Place a steamer basket in a pot or wok and add enough water to reach just below it. Arrange cauliflower in basket, cover, and steam over high heat for about 4 minutes, or until *al dente.* Place in a bowl and toss while still warm with olive oil, salt, and pepper. Just before serving, toss with vinegar or lemon juice.

NOTE: Look for creamy white cauliflower, with closely packed florets and green leaves at the base.

◆Cauliflower can be steamed a day ahead of time and refrigerated, but serve it at room temperature and adjust seasoning.

GRATED CARROT SALAD

If you own a food processor, this dish takes a minute to prepare. It is crunchy, lemony, colorful, and nutritious.   6 SERVINGS

6 medium carrots
About 1 tablespoon olive oil
About 1 tablespoon sugar

Juice of about ½ lemon, strained
Kosher salt
White pepper, freshly ground

I suggest you use a food processor.

Peel, trim, and grate carrots coarsely in a food processor fitted with the grating attachment. Toss with remaining ingredients.

NOTE: Buy small to medium carrots with leafy tops still intact. Large carrots tend to be woody.

◆This salad can be refrigerated overnight, but serve it at room temperature, readjusting the seasoning if necessary.

CUCUMBER SALAD

6 SERVINGS   A refreshing summer salad that is a good accompaniment to fish.

6 medium cucumbers
Kosher salt
1 to 2 tablespoons tarragon
   wine vinegar

1 to 2 tablespoons olive oil
White pepper, freshly ground
10 sprigs dill, snipped

I suggest you use a food processor.

Peel cucumbers, trim ends, cut in half lengthwise and remove seeds with a teaspoon. Slice thinly into half-rounds in a food processor fitted with the slicing attachment or by hand. Place in a sieve, sprinkle with 1 tablespoon kosher salt, and leave to drain for 30 minutes. (Salt drains some of the cucumber juices, leaving them limp but crisp.) Pat dry with paper towels. Toss with vinegar, olive oil, salt, pepper, and dill. (If you refrigerate this salad for any length of time, you may have to readjust the seasoning.)

NOTE: If Kirby cucumbers are available, try them; they are crisper.

If you are serving this salad with a dairy meal, combine cucumbers with several tablespoons sour cream or yogurt, just enough to coat.

EGGPLANT SALAD

4 SERVINGS   I like to serve this vegetable plain so that its delicate flavor may be savored.

2 medium eggplants, about 1
   pound each
Kosher salt

About ⅓ cup olive oil
Black pepper, freshly ground
Fresh lemon juice (optional)

Peel eggplants and cut into 1-inch cubes. Soak for about 1 hour in a large bowl of ice water to which 3 tablespoons of the kosher salt have been added. Drain, then squeeze gently in a dish towel to dry.

Preheat broiler. Line the broiler pan with foil and place eggplant cubes on it. Brush with half the olive oil and broil for about 5 minutes, or until light brown.

Turn cubes over with tongs and repeat. Let cool, then season with salt and pepper and a little lemon juice if you like.

NOTE: Select eggplants carefully: Look for glossy, unblemished, and firm skin. If they are very seedy, scrape off any seeds you can before broiling.

◆You can prepare this salad a day ahead of time, but serve it at room temperature and adjust the seasoning.

RED AND WHITE CABBAGE

I like to serve both cabbages together, but not combine them, since they absorb the dressing differently.

EACH SALAD SERVES 4

1 small head firm white cabbage, about 1½ pounds	2 tablespoons tarragon wine vinegar
1 small head firm red cabbage, about 1½ pounds	2 teaspoons Dijon-type mustard
About ¼ cup Mayonnaise (page 265)	1¾ tablespoons kosher salt
¼ cup olive oil	Black pepper, freshly ground

I suggest you use a food processor.

Discard limp and discolored outer cabbage leaves. Quarter cabbages and cut out center core. Shred each cabbage fine in a food processor fitted with the shredding attachment. Transfer shredded cabbages to separate bowls. Make a dressing with remaining ingredients. Toss each vegetable with half the dressing. Let stand for a few minutes, then toss again. Season well.

NOTE: Do not prepare these salads more than a day in advance, or they may lose some of their crunchiness.

For added flavor, add chopped scallions and parsley.

If you want to serve these salads with a dairy meal, make the dressing with mayonnaise and sour cream instead of oil.

ENDIVE, ARUGULA, AND ALFALFA SPROUT SALAD

I like to serve salad after the main course and have grown accustomed to that cleansing of the palate before dessert.

6 SERVINGS

2 bunches arugula	About ⅓ cup Vinaigrette
4 medium endives	Dressing (page 264)
About 3 ounces alfalfa sprouts	Black pepper, freshly ground

Discard most of the arugula stems. Wash leaves and spin dry. Trim endive bottoms and discard any discolored outer leaves. Separate the rest and wipe with a damp paper towel if necessary. (Endives rarely require further washing.) Trim flat ends of leaves and cut into wide julienne strips. Place arugula, endives, and alfalfa sprouts in a salad bowl and leave uncovered in the refrigerator. Just before serving, pour over some of the dressing and toss with your hands. Avoid drowning the leaves with dressing. Pass a pepper mill around the table.

NOTE: Arugula is sold in bunches, sometimes with the roots left on. After spin drying the leaves, spread them on paper towels and leave exposed to the air for a few minutes; they will dry completely. Wrap in a paper towel, place in a plastic bag, and refrigerate. They can be left overnight.

MUSHROOM SALAD

4 SERVINGS Do make this salad when white, firm fresh mushrooms are available. It is delicious with both fish and meat or as a first course.

¼ bunch Italian flat-leaf parsley or dill	About 3 tablespoons fresh lemon juice, strained
1 pound firm fresh mushrooms	Kosher salt
6 tablespoons olive oil	White pepper, freshly ground

Remove parsley stems; wash leaves, spin dry, and chop fine. Or snip dill with scissors into small bits. Wipe mushrooms with a damp paper towel. Trim stem ends if necessary. Slice mushrooms into paper-thin slices and place in a bowl. Toss with olive oil, lemon juice, and parsley or dill. Season with salt and pepper and serve right away.

NOTE: When buying mushrooms, look for white, very firm caps, with no opening between the cap and stem. If the mushrooms are not absolutely fresh, do not bother making this salad.

FLAGEOLET SALAD

8 TO 10 SERVINGS Flageolets are delicate green shell beans, like tiny limas. They are difficult to find fresh in the United States, but they are

available dried. This salad is a good accompaniment to other salads or to cold poultry or meats.

2 cups dried flageolets	2 tablespoons tarragon wine
¼ cup olive oil	vinegar
¼ bunch Italian flat-leaf	Kosher salt
parsley	White pepper, freshly ground

I suggest you use an enameled cast-iron saucepan with lid.

Place beans in a bowl with enough water to cover generously. Soak overnight. Drain and place in a saucepan with enough water to cover beans by about 2 inches. Bring to a boil and cook slowly, half covered, for about 1 hour, or until beans are tender. Drain and place in a large bowl. Toss with olive oil while still hot.

Remove parsley stems; wash leaves, spin dry, and chop fine. Toss beans with parsley, vinegar, salt, and pepper. After refrigeration, adjust seasoning.

NOTE: The dried flageolets sold in health food stores are generally fresher and more flavorful than those found in supermarkets.

◆You can make this salad a day in advance, but serve it at room temperature.

FUSILLI SALAD

I am very fond of all types of pasta. This simple salad can be   8 SERVINGS
made more elaborate and colorful by adding fresh steamed vegetables to it. The salad should be made a day ahead of time to allow the flavors to blend, but serve it at room temperature.

3 scallions, including green	1 pound dried imported fusilli
parts	or any other tubular pasta
1 small bunch Italian flat-leaf	½ cup strong Vinaigrette
parsley	Dressing (page 264)
Kosher salt	Black pepper, freshly ground

Trim scallions, wipe with a damp paper towel, and chop fine. Remove parsley stems; wash leaves, spin dry, and chop coarsely.

Bring 5 quarts water to a boil in a large pot. Add 2 tablespoons of the salt and all the pasta at once, stirring with a wooden spoon. Boil briskly for about 5 minutes, or until pasta is *al dente.* Test frequently to avoid overcooking; this pasta should be more *al dente* than usual. Drain well, shaking vigorously in a sieve.

Place pasta in a bowl and toss with some of the dressing, scallions, and parsley, using your hands. Cover well and refrigerate.

Before serving, toss salad with remaining dressing and season with salt and pepper. If you like, add fresh sweet peas, thinly sliced white radishes, steamed cubed zucchini, steamed broccoli florets, and any other vegetables you may prefer. Do not add the vegetables to the salad in advance, or they will discolor.

POTATO SALAD

6 TO 8 SERVINGS

VINAIGRETTE DRESSING:

2 tablespoons tarragon wine vinegar	1½ teaspoons kosher salt
1 teaspoon Dijon-type mustard	Black pepper, freshly ground
	½ cup olive oil

2½ pounds red new potatoes, about 2 inches in diameter	½ bunch Italian flat-leaf parsley
4 scallions, including green parts	Kosher salt
	Black pepper, freshly ground

I suggest you use a blender and a large stainless-steel collapsible steamer basket.

To make the dressing: Put vinegar, mustard, salt, and pepper in a blender. With motor on, dribble in oil through lid opening until thoroughly blended; set aside.

Scrub potatoes well and cut a thin strip of skin from center of each to keep skin from bursting.

Place a steamer basket in a pot or wok and add enough water to reach just below it. Arrange potatoes, preferably in a single layer, in basket and steam over medium-high heat for about 20 minutes, or until just tender. Test by piercing center with a thick sewing needles. (If you must cook potatoes in a double layer, switch layers after 10 minutes by bringing bottom layer to top.) Finally, lift out basket and cover loosely with a dish towel until potatoes are cool enough to handle.

While potatoes are steaming, trim scallions, wipe with a damp paper towel, and slice into thin rounds. Remove parsley stems; wash leaves, spin dry, and chop fine.

Cut potatoes into quarters or eighths, depending on their size. Toss lightly with dressing, scallions, and parsley. Season with salt and pepper. Potatoes will absorb dressing best when hot, giving the salad a special flavor.

NOTE: So-called new potatoes are not really new, but young, having not yet reached maturity. They should be even in size so that they all cook at the same time.

RICE SALAD

A favorite summer salad, which can be served with other salads or as an accompaniment to cold meats or poultry. I like to serve it plain or, at times, with chopped scallions, green peas, and green pepper cut into small cubes.

8 TO 10 SERVINGS

1½ cups long-grain rice (Uncle Ben's converted brand)
2½ cups cold water
About 2 tablespoons olive oil
½ bunch Italian flat-leaf parsley

About 1½ tablespoons tarragon wine vinegar
About 1 tablespoon kosher salt
White pepper, freshly ground

I suggest you use an enameled cast-iron saucepan with lid.

Combine rice and water in a saucepan. Cover and boil over very low heat for about 45 minutes to 1 hour, or until water has disappeared and rice is very soft, but not mushy. If all water has been absorbed and rice is still undercooked, add 1 to 2 tablespoons boiling water and boil for another few minutes. (It is important for rice grains to be soft; they harden when refrigerated.) Do not stir rice until it is ready and then only with a fork.

Empty rice into a large bowl. Using a fork, toss with olive oil. Let cool.

In the meantime, remove parsley stems; wash leaves, spin dry, and chop fine. Add vinegar and parsley to rice. Season with salt and pepper, toss, and refrigerate. If you like, add chopped scallions, green peppers, peas, or other vegetables now. Readjust seasoning before serving.

◆You can make this salad a day ahead of time, but be sure to bring it back to room temperature before serving.

TABBOULI SALAD

A lemony Middle Eastern salad. Wonderful served with other salads or with cold meat or poultry.

6 TO 8 SERVINGS

1 cup fine or medium-fine bulgur (cracked wheat)	¼ cup olive oil
1¾ cups boiling water	About ⅓ cup fresh lemon juice, strained
3 scallions, including green parts	Kosher salt
1 green pepper	Black pepper, freshly ground
¼ bunch Italian flat-leaf parsley	10 fresh mint leaves, chopped fine (optional)

Place bulgur (cracked wheat) in a large bowl and pour on boiling water. Let soak for about 30 minutes; water should be absorbed and grains should be fairly dry and fluffy. (If you have used a coarser grain of bulgur and all water is not absorbed, drain bulgur in a mesh sieve.)

Trim scallions, wipe with a damp paper towel, and chop fine. Remove ribs and seeds of green pepper and cut into fine cubes. Remove parsley stems; wash leaves, spin dry, and chop fine. Stir all ingredients into bulgur along with olive oil, lemon juice, salt, and pepper. Before serving, adjust seasoning; salad should be lemony. Add mint if you like.

NOTE: Bulgur (cracked wheat) can be found in health food stores, specialty shops, and most supermarkets. You can add other ingredients to this salad, such as peeled, seeded, and cubed tomatoes; chopped radishes; peeled, seeded, and cubed cucumbers. You can also add more parsley and mint.

◆You can make this salad a day ahead of time to allow the flavors to blend, but serve it at room temperature.

SALADE NIÇOISE

4 SERVINGS   Be as adventurous as you like with the ingredients. Have each one ready, but keep them separate. Just before serving, arrange all the ingredients attractively in a large glass bowl and toss with the dressing.

4 small red new potatoes	4 anchovy fillets
¼ pound fresh green beans	10 ounces tuna fish packed in oil, drained and separated into large pieces
1 cucumber	
1 green pepper	
2 scallions, including green parts	¼ pound feta cheese, separated into large pieces (optional)
2 medium ripe tomatoes	
1 medium head Boston lettuce or salad-bowl lettuce or a combination of both	About 8 black olives (Gaeta)
	4 eggs, hard-boiled and quartered

2 to 3 tablespoons capers
Italian flat-leaf parsley,
  chopped
Basil, chopped

Kosher salt
Black pepper freshly ground
½ cup strong Vinaigrette
  Dressing (page 264)

Steam potatoes in their jackets until *al dente;* let cool. Slice thin, then cover with plastic wrap to prevent discoloration.

Trim beans, steam until *al dente,* refresh with cold water, and drain.

Peel cucumber, trim ends (which are bitter), cut lengthwise, remove seeds with a teaspoon and discard. Cut into 2-inch pieces, then slice into ¼-inch julienne strips.

Wash and dry green pepper. Remove ribs and seeds and cut into strips.

Trim scallions and wipe with a damp paper towel. Cut into 2-inch pieces and slice into thin julienne strips.

Rinse, pat dry, core, and quarter tomatoes.

Separate salad greens; if leaves are too large, tear them gently. Wash leaves, spin dry, and spread on paper towels. Let stand for a few minutes, so the air can dry leaves further. Wrap them in paper towels, place in a plastic bag, and refrigerate. (Greens will remain crisp for several days if they are dried thoroughly.)

Rinse anchovy fillets and pat dry with paper towels.

To assemble the salad: Place lettuce in bottom of serving bowl and toss with some of the dressing. Arrange remaining ingredients on top and sprinkle lightly with salt and pepper. Toss at the table with some salad dressing and serve the rest on the side.

NOTE: To boil eggs, place them in a saucepan with cold water to cover. Bring to a boil over high heat and boil for 1 minute. Cover and remove from heat. Let stand for 20 minutes, pour off water, and let cool. I like hard-boiled eggs to be cooked but not too hard. After quartering eggs, keep them covered tightly with plastic wrap; they discolor when exposed to air.

If Boston or field lettuce is unavailable, use the white center leaves of romaine lettuce and combine with watercress.

If you wish to keep this salad pareve, omit the feta cheese.

Cakes and Cookies

BROWNIES

Everyone has his or her favorite brownie. These are moist, not too sweet, and light. They freeze very well.

THIRTY 2-INCH SQUARES

13 tablespoons (1 stick plus 5 tablespoons) sweet butter

1 cup plus 1 tablespoon sifted unbleached flour

5 ounces unsweetened chocolate, broken into small pieces

1 tablespoon instant coffee powder

1 teaspoon vanilla extract

4 eggs, at room temperature

½ teaspoon salt

Scant 1¾ cups sugar

1 cup walnuts, chopped coarse

I suggest you use the following: a 13-by-9-by-2-inch baking pan, a double boiler, and an electric mixer.

Melt 1 tablespoon of the butter and use half to brush bottom and sides of 13-by-9-by-2-inch baking pan. Line pan with a sheet of wax paper, which should extend several inches beyond short ends of pan. Brush remaining half tablespoon butter on wax paper. Dust evenly with 1 tablespoon of the flour and, holding onto the paper, invert pan and tap to shake off excess.

Place chocolate and remaining 12 tablespoons butter in top part of a double boiler. Set over simmering water until melted. Remove from heat and add instant coffee and vanilla, stirring until smooth. Let cool.

Preheat oven to 400°F. In an electric-mixer bowl, at medium speed, beat eggs with salt until foamy. Gradually add sugar and continue beating for 10 to 15 minutes; eggs will be very fluffy. Lower speed and dribble in cooled melted chocolate, continuing to mix until well combined.

Gradually fold in remaining flour and the walnuts with a rubber spatula, combining well after each addition. Pour batter into the prepared pan, spreading it evenly by tipping pan and letting batter roll.

Place in center of oven and immediately lower temperature to 350°F. Bake for 20 to 25 minutes. Test with a cake tester in the center; it should come out slightly moist. (Do not overbake.) Let cool on a rack for 5 minutes. Cover brownies with a large tray or jelly roll pan and invert.

Gently peel off wax paper. Cover brownies with original pan and invert again. Let cool completely before slicing, or refrigerate and then slice.

To slice: To slice brownies evenly, invert them onto a large cutting board and mark portions evenly with a ruler. Cut with a serrated knife.

NOTE: You can use a food processor fitted with the steel blade to chop walnuts coarsely.

Sift flour directly into the measuring cup.

◆You can freeze the brownies in a foil pan covered with foil and placed in a plastic bag.

ALMOND COOKIES

ABOUT 3 DOZEN COOKIES

Light and crisp.

6½ tablespoons sweet butter, at room temperature
6 tablespoons sugar
½ teaspoon vanilla extract

Scant ½ cup sifted unbleached flour
¾ cup almonds, blanched and sliced thin

I suggest you use two cookie sheets and an electric mixer.

Grease two cookie sheets with ½ tablespoon of the butter.

In an electric-mixer bowl, at medium speed, cream remaining 6 tablespoons butter, adding sugar gradually and continuing to beat until pale and fluffy, about 10 minutes. Lower speed and mix in vanilla and flour until combined. Fold in almonds and blend thoroughly.

Drop level teaspoonfuls of batter 1 inch apart onto the prepared cookie sheets. Flatten mounds slightly with a knife. Refrigerate for 15 minutes.

Preheat oven to 400°F. Bake one sheet at a time, in upper third of oven, for about 7 minutes, or until edges turn brown. Let cool for a few minutes to harden. Remove with a thin metal spatula to a cookie rack.

NOTE: Sift flour directly into the measuring cup.

Sliced blanched almonds are available in specialty stores. If not, blanch them yourself (page xxii), then slice.

Cookies keep well in a covered tin box, preferably in a cool place.

◆These cookies freeze well in a foil pan, with wax paper between the layers. Cover with foil and place in a plastic bag.

PALMIERS

->>>-

These cookies are traditionally made from leftover puff pastry dough. This is a different version, much easier to make. They are crisp, delicious, and keep very well in a tightly closed tin box in a cool place; or freeze them.

ABOUT
40 COOKIES

1½ cups unbleached flour	Grated rind of 1 lemon
½ pound (2 sticks) sweet butter, chilled, cut into small pieces	½ cup sour cream
	1 cup sugar

I suggest you use a food processor and two or three cookie sheets lined with foil.

Combine flour and butter in a food processor fitted with the steel blade until mixture resembles coarse crumbs. Add lemon rind and sour cream and blend until dough begins to form around the blade (just before it reaches the ball stage).

Turn dough out onto a sheet of wax paper, shaping it with the help of the paper into a smooth 4½-inch square. Dust lightly with flour, wrap in wax paper, and refrigerate for at least 3 hours or overnight.

Cut chilled dough into four equal pieces. Work with one piece at a time, and keep the rest refrigerated. Place a sheet of wax paper on a pastry board (preferably marble) and sprinkle with 2 to 2½ tablespoons of the sugar. Roll out a piece of dough over sugar, turning it often to absorb all the sugar. Make a rectangle 12½ inches long by 5½ inches wide. Trim edges to make them straight. On the long side, mark center lightly. Roll dough toward center from each short side; it should look like a scroll (1). Wrap in the same wax paper and chill in freezer for 30 minutes. Repeat with the remaining three pieces of dough, one at a time, using a fresh sheet of wax paper and the same amount of sugar each time.

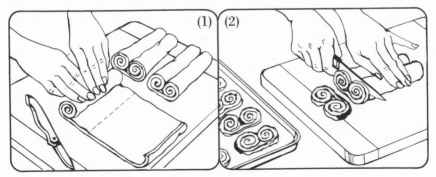

Preheat oven to 375°F. Unwrap first scroll of dough and spread about 1 tablespoon sugar on the wax paper. Cut scroll into ½-inch slices and dip both sides into sugar (2). Place slices, about 2 inches apart, on two or three foil-lined cookie sheets. Repeat with remaining dough scrolls. Bake palmiers for about 15 minutes, or until golden. Turn them over and bake for another 5 minutes. Let cool on racks.

NOTE: You can make these cookies either larger or smaller, as you wish.

◆To freeze palmiers, place them in a foil pan, cover with foil, and place in a plastic bag.

ROGELACH

32 COOKIES This Eastern European specialty looks like a miniature croissant, but tastes of sugar and cinnamon. Rogelach keep very well refrigerated or frozen.

1 recipe Cream Cheese Dough (page 245)
FILLING:
1 cup walnuts, chopped coarse   Scant ½ cup seedless dark
Generous ½ cup sugar   raisins
1 teaspoon ground cinnamon

I suggest you use two cookie sheets.

Make Cream Cheese Dough and divide it into two flat balls.
Combine walnuts, sugar, and cinnamon.
Preheat oven to 375°F. Work with one ball at a time, and keep the other refrigerated. On a lightly floured pastry board, with a floured rolling pin, roll out dough into a 15- or 16-inch circle, lifting dough and reflouring board as necessary. Sprinkle dough evenly with half the walnut mixture.
Cut circle into sixteen triangular pie-shaped sections and sprinkle with half the raisins (1). Roll each triangle tightly from the widest part to the

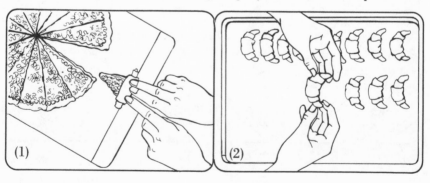

tip and curve slightly (2). Place rogelach on a cookie sheet. If some filling has fallen out while rolling, sprinkle it over rogelach, but remove raisins, since they will burn.

Proceed with second ball of dough in the same fashion. Bake cookies in upper third of oven for about 20 minutes, or until light brown. (Sometimes the bottom burns lightly because of the sugar; that is part of the traditional taste.) Let cool on a rack.

NOTE: A food processor fitted with the steel blade can be used to chop walnuts.

If you like larger rogelach, cut the circle of dough into fewer sections.

HAZELNUT–BUTTER WAFERS

➤➤➤

Lacy, crisp, and nutty; they are my favorite. They keep very well in a tightly covered tin box, in a cool place or frozen.

ABOUT 6 DOZEN COOKIES

1 cup hazelnuts
9 tablespoons (1 stick plus 1 tablespoon) sweet butter, at room temperature

½ cup sugar
3 tablespoons unbleached flour
2 tablespoons milk

I suggest you use the following: a food processor, an electric mixer, and two to four heavy cookie sheets.

Preheat oven to 350°F. Roast hazelnuts in oven in a single layer in a baking pan for about 15 minutes. Rub nuts well in a dish towel to remove skin. (Some skin will remain.) Let nuts cool, but keep oven hot. Coarsely chop in a food processor fitted with the steel blade.

Grease two to four cookie sheets with 1 tablespoon of the butter.

In an electric-mixer bowl, at medium speed, cream remaining 8 tablespoons butter, adding sugar gradually and continuing to beat until pale and fluffy, about 10 minutes. Fold in hazelnuts, flour, and milk with a rubber spatula until thoroughly combined.

Drop level ½ teaspoonfuls of batter 2 inches apart onto the prepared cookie sheets. Flatten mounds slightly with a knife. Bake one sheet at a time in center of oven for about 8 to 10 minutes, or until light brown. Let cool for a minute to harden, then remove gently to a cookie rack.

NOTE: If you do not have enough cookie sheets, just clean what you do have as you finish each batch.

◆You can freeze cookies in a foil pan with wax paper between the layers, covered with foil and placed in a plastic bag.

PECAN TARTLETS

5 DOZEN
TARTLETS

These miniature tartlets are a special treat for large parties. They are light, with a flaky pastry and a crunchy filling, and more substantial than most cookies. They freeze very well.

1 recipe Cream Cheese Dough
  (page 245)

FILLING:

2 eggs, at room temperature
1¼ cups dark brown sugar
3 tablespoons sweet butter,
  melted

1½ tablespoons sweet butter,
  melted

1 teaspoon vanilla extract
1⅓ cups pecans, chopped
  coarse

I suggest you use a 3-inch round cookie cutter and five aluminum muffin pans, each with twelve depressions about 1 ¾ inches across the top.

Preheat oven to 350°F. Cut dough into four pieces. Leave one piece at room temperature to soften until malleable, keeping the rest refrigerated.

Grease five muffin pans with butter, using a pastry brush.

On a lightly floured board, with a floured rolling pin, roll out each piece of dough as thinly as you can. Lift dough and reflour board and pin as necessary. With a cookie cutter, cut out circles and place in prepared muffin pans to form tiny containers. Gather scraps of dough and refrigerate them to be rolled out as you need more dough. Keep finished trays refrigerated.

To make the filling: In a small bowl, whisk eggs until foamy. Add sugar and mix with a wooden spoon until well combined. Stir in butter and vanilla.

Fill each tartlet shell with ¼ teaspoon chopped pecans, then add about 1 teaspoon egg-sugar mixture. Be sure not to fill tartlets to the very top, or filling will spill over dough and they will be difficult to unmold. Sprinkle tops with another ¼ teaspoon pecans.

Bake in center of oven for 20 to 25 minutes, or until edges are light brown. Let cool until easy to handle. Release edges slightly with a knife before unmolding. Place on a rack to cool thoroughly.

◆To freeze tartlets, place them in a foil pan with wax paper between the layers; cover with foil and place in a plastic bag.

LEMON LOAF

—>>>——————————————————————

A favorite tea cake with a lemony and moist flavor. It keeps very
well either refrigerated or frozen.

10 TO 12
SERVINGS

8½ tablespoons (1 stick plus
  ½ tablespoon) sweet butter,
  at room temperature
1 cup plus 1 tablespoon sifted
  unbleached flour

½ teaspoon baking powder
½ cup sugar
2 eggs, at room temperature
Grated rind of 1 lemon

GLAZE:
2 tablespoons confectioners'
  sugar

Juice of ½ lemon, strained

I suggest you use an electric mixer and a 9-by-5-inch loaf pan.

Preheat oven to 350°F. Grease a 9-by-5-inch loaf pan with ½ tablespoon
of the butter and dust evenly with 1 tablespoon of the flour. Invert pan and
tap to shake off excess.

Sift remaining flour and baking powder directly into measuring cup. In
an electric-mixer bowl at medium speed, cream remaining 8 tablespoons
butter, adding sugar gradually and continuing to beat until pale and fluffy,
about 10 minutes. With motor on, add eggs one at a time and lemon rind;
combine thoroughly. With a rubber spatula, fold flour gradually into batter
until blended. Pour batter into pan (it will only fill a quarter). Smooth top
and bake in center of oven for about 35 minutes. Test with a cake tester
in the center; it should come out dry, and top should be golden. (This is
not a high cake.) Let cool on a rack slightly, just until possible to unmold
and handle.

To glaze the loaf: Combine sugar and lemon juice until smooth. Loosen
sides of pan and unmold loaf onto a cake rack. Place a sheet of wax paper
beneath rack to catch drippings. Slowly spoon glaze over top. Let cool. Cut
into thin slices.

LEMON-MOUSSE TART

—>>>——————————————————————

A prebaked pastry shell is filled with a tart lemon mousse,
decorated with lemon rounds, and refrigerated for 24 hours.
Don't be afraid, the dough will not get soggy. Serve it at room
temperature.

10 TO 12
SERVINGS

DOUGH:

1 cup unbleached flour

¼ cup almonds, blanched and ground fine

Pinch salt

3 tablespoons sugar

7 tablespoons sweet butter, chilled

1 egg yolk mixed with 1 tablespoon bottled orange juice

1 egg white, lightly beaten

FILLING:

3 to 4 lemons

⅔ cup fresh lemon juice, strained (3 to 4 large lemons)

2 tablespoons cold water

2 teaspoons unflavored kosher gelatin

4 egg yolks

1 cup sugar

1 cup heavy cream, chilled

DECORATION:

1 firm lemon

½ tablespoon sweet butter, melted

I suggest you use the following: a food processor, a 10- to 11-inch quiche pan with removable bottom, and a double boiler.

To make the dough: Combine flour, almonds, salt, and sugar in a food processor fitted with the steel blade. Cut butter into small pieces and add to food processor along with egg yolk and orange juice. Blend until mixture resembles fine crumbs.

Turn out onto a pastry board (dough will appear dry) and knead lightly with the heel of your hand until you can gather dough into a smooth ball. Flatten ball, wrap in wax paper, and refrigerate for several hours or overnight. (Dough will keep refrigerated for several days.)

To roll out the dough: Remove dough from refrigerator and let rest until malleable. Roll out, on both sides, between two overlapping lightly floured sheets of wax paper. You will need two sheets on the bottom and two sheets on top, since a single sheet is not wide enough. Make a very thin circle, approximately 13 inches in diameter. Dough will spread more easily if you lift papers from time to time and, if necessary, dust lightly with flour. Lift top sheets and place back on dough. Turn dough over and remove what are now the top sheets. Roll dough loosely over rolling pin and unroll over a 10- to 11-inch quiche pan with removable bottom. (If dough breaks or cracks, don't worry about it, since it is very pliable, and you can easily repair it in pan.) With lightly floured thumb, press dough firmly into corners of mold, making sides thicker than bottom. Roll rolling pin over mold to cut off edges. Save scraps of dough, just in case you need them for patching after baking (see below). Prick bottom lightly with a fork and chill for about 1 hour, or until dough is firm.

Preheat oven to 350°F. Brush dough lightly with beaten egg white and bake on lowest rack of oven for about 20 minutes, or until it is golden and shrinks from sides of pan. Let cool on a rack. If dough cracks during baking, patch it with a little egg white and dough scraps, then return it to oven for a few minutes.

To make the filling: Have a large bowl of ice ready.

Grate rind of 3 lemons. Squeeze juice to obtain ⅔ cup and combine 2 tablespoons of the lemon juice and the cold water in a small saucepan. Sprinkle with gelatin and set aside. In top part of a double boiler, beat egg yolks, sugar, lemon rind, and remaining lemon juice with a whisk until blended. Set over simmering water and continue to beat until custard coats back of a metal spoon heavily, about 15 minutes. In the meantime, heat gelatin very slowly and stir until smooth. Add gelatin to custard, continuing to whisk vigorously until well blended.

Remove top part of double boiler and set over ice. Continue whisking vigorously until cool. Refrigerate until almost set (several hours), whisking once or twice to make the mousse light and fluffy. (Kosher gelatin tends to lump.)

In a well-chilled metal bowl, beat heavy cream until firm. Whisk into the almost-set custard until thoroughly blended. Chill mousse for several hours or until set. When shell is cool and the mousse is set, whisk vigorously again, fill crust, and smooth the top.

To make the decoration: Preheat oven to 375°F. Cut lemon into very thin rounds. With a serrated knife, trim rind and all but an extremely thin layer of pith (otherwise rounds will fall apart). Place lemon slices on a foil pan (lemon discolors metal), brush with melted butter, and bake for about 10 minutes, or until rounds are wilted. While still hot, transfer lemon slices to a plate and let cool. Decorate mousse with lemon slices and refrigerate overnight.

To serve: Place tart securely on an elevated object, such as a coffee can. Let rim fall down. Carefully slide tart to a flat serving platter or place two large, wide spatulas underneath it and transfer to a platter. Serve at room temperature.

CHOCOLATE ROLL

This soufflé-like chocolate roll was inspired by my good friend and teacher, Lilly Joss Reich.

10 TO 12
SERVINGS

CHOCOLATE ROLL:

1 tablespoon vegetable oil	5 eggs, at room temperature,
1 tablespoon instant coffee	separated
powder	¾ cup sugar
¼ cup boiling water	
5 ounces imported semisweet	
chocolate, broken into	
pieces	

FILLING:

1¼ cups heavy cream, chilled	Imported unsweetened cocoa
2 tablespoons confectioners'	powder
sugar	
1 tablespoon instant coffee	
powder	

I suggest you use the following: an 11-by-16-inch jelly roll pan, a double boiler, an electric mixer, and a damp towel.

To make the roll: Preheat oven to 400°F. Brush oil evenly over bottom and sides of an 11-by-16-inch jelly roll pan. Line pan with a 21-inch sheet of wax paper; it should extend several inches beyond short ends of pan. Brush oil over wax paper.

In top part of a double boiler set over simmering water, combine coffee powder, boiling water, and chocolate pieces. Stir from time to time until chocolate is melted and smooth. Remove from heat and let cool.

In an electric-mixer bowl, at medium speed, beat egg yolks, adding sugar gradually and continuing to beat until mixture is thick and bubbles appear, about 10 minutes. Lower speed and slowly pour in cooled chocolate. Blend thoroughly.

Beat egg whites until stiff. With a large spatula, fold a quarter of the whites into chocolate mixture until well combined. Now reverse the process, pouring chocolate over whites. Gently fold the two mixtures together, making a motion like a figure eight, until all the whites have disappeared. Do not overfold, or roll will be too heavy. Pour batter into pan, tipping pan to spread it evenly. Smooth the top.

Place in center of oven and immediately lower temperature to 350°F. Bake for 15 to 20 minutes. Do not overbake; top should be firm, but inside should be moist.

Cover roulade with a damp towel and let cool in refrigerator for about 30 minutes. Remove from refrigerator, take off towel, and leave at room temperature for a short while. (It is easier to peel off wax paper when roll is brought back to room temperature.)

To make the filling: Whip cream in a well-chilled metal bowl until it begins to hold a shape. Add sugar and beat until stiff. With a rubber spatula, fold in coffee powder and 1 tablespoon of the cocoa powder.

To assemble the roll: Invert roulade onto a double fold of wax paper, about 2 feet long. Remove pan and gently peel off wax paper. Trim cracked edges slightly. Cover roll with whipped cream. With the help of the wax paper, lift one long side of the cake and roll it up loosely like a jelly roll. Adjust the log shape with wax paper. (If roll cracks, do not worry about it.) Sift cocoa powder over top.

Slide two long, wide spatulas under short ends of roll and carefully lift it from wax paper to a serving platter. If roulade is not to be served immediately, cover it with wax paper to retain its log shape, and refrigerate. Serve at room temperature.

CHOCOLATE-MOUSSE TART

→》》》

A chocolate lover's delight. Even though I do not always wish to have a dessert at a meal's end, I succumb to this one. A prebaked cookie-crumb crust is filled with chocolate mousse, refrigerated overnight, and served the following day at room temperature.

10 TO 12 SERVINGS

CHOCOLATE-COOKIE-CRUMB CRUST:

About 11 ounces chocolate cookies

5½ tablespoons sweet butter, melted

FILLING:

½ pound imported semisweet chocolate, broken into small pieces

1½ tablespoons instant coffee powder

3 tablespoons boiling water

2 tablespoons imported unsweetened cocoa powder

3 tablespoons sweet butter, at room temperature

3 egg yolks, at room temperature

3 tablespoons sugar

2 tablespoons Grand Marnier

1 cup heavy cream, chilled

I suggest you use the following: a food processor, a 10- to 11-inch quiche pan with removable bottom, and a double boiler.

Preheat oven to 375°F. Place cookies, in batches, in a food processor fitted with the steel blade and process until smooth. Remove each batch to a bowl before placing in the next one.

Grease a 10- to 11-inch quiche pan with ½ tablespoon of the butter. Mix remaining 5 tablespoons butter with the crumbs. Put mixture into the prepared quiche pan, patting firmly with back of a spoon; start with bottom, making it thinner than sides. Set quiche pan on a thin, flat baking sheet or foil oven liner (it is easier to handle) and bake in center of oven for 10 minutes. Let cool completely.

To make the filling: Chop 2 ounces of the chocolate pieces into small chips in a food processor fitted with the steel blade.

In top part of a double boiler, combine coffee powder, boiling water, remaining 6 ounces chocolate pieces, and cocoa. Set over simmering water, cover until dissolved, then stir until smooth. Whisk in butter, 1 tablespoonful at a time, until blended. Transfer to a bowl.

Clean and dry top of double boiler and vigorously whisk together egg yolks, sugar, and Grand Marnier over simmering water until custard is thick, about 15 minutes. Remove from heat and whisk in chocolate until smooth. Refrigerate until cool. Beat heavy cream in a well-chilled metal bowl until stiff. With a rubber spatula, combine cream with the cooled chocolate and chocolate chips until thoroughly blended.

Fill the cooled crust and refrigerate overnight.

To serve: Place quiche pan on an elevated object, such as a coffee can, and let the rim fall down. Either slide pie to a flat serving platter or place two large, wide spatulas underneath and transfer to a platter.

CHOCOLATE SOUFFLÉ CAKE

10 TO 12
SERVINGS

Serve this light dessert with Crème Chantilly (page 261).

9½ tablespoons (1 stick plus 1½ tablespoons) sweet butter, melted but lukewarm

½ tablespoon unbleached flour

9 ounces imported extra-bittersweet chocolate, broken into pieces

6 eggs, at room temperature, separated

Scant ½ cup sugar

6 tablespoons cornstarch

I suggest you use the following: a 9-by-2½-inch springform pan, a double boiler, and an electric mixer.

Grease a 9-by-2½-inch springform pan with ½ tablespoon of the butter. Dust evenly with flour; invert pan and tap to shake off excess. Melt chocolate in top part of a double boiler, covered and set over simmering water. Let chocolate cool, then stir in remaining 9 tablespoons butter with a wooden spoon until well blended.

Preheat oven to 350°F. In an electric-mixer bowl, at high speed, beat egg whites until soft peaks form. Add sugar, 1 tablespoonful at a time, and continue to beat until all the sugar is incorporated. Beat egg yolks lightly with a fork. Add yolks to whites and continue to beat at same speed for 4 minutes.

Spoon cornstarch into a sifter and sift half of it over egg batter. Add half the chocolate and fold with a rubber spatula, making a motion like a figure eight and scraping batter from sides and bottom of bowl as if preparing a soufflé. Repeat with remaining cornstarch and chocolate. Be sure the final batter is well combined. Pour batter into the prepared pan, distributing it evenly. Bake in center of oven for 30 to 35 minutes. The inside of the cake will be moist and the center will appear loose. Let cool on a rack for 10 minutes.

To serve: Release edges of pan with a knife and remove outer ring. When cake is completely cool, loosen bottom with a knife and invert cake onto a platter. The bottom, now the top, will have a moist, soufflé-like texture. Serve with Crème Chantilly.

NOTE: Buy the best extra-bittersweet or bittersweet chocolate you can find.

Chocolate tends to be heavy; therefore, when combining with the eggs, reach to the bottom of the bowl with a rubber spatula to make sure that all the ingredients are completely combined.

GÉNOISE

A variation of the classic génoise, or sponge cake, with a sprinkling of chocolate. Follow the technique carefully; it is well worth the effort.

12 TO 14 SERVINGS

½ tablespoon sweet butter, melted
1 tablespoon unbleached flour
3 ounces semisweet chocolate, broken into pieces
1½ cups plus 1 tablespoon sifted unbleached flour
2 tablespoons cornstarch

4 whole eggs plus 4 egg yolks, at room temperature
Boiling water
1 cup sugar
1 teaspoon vanilla extract
Grated rind of 1 lemon
½ pound (2 sticks) sweet butter, clarified (page xvi)

I suggest you use the following: a 10-inch gugelhupf pan, a food processor, and an electric hand beater.

Preheat oven to 350°F. Grease a 10-inch gugelhupf pan with melted butter and dust with 1 tablespoon of the flour. Invert pan and tap to shake off excess.

Coarsely chop chocolate pieces in a food processor fitted with the steel blade.

Sift together flour and cornstarch directly into measuring cup, then return to sifter.

Rinse a large bowl with hot water and dry well. Break eggs and egg yolks into warm bowl and set inside another bowl filled with boiling water. With an electric hand beater, beat eggs at medium speed, adding sugar gradually until thick, pale yellow, and triple in volume, about 10 to 15 minutes. Keep adding boiling water to bowl to keep temperature constant. Stir in vanilla and lemon rind. Remove bowl from hot water.

With sifter, sprinkle one third of the flour on top of egg mixture, folding it gently with a large rubber spatula. When almost combined, dribble in one third of the butter, folding it gently. Try to catch butter before it falls to bottom of batter. Repeat in the same fashion with the remaining flour and butter. Do not add flour and butter in more than three or four batches, or cake will be overfolded.

Pour half the batter into the prepared mold, sprinkle with chopped chocolate, and cover with remaining batter.

Bake in oven on lowest rack for about 45 minutes, or until cake is golden, springy to the touch, and shrinking from sides of pan. Invert at once onto a cake rack to let cool.

NOTE: Eggs are beaten over hot water to make them airier.
When no longer fresh, Génoise is delicious toasted.

CHEESECAKE

12 GENEROUS
SERVINGS

This Polish cheesecake is not overly sweet and has a pleasant, noncreamy texture.

DOUGH:

1 cup unbleached flour	8 tablespoons (1 stick) sweet
2 tablespoons sugar	butter, chilled

1 egg white, lightly beaten

FILLING:

2½ pounds farmer cheese	Seedless golden raisins or
3 ounces cream cheese	slivered blanched almonds
1 cup sour cream	(optional)
Generous ¾ cup sugar	4 eggs, at room temperature
Grated rind of 1 lemon	¼ cup unbleached flour
1 tablespoon fresh lemon juice	Sweet butter
1 teaspoon vanilla extract	

I suggest you use a food processor and a 10-by-2½-inch springform pan.

To make the dough: Combine flour and sugar in a food processor fitted with the steel blade. Cut butter into small pieces, add to flour, and blend until mixture resembles coarse crumbs. Turn dough out onto a pastry board and combine with your hands into a smooth ball. Roll dough out, on both sides, between two sheets of lightly floured wax paper into a 12-inch round. (Do not worry if circle is uneven; you can fix it in pan.) Dough will spread more easily if you lift papers from time to time. Remove top sheet of wax paper and place it back on dough. Turn dough over and remove what is now the top sheet. Roll dough very loosely over rolling pin and unfold over a 10-by-2½-inch springform pan. Fit firmly into pan, fixing any cracks with your fingers, and form an even 1½- to 2-inch border. Prick bottom lightly with a fork and chill for about 1 hour.

Preheat oven to 350°F. Brush dough lightly with beaten egg white and bake on lowest rack of oven for about 20 minutes, or until it is golden and shrinks from sides of pan. Let cool.

To make the filling: Preheat oven to 350°F. Place farmer cheese, cream cheese, sour cream, and sugar, in batches, in a food processor fitted with the steel blade. Process until mixture is just combined. Transfer each batch to a bowl before proceeding with the next one. Stir in lemon rind, lemon juice, and vanilla. Add raisins or almonds if you wish. With a rubber spatula, fold in one egg at a time, then flour until thoroughly blended. Lightly grease uncovered sides of pan. Pour filling into shell and smooth the top.

Bake on lowest rack of oven for 30 minutes. Transfer cake to center of oven and bake for another 30 minutes. Turn off heat and leave cake in oven until oven is completely cool. Remove cake and let cool completely on a rack. Release sides with a knife and remove rim. Loosen bottom with a knife. Slide two large spatulas under cake and transfer to a serving platter.

NOTE: If you prefer a smoother filling, blend longer in the food processor.

Cheesecake keeps fresh for many days refrigerated, but the dough loses some of its crispness.

POT CHEESE SQUARES

An Eastern European specialty with a coarsely textured cheese filling. The squares keep very well refrigerated and the dough remains crisp. Be sure to dry the pot cheese well.

THIRTY
1½-INCH
SQUARES

DOUGH:

1½ cups unbleached flour
½ cup almonds, blanched and
  ground fine
Pinch salt
¼ cup sugar
10 tablespoons (1 stick plus 2
  tablespoons) sweet butter,
  chilled

1 egg yolk combined with 1½
  tablespoons bottled orange
  juice

1 egg white, lightly beaten

FILLING:

1¾ pounds pot cheese

Generous ½ cup sugar

3 eggs, at room temperature,
 separated

1 tablespoon vanilla extract

Grated rind of 1 lemon

1 tablespoon fresh lemon
 juice, strained

½ cup seedless golden raisins
 or slivered blanched
 almonds

I suggest you use a food processor and a 13-by-9-by-2-inch baking pan.

To make the dough: Combine flour, almonds, salt, and sugar in a food processor fitted with the steel blade. Cut butter into small pieces. Add butter and egg yolk–orange juice mixture to food processor and blend until mixture resembles fine crumbs. Turn out onto a pastry board (it will be dry) and work with your hands until you can gather dough into a smooth ball. Flatten ball, wrap in wax paper, and refrigerate for several hours or overnight. (Dough will keep refrigerated for several days.)

To roll out the dough: Remove dough from refrigerator and let rest until malleable. Roll out, on both sides, between two lightly floured sheets of wax paper, into an approximately 11-by-15-inch rectangle. Dough will spread more easily if you lift papers from time to time. Remove top sheet of wax paper and place it back on dough. Turn dough over and remove what is now the top sheet. Roll dough loosely over rolling pin and unfold over a 13-by-9-by-2-inch baking pan. Fit firmly into pan, fixing any cracks with fingers. Shape sides, making them about 1½ inches high. Prick bottom lightly with a fork and chill for 1 hour.

Preheat oven to 350°F. Brush dough lightly with beaten egg white. Bake on lowest shelf of oven for 20 to 25 minutes, or until it is golden and shrinks from sides of pan. Let cool a bit on a rack.

To drain the pot cheese: Place pot cheese in a mesh sieve and set over a bowl. Cover cheese with wax paper and weight down with a plate and a heavy object, such as a large can. Allow to drain for several hours or overnight in refrigerator. Pat dry with paper towels.

To make the filling: Place dried pot cheese, sugar, egg yolks, vanilla, lemon rind, and lemon juice in food processor fitted with the steel blade. Process until just combined (filling should have a coarse texture); transfer to a bowl. Beat egg whites until stiff. With a rubber spatula, fold egg whites into cheese mixture. Add raisins or almonds. Spread filling in shell and smooth top.

Bake on lowest rack of oven for about 35 minutes, or until top feels firm. Let cool. Cut into squares. (It is easier to do this after it has been refrigerated for a short while.)

WALNUT TART

->>>————————————————————————————————————

A treat for the nut lover. Serve it with Crème Chantilly (page 261).

1 10- to 11-inch prebaked pie shell (page 243)

FILLING:

2 cups walnuts	Scant ¾ cup sugar
1¼ teaspoons instant coffee powder	⅓ teaspoon salt
¼ cup boiling water	2 eggs, at room temperature
8 tablespoons (1 stick) sweet butter, at room temperature	

GLAZE:

1 tablespoon instant coffee powder	Scant ½ cup confectioners' sugar
2 tablespoons boiling water	1 teaspoon vanilla extract

I suggest you use a food processor and an electric mixer.

Preheat oven to 350°F. Roast walnuts in oven in a single layer in a baking pan for 10 minutes. Let cool. Chop very coarsely in a food processor fitted with the steel blade.

Dissolve coffee powder in boiling water; let cool.

Increase oven to 375°F.

To make the filling: In an electric-mixer bowl, at medium speed, cream butter, adding sugar gradually and continuing to beat until light and fluffy, about 10 minutes. With motor on, add salt, one egg at a time, and coffee liquid. Mix until well blended. With a rubber spatula, mix in walnuts.

Spoon filling into prebaked shell and smooth the top. Bake on lowest rack of oven for about 25 minutes, or until top is firm to the touch. Let cool on a rack.

To make the glaze: While tart is baking, mix all glaze ingredients in a small saucepan and keep warm.

Glaze tart with a pastry brush as soon as it comes out of oven.

To serve: Place tart securely on an elevated object, such as a coffee can. Let rim fall down. Either slide tart to a flat serving platter or place two large, wide spatulas underneath and transfer to a platter. Serve with Crème Chantilly on the side.

NOTE: If you are serving the tart without Crème Chantilly, you may wish to reduce the sugar in the filling to ⅔ cup.

I like to use dark quiche pans; they are better conductors of heat.

◆If you like, the tart can be made a day ahead of time and refrigerated. The dough will not get soggy. But be sure to serve it at room temperature.

PECAN PIE

10 TO 12 SERVINGS A popular treat with a flaky crust and a crunchy filling. Serve it with Crème Chantilly (page 261).

1 recipe Cream Cheese Dough (page 245)
FILLING:

Scant 1 cup dark corn syrup	1 teaspoon vanilla extract
Scant 1 cup sugar	1 to 2 tablespoons dark rum
4 tablespoons (½ stick) sweet butter	2 cups pecan halves or combination of halves and
4 eggs, at room temperature	broken pieces

I suggest you use a 10- to 11-inch quiche pan with removable bottom.

Leave dough at room temperature until malleable. On a floured pastry board, with a floured rolling pin, roll out into a 13- to 14-inch round. Reflour pastry board and rolling pin as needed. Roll dough loosely over rolling pin and unroll over a 10- to 11-inch quiche pan. Fit dough into pan, pressing well into corners and shaping border. Let a bit of dough extend over edges. Roll rolling pin over edges to trim excess dough. Refrigerate shell while preparing filling.

To make the filling: Preheat oven to 350°F. In a small saucepan, boil corn syrup and sugar, stirring until sugar is dissolved. Add butter.

In a large bowl, whisk eggs lightly and gradually beat in sugar syrup, vanilla, and rum. Pour mixture into pie shell and scatter pecans over it.

Bake in center of oven for 30 minutes, then transfer to lowest rack for another 20 to 25 minutes, or until filling is firm. Let cool on a rack.

To serve: Place quiche pan securely on an elevated object, such as a coffee can, and let the rim fall down. Either slide pie to a flat serving platter or place two large, wide spatulas underneath and transfer to a serving platter. Serve with Crème Chantilly that has not been flavored with liqueur and that has a reduced sugar content.

NOTE: I use Saint James rum, imported from Martinique.

I prefer to bake in dark quiche pans; they are better conductors of heat.

SOUR-CREAM POUND CAKE

17 tablespoons (2 sticks plus 1 tablespoon) sweet butter, at room temperature
2 cups plus 1½ tablespoons sifted unbleached flour
Scant 1½ cups sugar

4 eggs, at room temperature
½ teaspoon baking soda
½ teaspoon salt
½ cup sour cream, at room temperature

2 LOAVES,
EACH
SERVING 12

I suggest you use an electric mixer and two 9-by-5-inch loaf pans.

Preheat oven to 325°F. Grease two 9-by-5-inch loaf pans with 1 tablespoon of the butter. Dust evenly with 1½ tablespoons of the flour. Invert pans and tap to shake off excess.

In an electric-mixer bowl, at medium speed, cream butter, adding sugar gradually and continuing to beat until pale and fluffy, about 10 minutes. Add eggs, one at a time, blending well after each addition. Sift together flour, baking soda, and salt directly into measuring cup. With a rubber spatula, fold small amounts of flour mixture and sour cream into batter until well combined.

Divide batter equally between the two prepared pans and bake in center of oven for about 40 to 45 minutes, making sure pans do not touch. Test with a cake tester in the center; it should come out dry. Let cool on a rack. Loosen sides with a knife before unmolding.

NOTE: For variety and texture, you can add raisins, currants, or chocolate morsels. You can also glaze loaves while still warm with a mixture of fresh lemon juice and confectioners' sugar.

Pound cake remains fresh and moist for several days, refrigerated. Not-so-fresh pound cake can be toasted.

HEAVY-CREAM POUND CAKE

A variation of Sour-Cream Pound Cake (above), equally delicious but with a different texture.

2 LOAVES,
EACH
SERVING 12

1 tablespoon sweet butter
3 cups plus 1½ tablespoons sifted unbleached flour
4 teaspoons baking powder
½ teaspoon salt

2 cups heavy cream
1¾ cups sugar
1 teaspoon vanilla extract
4 eggs, at room temperature

I suggest you use an electric mixer and two 9-by-5-inch loaf pans.

Preheat oven to 325°F. Grease two 9-by-5-inch loaf pans. Dust evenly with 1½ tablespoons of the flour. Invert pans and tap to shake off excess.

Sift together flour, baking powder, and salt directly into a large measuring cup. In an electric-mixer bowl, at medium speed, whip heavy cream until cream begins to hold a shape (do not overbeat). With motor on, gradually add sugar, vanilla, and eggs, one at a time, until well blended. With a rubber spatula, fold in small amounts of flour mixture at a time until no traces of flour are visible.

Divide batter evenly among the two prepared pans. Bake in center of oven for 55 to 60 minutes, making sure pans do not touch.

Test with a cake tester in the center; it should come out dry. Let cool on a rack. Loosen sides with a knife before unmolding.

◆This cake remains fresh for many days, either refrigerated or frozen.

TARTE TATIN
(UPSIDE-DOWN APPLE TART)

8 TO 10
SERVINGS

A winter dessert of French origin. Caramelized apple slices are arranged in a quiche pan and covered with a piecrust. After baking, the tart is inverted onto a platter so that the top becomes the bottom. It is best served warm with Crème Chantilly (page 261) on the side. The combination of the warm dessert and the cold cream is quite delightful.

1 recipe Pâte Brisée (page 243)
CARAMEL:
½ cup sugar   ¼ cup cold water
FILLING:
7 medium apples (Golden   4 tablespoons (½ stick) sweet
   Delicious), about 3 pounds   butter, melted
¼ cup sugar

Unbleached flour
GLAZE:
1 egg white, lightly beaten

I suggest you use the following: a small copper saucepan, a 10- or 11-by-2½-inch quiche pan or round baking pan without removable bottom, and a jelly roll pan.

To make the caramel: Keep quiche pan near the stove. Combine sugar and water in a copper saucepan. Boil over medium-high heat, without stirring, until sugar turns medium brown. Do not let it get too dark, since it burns very quickly. Pot holder in hand, pour syrup immediately into a 10- or 11-by-2½-inch quiche pan. Tip pan to let it spread evenly. If some of the bottom is not covered, don't worry about it. (When working with caramel, speed is essential because the syrup turns hard. Be careful not to burn your hands.)

To make the filling: Preheat oven to 375°F. Peel, core, and slice apples into ½-inch wedges. Place apples, overlapping, in a jelly roll pan. Sprinkle with sugar and butter. Bake in upper third of oven for 10 minutes. (Apples will still be undercooked.)

Preheat broiler. Broil apples very close to heat source for about 5 minutes, or until golden. Watch apples, since those coated with too much sugar may burn. Let cool, then drain of accumulated liquid.

Arrange apples in the quiche pan. Overlap them in a circle in an orderly fashion, because when the tart is inverted, the bottom will be the top.

To roll out the dough: Remove dough from refrigerator and let rest until malleable. Roll out, on both sides, between two overlapping sheets of lightly floured wax paper. You will need two sheets on the bottom and two sheets on top, since a single sheet is not wide enough. Make a very thin circle, approximately 13 inches in diameter. Dough will spread more easily if you lift papers from time to time and, if necessary, dust lightly with flour. Lift top sheets and place back on dough. Turn dough over and remove what are now the top sheets. Roll dough loosely over rolling pin and unroll over apples. Roll rolling pin over top of mold to remove excess dough. Tuck in edges with a knife. Brush top lightly with egg white. Prick dough in a few places to release steam.

Bake in upper third of oven for about 20 minutes, or until top is golden. Let cool for a minute. Invert onto a flat platter; leave pan in place for a few seconds, then tap and remove. You must invert tart while still hot; otherwise apples will stick to pan as sugar cools and hardens. Serve with Crème Chantilly on the side.

NOTE: If you do not have a copper saucepan, use any heavy one.

DACQUISE

For this torte, three hazelnut meringue rounds are made to sandwich a mocha buttercream filling. Do not be discouraged by the seeming complexity of the preparation. Each step can be done in advance, and the entire cake can be assembled a day ahead of time and refrigerated. Special equipment is, however, necessary.

12 SERVINGS

MERINGUES:

7 ounces hazelnuts, about 1½ cups

½ cup cold water

1¼ cups sugar

5 egg whites, at room temperature

MOCHA BUTTERCREAM:

1½ tablespoons instant coffee powder

2 teaspoons boiling water

¼ pound imported bittersweet chocolate, broken into small pieces

2 tablespoons brandy (Cognac)

½ pound (2 sticks) sweet butter, at room temperature

⅓ cup cold water

Scant ½ cup sugar

5 egg yolks, at room temperature

I suggest you use the following: a food processor, three heavy cookie sheets, a small copper saucepan, a candy thermometer, a 1½- to 2-quart double boiler, an electric hand beater, and an electric mixer.

Preheat oven to 350°F. Roast hazelnuts in oven in a single layer on a baking pan for about 15 minutes, or until nuts are lightly colored and skins have blistered. Wrap in a towel and rub hard to remove as much skin as possible. (Some will remain.)

Chop nuts coarsely, in batches, in a food processor fitted with the steel blade. Remove each batch before chopping the next one. Empty chopped nuts into a mesh sieve and shake to remove nut powder; set aside.

Cut out three 9-inch rounds of heavy foil and place on three heavy cookie sheets.

To make the meringues: Combine water and sugar in a small copper saucepan. Boil over high heat, without stirring, until syrup reaches the thread stage, 230°F on a candy thermometer. Leave thermometer in syrup while it is boiling.

While sugar syrup is boiling, boil water in bottom part of a double boiler, then leave to simmer.

Also at the same time, beat egg whites in top part of double boiler with an electric hand beater until stiff. When sugar syrup is ready, pour in a slow stream over egg whites, beating them constantly. Set mixture over simmering water and continue beating, rotating whisk all around the pot for 15 to 20 minutes, or until whites are very, very stiff. (They will continue rising as they cook.) Remove from heat and continue beating until whites are lukewarm.

Preheat oven to 140°F if electric, 150° if gas, or whatever the lowest temperature your oven can maintain. With a rubber spatula, fold hazelnuts into whites until thoroughly combined. Divide meringue equally among the three circles and spread. Smooth tops and neaten edges. Try to make at least one perfect circle, which will be the top layer. Leave meringues in oven for 15 hours to dry out completely. I generally prepare them late in the afternoon to have them ready in the morning.

When meringues are thoroughly dry, gently peel off foil and let cool on racks. If you are not using meringues the same day, wrap them carefully in foil and leave in a cool place for up to a week.

To make the mocha buttercream filling: Dissolve coffee powder in boiling water. In top part of double boiler combine coffee liquid and chocolate. Set over simmering water, cover, and melt until smooth. Add brandy (Cognac) and let cool.

In an electric-mixer bowl, at medium speed, cream butter until very pale and creamy, about 10 minutes. Transfer to a bowl and wash and dry mixer bowl.

Combine water and sugar in a copper saucepan. Boil over high heat, without stirring, until sugar reaches 230°F on a candy thermometer. While sugar is boiling, beat yolks in electric mixer until frothy. When sugar syrup is ready, dribble very slowly into yolks, continuing to beat at high speed until outside of bowl feels cool to the touch. (As mixture cools, it will become thick and light.) At the same speed, beat in creamed butter, one tablespoonful at a time. Then add chocolate until thoroughly combined. Buttercream will be smooth and thick. (Be sure that sugar syrup does not reach over the 230°F mark, or it will not absorb into yolks but will form sugar crystals instead. If syrup has not reached the 230° mark, no amount of beating will make yolks thick.)

Buttercream can be refrigerated for several days, but bring it back to room temperature when ready to use. It can also be frozen, then defrosted in the refrigerator.

To complete the final assembly: Spread equal amounts of filling over two of the meringue rounds and sandwich them together. Cover with the third round. Spread remaining cream over sides, leaving top plain. Slide a large spatula underneath and transfer to a platter. Refrigerate, but return to room temperature to serve.

NOTE: If you do not have a copper saucepan, use a heavy one.

YOGURT PIE
WITH ZWIEBACK–WALNUT CRUST

The discovery of this refreshing low-calorie summer dessert surprised me: I never thought one could make a yogurt pie. Serve it cold.

8 SERVINGS

CRUST:

5 tablespoons sweet buter, melted

11 zwieback toasts or enough to make about 1 cup fine crumbs

½ cup walnuts

3 tablespoons sugar

FILLING:

2 eggs, at room temperature, separated

2 cups rich plain yogurt (Brown Cow Farm or Colombo brand)

Grated rind of 1 lemon

1 tablespoon lemon juice, strained

½ cup sugar

1½ tablespoons unbleached flour

⅛ teaspoon salt

I suggest you use a food processor, a 9-inch quiche pan with removable bottom, and a thin, flat baking sheet or foil oven liner.

To make the crust: Preheat oven to 350°F.

Set a 9-inch quiche pan with removable bottom on any flat sheet and grease with 1 tablespoon of the butter. (It will be easier to handle the crust.)

Break zwieback toasts into small pieces and grind fine in a food processor fitted with the steel blade; transfer to a bowl. Grind walnuts medium fine in food processor and combine with zwieback crumbs. Mix well with sugar and remaining 4 tablespoons butter.

Pat crumbs firmly and evenly into pan with back of a small spoon, forming sides first and making them thicker than bottom.

Bake in center of oven for 15 minutes. Let cool.

To make the filling: Beat egg yolks lightly with a fork in a medium bowl. Add yogurt, lemon rind, lemon juice, sugar, and flour and mix well.

Beat egg whites with salt until stiff.

With a rubber spatula, gently fold egg whites into yogurt mixture until all the whites have disappeared.

Pour filling into crust and bake pie on a flat baking sheet or foil oven liner in center of oven for 35 to 40 minutes, or until top is set and golden. Let cool.

To serve: Release edges carefully with a knife.

Place pan securely on an elevated object, such as a coffee can, and let the rim fall down. Carefully slide two large, wide spatulas underneath and transfer to a serving platter. Refrigerate pie until ready to serve.

◆The pie can be baked a day in advance, but the crust will get a bit soggy.

APPLE–NUT CAKE

————————————————————

Moist and not too sweet. It keeps fresh for many days refrigerated and freezes very well.

ABOUT
3 DOZEN
1 ½-INCH
SQUARES

8½ tablespoons (1 stick plus
 ½ tablespoon) sweet butter,
 at room temperature
2 cups plus 1 tablespoon
 sifted unbleached flour
1 cup sugar
2 eggs, at room temperature
½ teaspoon baking soda
½ teaspoon baking powder

3½ tablespoons sour cream,
 at room temperature
1 teaspoon vanilla extract
2 small McIntosh apples,
 peeled, cored, and chopped
 fine
1 cup walnuts, chopped coarse

*I suggest you use an electric mixer and a 9-by-9-by-1¾-inch
baking pan.*

Preheat oven to 350°F. Grease a 9-by-9-by-1¾-inch baking pan with ½
tablespoon of the butter and dust evenly with 1 tablespoon of the flour.
Invert pan and tap to shake off excess.

In an electric-mixer bowl, at medium speed, cream remaining 8 tablespoons butter, adding sugar gradually and continuing to beat until pale and
fluffy, about 10 minutes. With the motor on, add eggs, one at a time, until
thoroughly blended. Sift together flour along with baking soda and baking
powder directly into measuring cup. With a rubber spatula, fold small
amounts of flour into batter, alternating with sour cream. Combine well after
each addition. Add vanilla, apples, and walnuts. Spoon batter into pan and
smooth the top. Bake in center of oven for about 45 to 50 minutes. Test
with a cake tester in the center; it should come out dry. Let cool on a rack.
Loosen sides with a knife before unmolding.

NOTE: You can chop both apples and walnuts in a food processor fitted
with the steel blade.

TUILES (ROOF-TILE NUT COOKIES) I

ABOUT
1 DOZEN
3-INCH TUILES

Tuiles are French butter-almond cookies, whose shape resembles the terra-cotta tiles found on the roofs of Mediterranean houses. They are traditionally made with butter and cream and are very thin, crisp, and delicate. I have adopted two pareve versions, which I serve with sorbets or poached fruit.

1 egg, at room temperature
¼ cup sugar
1 tablespoon unbleached flour
¼ cup almonds, blanched and
   sliced or chopped coarse

½ tablespoon unsalted
   margarine

I suggest you use the following: two or three heavy cookie sheets; a thin, flexible metal spatula; and a thin rolling pin or thin bottle.

Preheat oven to 400°F. Place eggs, sugar, flour, and nuts in a small bowl. Mix with a wooden spoon until just blended. Let rest for 5 minutes.

Grease two or three thoroughly cleaned heavy cookie sheets with margarine. (It will be easier to remove the rounds if the cookie sheets are absolutely clean and heavy.)

Drop batter by teaspoonfuls onto cookie sheets. With the back of a small spoon, spread mounds evenly into very thin circles, about 3 inches in diameter, allowing no more than about six rounds to a cookie sheet. Bake in center of oven for about 5 minutes, or until edges are beginning to brown.

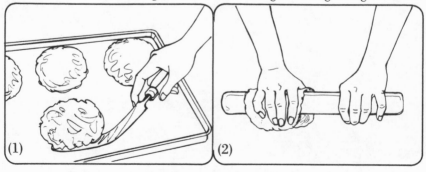

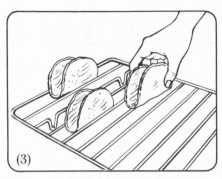

(3)

Watch them carefully, since they burn easily. Immediately loosen circles by sliding a spatula bit by bit under each round (1). Place each one over a thin rolling pin or bottle and press gently (2). They will form into a tuile shape (3). (If you have difficulty releasing the rounds, return them to the oven for a few seconds to reheat and try again.)

To cool them further, place them, edges up, on a cookie rack. They keep for a long time placed one on top of the other in a tightly covered tin box, preferably in a cool place.

TUILES II

6 tablespoons unsalted margarine, at room temperature	2 eggs, at room temperature	ABOUT
	½ cup unbleached flour	3 TO 4 DOZEN
	½ teaspoon almond extract	3-INCH TUILES
Scant ¾ cup dark brown sugar	Scant ¾ cup walnuts, chopped coarse	

I suggest you use the following: a food processor; two to five heavy cookie sheets; a thin, flexible metal spatula; and a thin rolling pin or thin bottle.

Preheat oven to 325°F. Grease two to five cookie sheets with 1 tablespoon of the margarine.

Cream remaining 5 tablespoons margarine in a food processor fitted with the steel blade. Gradually add sugar until well combined and smooth. With motor on, add one egg at a time, flour, and almond extract until thoroughly blended. Transfer batter to a bowl; it will be very thin.

Drop batter by teaspoonfuls, 2 inches apart, onto the prepared cookie sheets. Sprinkle each round generously with chopped walnuts.

Bake in center of oven for about 8 to 10 minutes, or until edges turn light brown. Proceed in the same fashion as in the preceding recipe.

NOTE: I chop walnuts in a food processor fitted with the steel blade.

If you do not have enough cookie sheets, just clean what you do have as you finish each batch.

If you do not wish to shape these cookies into tuiles, just leave them as round wafers.

NUTTY CHOCOLATE MERINGUE SQUARES

4 TO 5
DOZEN
1 ½-INCH
SQUARES

These small crunchy cookies freeze very well and are nice to have on hand.

MERINGUE:

½ pound walnuts, about 2 cups

1 tablespoon unsalted margarine, melted

1 tablespoon unbleached flour

¼ pound semisweet chocolate, broken into small pieces

5 egg whites, at room temperature

Pinch salt

Scant 1 cup superfine sugar

1 teaspoon vanilla extract

ICING:

¼ pound semisweet chocolate, broken into small pieces

1 ounce unsweetened chocolate, broken into small pieces

2 tablespoons instant coffee powder

¼ cup boiling water

2 tablespoons sugar

8 tablespoons (1 stick) unsalted margarine, at room temperature

1 egg yolk, at room temperature

I suggest the following: a food processor, an 11-by-16-inch jelly roll pan, an electric mixer, and a double boiler.

To make the meringue: Preheat oven to 350°F. Roast walnuts in oven in a single layer on a baking sheet for 10 minutes. Let cool. Chop medium coarse, in a food processor fitted with the steel blade.

Use half the margarine to coat the bottom and sides of an 11-by-16-inch jelly roll pan. Line pan with a 21-inch-long sheet of wax paper; ends will extend over shorter sides of pan. Brush wax paper with remaining margarine and dust evenly with flour. Holding on to paper, invert pan and tap to remove excess flour.

Preheat oven to 300°F. Place chocolate in top part of a double boiler. Cover and set over simmering water until melted and smooth. Remove and let cool.

In an electric-mixer bowl, at high speed, beat whites until frothy. Add salt and beat again until whites hold soft peaks. Gradually add sugar, continuing to beat until meringue is stiff and glossy. Add vanilla.

With a rubber spatula, fold a quarter of the whites into the chocolate. Reverse the process, folding chocolate into whites. Add walnuts and combine thoroughly. Transfer batter to prepared pan, spreading it evenly and smoothing the top.

Bake in center of oven for 45 minutes. Let cool on a cake rack until lukewarm. Invert meringue onto a large tray or baking sheet. Gently peel off wax paper, cover meringue with a jelly roll pan, and invert back.

To make the icing: While meringue is baking, place chocolate, coffee powder, boiling water, and sugar in top part of a double boiler. Set over simmering water until melted and smooth. Remove from heat and whisk in margarine, 1 tablespoonful at a time, until thoroughly blended. Whisk in egg yolk. Let cool.

Pour icing evenly over meringue and smooth over the top. Place in refrigerator until cold. With a serrated knife, cut meringue into 1½-inch squares. (Do it carefully, since meringue has a tendency to crack.)

◆To freeze these cookies, place them in a foil pan with wax paper between the layers. Cover with foil and place in a plastic bag.

ORANGE-FLAVORED ALMOND COOKIES
➤➤➤

Easy, quick to make, not too sweet, and crunchy. They keep very well stored in an airtight tin box, preferably in a cool place. They also freeze very well.

ABOUT
20 COOKIES

Generous ½ cup almonds, blanched
1¼ tablespoons unsalted margarine, at room temperature
½ cup plus ½ tablespoon cake flour

⅓ cup sugar
1 egg, at room temperature
1 tablespoon Grand Marnier
Grated rind of 1 orange

I suggest you use a food processor and a cookie sheet.

Chop almonds in a food processor fitted with the steel blade until they resemble coarse grains; set aside.

Preheat oven to 275°F. Grease a cookie sheet with ¼ tablespoon of the margarine and dust with ½ tablespoon of the flour. Invert pan and tap to shake off excess.

Place remaining 1 tablespoon margarine, remaining ½ cup flour, and sugar in food processor and combine. Add almonds and all remaining ingredients and process until well blended.

Drop batter by ½ tablespoonfuls, 1 inch apart, onto a cookie sheet. Bake in center of oven for 15 to 20 minutes, or until tops feel firm to the touch. Let cool on a rack.

HONEY–NUT BALLS

ABOUT
6 DOZEN
COOKIES

Easy to make, nutritious, not too sweet, and crunchy. They keep fresh for a long time; they also freeze very well.

½ pound almonds, about 1¾ cups

½ pound walnuts, about 2 cups

1 tablespoon fresh lemon juice, strained

1 tablespoon fresh or bottled orange juice

Grated rind of 1 lemon

Grated rind of 1 orange

½ cup honey

3 egg whites, at room temperature, lightly beaten

1 to 1¼ cups unbleached flour

½ tablespoon unsalted margarine

Confectioners' sugar

I suggest you use a food processor and two cookie sheets.

Preheat oven to 350°F. Roast almonds and walnuts in oven in a single layer in a baking pan for about 10 minutes; let cool.

Coarsely chop almonds and walnuts separately in a food processor fitted with the steel blade. (Walnuts are softer.) Place in a bowl with juices, rinds, honey, and egg whites. Mix well. Add flour gradually, mixing with a wooden spoon to form a thick, but not stiff, mixture.

Reduce heat to 250°F. Grease two cookie sheets with margarine and dust with remaining 1 tablespoon flour. Invert pans and tap to shake off excess.

Roll generous teaspoonfuls of the mixture into balls between damp (not wet) palms. (You may have to rinse your hands from time to time.) Place on cookie sheets and bake for about 10 to 15 minutes, or until tops feel firm to the touch. Let cool on racks. Sprinkle with confectioners' sugar.

You can keep these stored in a tightly covered container, preferably in a cool place.

MICHEL FITOUSSI'S TULIPES

ABOUT
14 BASKETS

I have enjoyed most of the cooking classes I've attended but have not always found recipes I could adopt to my style of entertaining. This one was a real find, taught by Michel Fitoussi in the De Gustibus series. These wafer-thin, crisp cookie baskets can be filled with ice cream, sorbet, or mousse. My favorite way of serving this delightful dessert is, just before serving, to coat individual plates with raspberry sauce, fill the baskets with Frozen Raspberry Mousse (page 234), then place the filled tulipes on the sauce. They keep for days in an airtight tin box in a cool place.

TULIPES:

2 eggs, at room temperature	2 tablespoons unbleached flour
½ cup sugar	1 tablespoon unsalted
½ cup almonds, blanched and	margarine
sliced or chopped coarse	

RASPBERRY SAUCE:

Two 10-ounce packages frozen	2 tablespoons framboise
raspberries, thawed	(raspberry liqueur)

I suggest you use the following: two to five heavy cookie sheets; a thin, flexible metal spatula; three Chinese soup bowls, approximately 4 ½ inches across the top and 2 ½ inches across the bottom; and a blender.

To make the tulipes: Preheat oven to 400°F. Place eggs, sugar, nuts, and flour in a small bowl. Mix with a wooden spoon until just blended. Let batter rest for 5 minutes while you grease thoroughly clean cookie sheets with margarine. (It will be easier to remove the rounds if the cookie sheets are absolutely clean and heavy.)

Drop generous tablespoonfuls of batter onto a cookie sheet. With the back of a small spoon, spread each mound evenly into a very thin circle about 5 inches in diameter. Allow no more than three rounds to a cookie sheet.

Bake in center of oven for about 5 minutes, or until edges begin to brown. Watch them carefully, since they burn easily. Immediately loosen circles by sliding a spatula, bit by bit, under each round. Do it quickly, since they

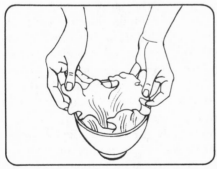

harden as they cool and are tricky to release. (If you have an upright oven, set cookie sheets on open oven door to keep them warm longer.) If you are having difficulty releasing the rounds, return them to the oven for a few seconds to reheat, then try again. Remove baskets to a rack to cool further. Fit rounds, loosened side down, into Chinese soup bowls to shape.

To make the sauce: Pour off 2 tablespoons syrup from each package of thawed frozen raspberries. Puree rest in a blender until smooth. Strain through a mesh sieve, pushing on solids with back of a wooden spoon; discard seeds. Refrigerate sauce in a covered jar. Just before serving, stir in framboise, and serve immediately.

NOTE: If you do not have enough cookie sheets, just clean what you do have as you go.

Chinese soup bowls are inexpensive and easily available, but any similar bowl will do.

HAZELNUT CRISPS

ABOUT
6 DOZEN
COOKIES

You will appreciate these cookies and find them easy to make and serve. They are very thin, crisp, light, and go well with sorbets, ice creams, poached pears, and fresh fruit. They also keep very well stored in a tightly covered tin box, preferably in a cool place, or you can freeze them.

Generous ¾ cup hazelnuts, about 5 ounces

About 6 tablespoons unsalted margarine

1 cup less 2 tablespoons sugar

4 egg whites, at room temperature

Grated rind of 1 lemon

⅔ cup cake flour

I suggest you use the following: a food processor; an electric mixer; two to six heavy cookie sheets; and a thin, flexible metal spatula.

Preheat oven to 350°F. Roast hazelnuts in oven in a single layer in a baking pan for 10 to 15 minutes. Rub nuts well in a dish towel to remove skin (some will remain). Let cool, then chop coarsely in a food processor fitted with the steel blade.

Grease two to six heavy cookie sheets with some of the margarine.

In an electric-mixer bowl, at medium speed, cream remaining 5 tablespoons margarine, adding sugar gradually and continuing to beat until pale and thick, about 10 minutes. Beat egg whites lightly with a fork and add to sugar-margarine mixture in a slow stream until well blended. With a rubber spatula, fold in hazelnuts, lemon rind, and flour, 1 tablespoonful at a time, until thoroughly combined. Drop level teaspoonfuls of batter 2 inches apart onto prepared cookie sheets. Bake one sheet at a time in center of oven for 8 to 10 minutes, or until edges turn light brown.

Work as quickly as possible to loosen circles by sliding a metal spatula or knife under them. Release all the cookies first, then place on a rack to cool. They harden as they cool and become tricky to remove. If that happens, return them to the oven for a few seconds to reheat, then try again.

NOTE: If you do not have enough cookie sheets, just clean what you do have as you go.

◆I freeze these cookies in a foil pan, covered with foil and placed in a plastic bag.

CHOCOLATE–ALMOND TRUFFLES

>>>

After a month of experimentation, I stumbled on this almost noncaloric, pareve sweet, which actually improves with time. I always have them in the freezer; they take only a few minutes to defrost.

ABOUT
4 DOZEN
TRUFFLES

1 cup almonds
¼ pound imported semisweet chocolate, broken into small pieces
2 egg yolks, at room temperature

½ cup sugar
Generous 1 tablespoon dark rum
3 tablespoons imported unsweetened cocoa powder

I suggest you use a food processor.

Preheat oven to 350°F. Roast almonds in oven in a single layer in a baking pan for about 10 minutes; let cool.

Coarsely chop almonds and chocolate in a food processor fitted with the steel blade. Add egg yolks, sugar, and rum. Process until mixture is medium fine and moist enough to shape into small balls. Roll level teaspoonfuls of mixture into balls between your palms. (If mixture is too dry and does not hold together, repeat the processing; if still too dry, add a few drops of egg white and process again. If hands get too sticky, rinse them.) Spread cocoa on a sheet of wax paper and roll each ball to coat completely.

To store, place truffles in a small foil pan, sprinkle with whatever cocoa has not been absorbed, cover with plastic wrap, then foil, and refrigerate. If you prefer to freeze the truffles, place them also in a plastic bag.

NOTE: I use Saint James rum, made in Martinique.
Use the best imported chocolate you can find.

CHOCOLATE COOKIES

>>>

This is a very easy cookie to make, and if you have children, they can help. They freeze very well and, strangely enough, taste better when eaten straight from the freezer.

ABOUT
7 DOZEN

½ pound (2 sticks) plus 1 tablespoon unsalted margarine, at room temperature
⅔ cup sugar
2 eggs, at room temperature

¾ cup imported unsweetened cocoa powder
⅔ cup unbleached flour
1 teaspoon vanilla extract
1¼ cups walnuts, chopped very coarse

I suggest you use an electric mixer and four to five cookie sheets.

Preheat oven to 375°F. Grease four to five cookie sheets with margarine.

In an electric-mixer bowl, at medium speed, cream remaining ½ pound margarine, adding sugar gradually and continuing to beat until light and fluffy, about 5 minutes. Beat eggs well with a fork and add, in a slow stream, to sugar-margarine mixture. Reduce speed and slowly add cocoa, flour, and vanilla until thoroughly blended.

Drop level ½ tablespoonfuls of batter, 1 inch apart, onto cookie sheets and sprinkle generously with walnuts. Bake in center of oven for about 6 minutes, or until firm. Let cool on a rack.

NOTE: If you like, you can make the cookies larger.

If you do not have enough cookie sheets, just clean what you do have as you go.

◆To freeze, place cookies in a foil pan with wax paper between the layers, cover with foil, then place in a plastic bag.

CARROT LOAF

2 LOAVES, EACH SERVING 12

When my children were small, I made this cake all the time. It is nutritious, easy to prepare, and remains fresh for many days, refrigerated. It also freezes very well.

6 medium carrots, peeled and trimmed	Scant 1¾ cups sugar
1½ cups walnuts	¾ teaspoon baking powder
1 cup plus ½ tablespoon corn oil	¼ teaspoon baking soda
2 cups plus 1½ tablespoons sifted unbleached flour	1 teaspoon salt
	4 eggs, at room temperature
	2 teaspoons ground cinnamon

I suggest you use a food processor and two 9-by-5-inch loaf pans.

Preheat oven to 350°F. Coarsely grate carrots in a food processor fitted with the grating attachment. You should have about 3 cups tightly packed grated carrots. Set aside.

Coarsely chop walnuts in food processor fitted with the steel blade. Set aside.

Grease two 9-by-5-inch loaf pans with ½ tablespoon of the oil. Dust evenly with 1½ tablespoons of the flour. Invert pans and tap to shake off excess.

Combine remaining 1 cup oil and the sugar in a large bowl. Stir with a wooden spoon for about 5 minutes, or until sugar is thoroughly mixed. Sift together flour along with baking powder, baking soda, and salt directly into a measuring cup.

To oil-sugar mixture add small amounts of flour alternately with 1 egg at a time, mixing well with a wooden spoon after each addition. Fold in carrots, walnuts, and cinnamon until well blended.

Divide batter equally between the two prepared pans. Bake in center of oven for 50 to 60 minutes, making sure pans do not touch.

Test with a cake tester in the center; it should come out dry. (Carrot loaves will not rise to top of pan.) Let cool on a rack. Loosen sides with a knife before unmolding.

ZUCCHINI LOAF

->>>

3 medium zucchini, about 1¼ pounds	1½ cups sugar	2 LOAVES, EACH SERVING 12
1½ cups walnuts	½ teaspoon baking powder	
1 cup plus ½ tablespoon corn oil	¾ teaspoon baking soda	
2 cups plus 1½ tablespoons sifted unbleached flour	1 teaspoon salt	
	4 eggs, at room temperature	
	1 teaspoon vanilla extract	
	2 teaspoons ground cinnamon	

I suggest you use a food processor and two 9-by-5-inch loaf pans.

Preheat oven to 350°F. Wash zucchini, pat dry with paper towels, and trim ends. Coarsely grate zucchini in a food processor fitted with the grating attachment. Wring out in a dish towel, in small batches, to remove moisture. You should have about 2¾ cups tightly packed grated zucchini. Set aside.

Coarsely chop walnuts in a food processor fitted with the steel blade. Set aside.

Grease two 9-by-5-inch loaf pans with ½ tablespoon of the oil. Dust evenly with 1½ tablespoons of the flour. Invert pans and tap to shake off excess.

Combine remaining 1 cup oil and the sugar in a large bowl. Stir with a wooden spoon for about 5 minutes, or until sugar is thoroughly mixed. Sift together flour with baking powder, baking soda, and salt directly into a measuring cup.

To oil-sugar mixture add small amounts of flour alternately with 1 egg at a time, mixing well with a wooden spoon after each addition. Fold in vanilla, cinnamon, zucchini, and walnuts until well blended.

Divide batter equally between the two prepared pans. Bake in center of oven for 50 to 60 minutes, making sure pans do not touch. Test with a cake tester in the center; it should come out dry. (Zucchini loaves will not rise to top of pan.) Let cool on a rack. Loosen sides with a knife before unmolding.

PUFF-PASTRY APPLE STRIPS

2 STRIPS,
EACH
SERVING
4 TO 6

An adaptation of a classic French dessert. Serve it either warm or at room temperature.

1 recipe Puff Pastry dough
(page 249)

FILLING:
Generous 1 cup almonds
4 tablespoons (½ stick)
unsalted margarine, at room
temperature
½ cup sugar
1 egg, at room temperature

1 egg yolk mixed with 1
teaspoon cold water

1 teaspoon vanilla extract
2 tablespoons dark rum
¾ cup apricot jam
5 medium apples (Granny
Smith or Cortland)

I suggest you use the following: two heavy cookie sheets, metal pie weights, a food processor, and an electric mixer.

Make the puff pastry dough in advance. If it is frozen, defrost in the refrigerator overnight. Cut dough in half; keep one piece refrigerated. On a lightly floured marble surface, with a floured rolling pin, roll dough out into an approximately 10-by-16-inch rectangle. (If dough sticks, dust lightly with flour.) Roll dough loosely over a rolling pin and unroll over a heavy cookie sheet. Refrigerate or freeze for 10 minutes. Roll out other piece of dough in the same fashion.

Trim rectangles to make them straight. Cut two 1-inch-wide strips of dough from long sides of rectangles; you will have four strips of dough. Brush water over long edges and attach strips to form a border, leaving shorter sides free. Prick bottom with a fork and refrigerate shells for 1 hour or freeze for 30 minutes.

Preheat oven to 425°F. Line bottom of strips with foil. Weigh foil down with pie weights (or rice or beans kept expressly for this purpose). Brush egg yolk and water mixture over border. Bake for 15 minutes. Remove weights and foil and let cool.

To make the filling: Preheat oven to 350°F. Roast almonds in oven in a single layer in a baking pan for 10 minutes; let cool. Chop coarsely in a food processor fitted with the steel blade.

In an electric-mixer bowl, at medium speed, cream margarine, adding sugar gradually and continuing to beat until fluffy, about 5 minutes. Add egg, vanilla, and rum and continue mixing until blended. Combine thoroughly with almonds.

In a small saucepan, gently heat apricot jam. Strain through a mesh sieve, pushing on solids with a wooden spoon; discard residue. Return strained jam to saucepan.

Preheat oven to 400°F. Peel, core, and slice apples very thin. Spread bottom pastry with almond filling. Cover with overlapping rows of apples, laying them crosswise for easier slicing. Brush top with heated apricot jam. Bake for 15 minutes, or until apples are almost soft. While strips are still warm, slice into 4 to 6 servings.

NOTE: I use Saint James dark rum, imported from Martinique.

◆Apple tarts can be baked earlier in the day and reheated.

PUFF-PASTRY TORTE WITH PRALINE FILLING

->>>

Ever since I learned how to make pareve puff pastry, I have been fascinated by its many uses. This wonderful torte with a distinct almond flavor can be made a day ahead of time and refrigerated. Serve it at room temperature.

10 TO 12 SERVINGS

1 recipe Puff Pastry dough (page 249)
ALMOND PRALINE:
1 cup almonds, blanched
Vegetable oil
¾ cup sugar

⅓ cup plus 2 tablespoons cold water

FILLING:
12 tablespoons (1½ sticks) unsalted margarine, at room temperature
2 tablespoons sugar
2 egg yolks, at room temperature

1 teaspoon almond extract
2 tablespoons brandy (Cognac)

I suggest you use the following: four heavy cookie sheets, a small copper saucepan, a blender, and an electric mixer.

To roll out the dough: Make the puff pastry in advance. If it is frozen, defrost in the refrigerator overnight. Cut dough into three equal pieces. Work with one piece at a time, keeping the rest refrigerated.

On a lightly floured marble surface, with a lightly floured rolling pin, roll out one piece of dough into a very thin square, approximately 11 by 11 or 12 by 12 inches. (Dough is elastic and may shrink while rolling; just apply pressure with rolling pin and dust lightly with flour as needed.) Roll dough loosely over rolling pin and unroll on a heavy cookie sheet. If dough shrinks as it is placed on cookie sheet, remove and roll again, or else stretch it with your hands. Do not be afraid of this dough. Remember, it will also shrink as it bakes, and you need three 10-inch rounds. Roll out rest of dough in the same fashion. Prick well with a fork to prevent it from puffing up too much and place cookie sheets in refrigerator for 1 hour, or else freeze for 30 minutes.

Preheat oven to 400°F. Bake sheets in center of oven for 10 to 15 minutes, or until golden. Let cool. Using a pot lid as a guide, cut out three 10-inch circles.

To make the praline: Preheat oven to 350°F. Roast almonds in oven in a single layer in a baking pan for about 10 to 15 minutes, or until golden and crackling. Keep almonds near the stove.

Lightly grease a cookie sheet with vegetable oil and keep it near the stove.

Combine sugar and water in a copper saucepan. Boil over medium-high heat, without stirring, until sugar turns medium brown. Do not let it get too dark; it burns very quickly. Drop almonds into sugar syrup all at once. Pot holder in hand, pour immediately onto oiled cookie sheet. It will harden as it cools. Break into small pieces and pulverize in a blender; you should have about 2 cups. (Praline powder keeps for several weeks, refrigerated in a covered glass jar.)

To make the filling: In an electric-mixer bowl, at medium speed, cream margarine, adding sugar gradually and continuing to beat until pale and fluffy, about 5 minutes. Add egg yolks and blend. With a rubber spatula, fold in 1½ cups of the praline powder, almond extract, and brandy (Cognac) until thoroughly combined.

To assemble the torte: Select even circles for bottom and top of torte. Spread some of the filling over two circles and cover with the third. (If the middle circle is uneven, fix it with leftover scraps of dough.) Spread remaining filling over top and sides of the cake. Sprinkle top and sides with remaining ½ cup praline powder. Refrigerate.

NOTE: If you do not have a copper saucepan, use any heavy one.

If you make the puff pastry dough and the filling with butter, the dessert will be flakier and richer.

◆You can make the filling ahead of time and refrigerate it, but bring it back to room temperature before assembling the torte.

ALMOND TORTE WITH
APRICOT–CHOCOLATE ICING

>>>

Many years ago I took classes with Lilly Joss Reich, author of *The Viennese Pastry Cookbook*, who introduced me to flourless nut tortes. This wonderful dessert is easy to make and light, with a crunchy texture. It stays moist for many days and freezes very well.

10 TO 12
SERVINGS

¾ pound almonds, about 2 generous cups
½ tablespoon unsalted margarine
½ tablespoon unbleached flour

5 eggs, at room temperature, separated
Generous ½ cup sugar
1 teaspoon almond extract

ICING:

½ cup apricot jam
3½ ounces semisweet chocolate, broken into small pieces
1 tablespoon boiling water

1 tablespoon instant coffee powder
4½ tablespoons unsalted margarine, at room temperature

I suggest you use the following: a food processor, a 9-by-2½-inch springform pan, an electric mixer, and a double boiler.

Preheat oven to 350°F. Roast almonds in oven in a single layer in a baking pan for about 10 minutes. Let cool. Measure out ¼ cup for garnish; set aside. Grind the rest medium fine in a food processor fitted with the steel blade.

Grease a 9-by-2½-inch springform pan with margarine, and dust evenly with flour. Invert pan and tap to shake off excess.

In an electric-mixer bowl, at medium speed, beat egg yolks, adding sugar gradually and continuing to beat until pale and thick, about 10 minutes. Stir in almond extract.

Beat egg whites at high speed until stiff. With a rubber spatula, fold half the ground nuts and a quarter of the egg whites into batter until well blended. Repeat with remaining nuts and another quarter of the whites. Now reverse the process, pouring the batter over the remaining whites. Gently fold the two mixtures together, using a motion like a figure eight, until all the whites have disappeared. Be careful not to overfold. Pour batter into the prepared pan and smooth the top.

Bake in center of oven for about 25 minutes. Test with a cake tester in the center; it should come out dry. Do not overbake. Let cool on a rack. (Cake may drop a bit.) Release sides with a knife and remove rim. Loosen bottom with a knife and invert to a platter to be iced. (The bottom will now be the top.) Or, if you like, cover cake with foil and leave to be iced the following day.

To make the icing: In a small saucepan, heat jam gently. Strain through a mesh sieve, pushing on solids with a wooden spoon; discard residue. Coat top of cake with jam.

Place chocolate in top part of a double boiler. Cover and set over simmering water until melted and smooth.

While chocolate is melting, use boiling water to dissolve coffee powder. Remove chocolate from heat and whisk in coffee liquid and margarine, 1 tablespoonful at a time, until smooth. If icing is very thin, let stand at room temperature to thicken slightly. Place pieces of wax paper beneath edges of torte to catch icing driblets. Pour icing over top of cake, tilting platter to distribute it evenly and let chocolate run down the sides. Let stand for a few minutes to set, then smooth dribbles with a knife, adding any leftover chocolate from pan and wax paper to cover sides completely.

When icing is set, sprinkle top with reserved chopped almonds. When icing is firm, remove wax paper.

To make the garnish: Cut the reserved ¼ cup almonds into small bits with a knife and toast until golden.

POPPY SEED CHOCOLATE TORTE

10 TO 12 SERVINGS

Another flourless torte: This one is made with poppy seeds, which are frequently used in Eastern European countries, but are not very popular here. This torte stays moist for many days and freezes very well.

2 ounces semisweet chocolate, broken into small pieces

2 cups plus 2 tablespoons ground poppy seeds, about 6 ounces

8½ tablespoons (1 stick plus ½ tablespoon) unsalted margarine, at room temperature

½ tablespoon unbleached flour

Generous ½ cup sugar

6 eggs, at room temperature, separated

½ teaspoon vanilla extract

ICING:

3½ ounces semisweet chocolate, broken into small pieces

1 tablespoon instant coffee powder

1 tablespoon boiling water

4½ tablespoons unsalted margarine, at room temperature

I suggest you use the following: a food processor, a 9-by-2 1/2-inch springform pan, an electric mixer, and a double boiler.

Grind chocolate fine in a food processor fitted with the steel blade. Combine with 2 cups of the poppy seeds. Set aside rest of poppy seeds for garnish.

Grease a 9-by-2 1/2-inch springform pan with 1/2 tablespoon of the margarine and dust evenly with flour. Invert pan and tap to shake off excess.

Preheat oven to 350°F. In an electric-mixer bowl, at medium speed, cream remaining 8 tablespoons margarine, adding sugar gradually and continuing to beat until pale and fluffy, about 5 minutes. Add egg yolks, one at a time, until well blended. Stir in vanilla.

Beat egg whites at high speed until stiff. With a rubber spatula, fold half of the poppy seed mixture and a quarter of the egg whites into batter until well blended. Repeat with remaining poppy seeds and another quarter of the whites. Now reverse the process, pouring batter over whites. Gently fold the two mixtures together, using a motion like a figure eight, until all the whites have disappeared. Be careful not to overfold. Pour batter into the prepared pan and smooth the top.

Bake in center of oven for about 35 minutes. Test with a cake tester in the center; it should come out dry. Let cool on a rack. The cake will drop a bit. Release sides with a knife and remove rim. Loosen bottom with a knife and invert onto a platter to be iced. (The bottom will now be the top.) Or, if you like, cover the cake with foil and leave to be iced the following day.

To make the icing: Place chocolate in top part of a double boiler. Cover and set over simmering water until melted and smooth.

While chocolate is melting, dissolve coffee powder in boiling water. Remove chocolate from heat and whisk in coffee liquid and margarine, one tablespoonful at a time, until smooth. If icing is very thin, let stand at room temperature to thicken slightly. Place pieces of wax paper beneath edges of torte to catch icing driblets. Pour icing over top of cake, tilting platter to distribute it evenly and let chocolate run down the sides (1). Let stand for a few minutes to set, then smooth dribbles with a knife, adding any leftover chocolate from pan and wax paper to cover sides completely (2).

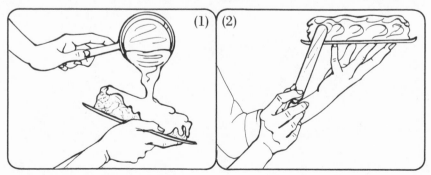

When icing is set, sprinkle top with remaining 2 tablespoons poppy seeds. When icing is firm, remove wax paper.

NOTE: Whole poppy seeds are available in specialty stores. They will grind them for you. You can keep ground poppy seeds refrigerated for several weeks and frozen for several months.

If you like, you can make this torte with butter; it has a wonderful flavor.

Desserts

RASPBERRIES WITH CRÈME FRAICHE

This homemade version of Crème Fraiche is a reasonable facsimile of the French one. Sour cream acts as the fermenting agent in the heavy cream and thickens it. Crème Fraiche makes a wonderful topping on any berry, but my favorite are raspberries.

CRÈME FRAICHE:

1 cup heavy cream
2 tablespoons sour cream

About 1 to 2 tablespoons
confectioners' sugar

1½ pints fresh raspberries

Combine heavy cream and sour cream in a covered glass jar. Shake mixture for about 2 minutes as if you were shaking a cocktail. Let mixture stand at room temperature for at least 8 hours, or overnight; it will thicken. Sweeten with confectioners' sugar to taste. Mix and refrigerate. Crème Fraiche keeps fresh for at least a week.

To serve: Pick over raspberries (never wash them). Divide among individual plates. Serve Crème Fraiche on the side.

NOTE: If the temperature in the room is colder than 75°F, it will take longer to thicken the cream.

If you have some Crème Fraiche left, add more heavy cream to it and you will make even more.

STRAWBERRIES WITH ZABAGLIONE–CREAM SAUCE

A perfectly elegant dessert, which I learned many years ago in Michael Field's cooking class. Serve it at room temperature.

7 egg yolks, at room
    temperature
¾ cup sugar
Scant 1 cup imported very
    dry cocktail sherry or
    kosher cream sherry

1 cup heavy cream, chilled
3 to 4 pints fresh strawberries

I suggest you use a 1½- to 2-quart double boiler and a large crystal or glass serving bowl.

Have a large bowl of ice ready.

In top part of a double boiler, whisk egg yolks, sugar, and sherry until well blended.

Set top over simmering water and whisk continuously until sauce is as thick as light custard. (Do not stop whisking; the sauce may curdle.) Remove top and set it over ice, whisking continuously until sauce is cool to the touch.

Beat cream in a well-chilled metal bowl until stiff. Fold cream into sauce with a rubber spatula until well blended. Pour into serving bowl, cover tightly with plastic wrap, and refrigerate until ready to serve.

Rinse strawberries, hull, and pat dry with paper towels. Remove sauce from refrigerator, top with upright strawberries, and serve.

◆The sauce can also be made a day ahead of time without any loss of flavor or texture, but be sure to whisk it again. If you wish to prepare the strawberries several hours before serving them, leave them upside down on their stem sides on paper towels to keep dry.

STRAWBERRY BAVARIAN WITH BLACKBERRY SAUCE

12 SERVINGS A fabulous combination of flavors and an elegant finale to a light meal. This dessert must be made a day ahead of time.

5 eggs, at room temperature,
    separated
Scant ¾ cup sugar
2 teaspoons cornstarch
1 cup milk, well heated
½ cup fresh orange juice,
    strained
SAUCE:
1 pint fresh blackberries
2 to 3 tablespoons sugar

1 tablespoon unflavored
    kosher gelatin
2 pints fresh strawberries
1 cup heavy cream, chilled

1 tablespoon Grand Marnier

I suggest you use the following: a double boiler, a blender, and a 2-quart (preferably glass) soufflé dish.

Have a large bowl of ice ready.

In top part of a double boiler, whisk egg yolks, sugar, and cornstarch. Whisk in milk and set over simmering water. Continue whisking until custard is thick enough to coat a metal spoon heavily, about 10 to 15 minutes. While whisking custard, combine orange juice and gelatin in a small saucepan. Heat slowly and stir until dissolved. Add gelatin to custard, whisking vigorously until thoroughly blended. Transfer to a bowl and set over ice. Continue whisking frequently until cool.

Beat egg whites until stiff. Whisk egg whites into cooled custard and blend thoroughly. Refrigerate custard until it begins to set (several hours). From time to time whisk again harder to make it light and fluffy.

In the meantime, rinse strawberries, hull, and pat dry with paper towels. Puree, in batches, in a blender until smooth; set aside.

Beat heavy cream in a well-chilled metal bowl until stiff. Whisk strawberry puree into almost-set custard. Fold in whipped cream with a rubber spatula and blend well.

Pour mousse into a 2-quart soufflé dish or glass or crystal bowl. Cover tightly with plastic wrap and refrigerate overnight.

Serve directly from refrigerator with sauce on the side or on sauce-covered plates.

To make the sauce: Do not rinse blackberries, just pick them over. Puree in blender until smooth. Strain through a mesh sieve, pushing on solids with a wooden spoon; discard residue. Combine with sugar to taste. Refrigerate in a covered container. Combine with Grand Marnier just before serving.

NOTE: If blackberries are unavailable, substitute strawberries and adjust sugar proportions.

APPLE MOUSSE

Make this silky-textured dessert during the autumn, when apples are at their best. You can make it in a charlotte mold or serve it in a glass or crystal bowl. It must be prepared a day ahead of time to chill thoroughly.   12 SERVINGS

Vegetable oil	1½ cups milk, well heated
8 medium McIntosh apples	½ cup fresh orange juice,
4 egg yolks, at room	strained
temperature	1 tablespoon unflavored
2 teaspoons cornstarch	kosher gelatin
¾ cup sugar	1 cup heavy cream, chilled

I suggest you use the following: a 2-quart tinned-steel charlotte mold, an enameled cast-iron saucepan, and a double boiler.

If you are using a charlotte mold, oil sides lightly with vegetable oil. Cut a sheet of wax paper to cover bottom of mold exactly. Wash, core, and cut apples into small pieces. Place in a saucepan and cook slowly, covered, until apples are very soft. From time to time, stir with a wooden spoon and be careful not to scorch the bottom of the pan.

Strain apples, in batches, through a mesh sieve, pushing on solids with a wooden spoon and discarding residue each time. (You should have about 3½ cups strained apple puree.)

Have a large bowl of ice ready.

In top part of a double boiler, whisk egg yolks, cornstarch, and sugar. Whisk in milk and set over simmering water. Continue whisking until custard is thick enough to coat a metal spoon heavily. While whisking custard, combine orange juice and gelatin in a small saucepan. Heat slowly and stir until dissolved and smooth. Whisk into custard until thoroughly blended.

Transfer custard to a bowl, set over ice, and whisk frequently until cool. Refrigerate until custard begins to set (several hours). From time to time, whisk again to make it light and fluffy.

Beat heavy cream in a well-chilled metal bowl until stiff. Whisk apple puree into the almost-set custard. With a rubber spatula, fold in cream and combine thoroughly. Pour into charlotte mold, cover tightly with plastic wrap, and refrigerate overnight.

To unmold: It is a little tricky to unmold the mousse. Loosen the sides, pushing the blade of a knife all the way down to the bottom of the mold. Dip mold into very hot water and leave for a few seconds. Dry bottom and invert onto a flat nonmetal platter. Tap mold; if you hear a little noise, the mousse will unmold. Leave mold on for 10 minutes, then lift. If you are not successful, repeat several times in the same fashion. If you have unmolded the mousse and it does not hold its shape at all, just serve it in individual goblets or a crystal bowl.

MOCHA MOUSSE

This dessert is so easy to make that it is difficult to believe that it can be so good. Make it a day ahead of time to chill properly.

8 TO 10 SERVINGS

4 egg yolks
½ cups sugar
2 cups half and half or light cream
1 tablespoon instant coffee powder
2 ounces semisweet chocolate, broken into small pieces

¾ tablespoon unflavored kosher gelatin
2 tablespoons brandy (Cognac)
1 tablespoon finely ground coffee beans
1 cup heavy cream, chilled

I suggest you use an enameled cast-iron saucepan and a 1½-quart soufflé dish, preferably glass, or any crystal bowl.

Have a large bowl of ice ready. In a saucepan, whisk egg yolks, sugar, and half and half or light cream. Add coffee, chocolate, and gelatin. Whisk over medium heat until custard is hot and smooth. Pour into a bowl and set over ice, whisking custard frequently until cool.

Stir in brandy (Cognac) and ground coffee beans. Refrigerate custard until it begins to set, whisking from time to time to make it fluffy and light.

Beat heavy cream in a well-chilled metal bowl until stiff. Whisk cream into custard and pour into a soufflé dish. Cover tightly with plastic wrap and refrigerate overnight. Serve at room temperature.

MOUSSE WITH CHESTNUTS AND LADYFINGERS

A beautiful dessert with a velvety texture and the delicate flavor of kirsch. It is decorated with ladyfingers and unmolded. Make it a day ahead of time to chill.

10 TO 12 SERVINGS

5 egg yolks, at room temperature
Scant ½ cup sugar
1¼ cups milk, well heated
¼ cup plus 2 tablespoons kirsch
1 tablespoon unflavored kosher gelatin

1 teaspoon vanilla extract
18 "double" store-bought ladyfingers, two 3-ounce packages
½ cup apricot jam
1½ cups heavy cream, chilled
10-ounce jar brandied chestnut pieces, drained

I suggest you use a double boiler and a 2-quart tinned-steel char-lotte mold.

Have a large bowl of ice ready. In top part of a double boiler, whisk egg yolks and sugar. Whisk in hot milk and set over simmering water. Continue whisking until custard is thick enough to coat a metal spoon heavily. While whisking custard, combine ¼ cup of the kirsch and gelatin in a small saucepan. Heat slowly and stir until dissolved. Add gelatin to custard, whisking vigorously until smooth. Stir in vanilla.

Transfer custard to a bowl and set over ice. Whisk frequently until cool. Refrigerate custard until it begins to set (several hours). From time to time, whisk again to make it light and fluffy.

In the meantime, cut a sheet of wax paper and fit it into bottom of mold. In order to have a design on top of mousse, separate one "double" la-dyfinger and cut out four balls with a melon scooper. Separate another three ladyfingers, trim ends into a V shape, and arrange trimmed la-dyfingers in a petallike design with the four balls in between on the wax paper. Separate eight more ladyfing-ers and line sides of mold, sugared side against mold. Sprinkle all the ladyfingers with remaining 2 tablespoons kirsch.

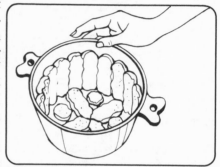

Heat apricot jam gently in a small saucepan. Strain through a mesh sieve, pushing on solids with a wooden spoon; discard residue. Let cool.

Beat heavy cream in a well-chilled metal bowl until stiff. With a rubber spatula, combine almost-set custard with whipped cream and chestnut pieces. Pour half the mousse into the mold and cover with a layer of single ladyfingers. Spread apricot jam over them and then spread on remaining mousse. Finally, top mousse with additional single ladyfingers. (You may have some left over.) Cover tightly with plastic wrap and refrigerate over-night.

To unmold: Loosen sides with a knife, pushing the blade all the way down to the bottom of the mold. Invert onto a flat nonmetal platter; tap all along mold and lift off. Remove wax paper.

NOTE: I use imported Raffeto-brand brandied marron pieces. They are available in specialty stores.

AMANDA'S LEMON ICE CREAM

➤➤➤
___

One of the simplest of recipes. I am indebted to my friend Amanda for sharing this wonderful recipe with me.

6 TO 8 SERVINGS

2 cups heavy cream
Scant 1 cup sugar
Grated rind of 2 lemons

⅓ cup fresh lemon juice, strained

Combine cream and sugar in a large bowl and let it rest for a few minutes. Stir with a wooden spoon until sugar is dissolved. Add lemon rind and juice and mix well. Pour into a container or soufflé dish. Cover dish tightly with plastic wrap and freeze overnight.

This ice cream freezes quite hard. Transfer to refrigerator 30 minutes before serving to soften a bit.

MOCHA CHIP ICE CREAM

➤➤➤
___

What fun and what little effort it is to make your own ice cream.

ABOUT 1½ QUARTS

¼ pound imported semisweet chocolate, broken into small pieces
1 cup milk
2 tablespoons instant coffee powder

1 cup sugar
⅛ teaspoon salt
3 egg yolks
3 cups heavy cream
3 to 4 ounces semisweet chocolate morsels

I suggest you use a food processor, a small enameled cast-iron saucepan, and an electric ice-cream maker.

Grate chocolate in a food processor fitted with the steel blade; set aside.

Rinse a small saucepan with cold water. Pour in milk and scald it (that is, heat to boiling point, but do not boil).

Remove from heat and stir in coffee powder, ½ cup of the sugar, and salt. Beat egg yolks with a fork and add remaining ½ cup sugar to them. Whisk egg yolks into milk mixture.

Place over medium heat and whisk vigorously and continuously until mixture is thick enough to coat a metal spoon heavily. Add 1 cup of the cream and let cool a bit.

Drape a thin muslin towel or thin piece of cloth over a bowl and strain the mixture. (You may have to wring the cloth at the end.) Stir in grated chocolate and remaining 2 cups heavy cream. Let cool.

Add chocolate morsels, pour into bowl of an electric ice-cream maker, and follow instructions. (If you like, you can drop chocolate bits through the opening in the cover instead, after ice cream has chilled for a few minutes.)

Freeze in a covered container.

NOTE: If you prefer, you can make your own chocolate chips by placing semisweet chocolate, broken into small pieces, in a food processor fitted with the steel blade.

ALMOND PRALINE ICE CREAM

ABOUT
1 QUART

PRALINE (NUT BRITTLE):

½ cup almonds, blanched   ½ cup sugar

Vegetable oil   ⅓ cup water

CARAMEL:

2 cups heavy cream   ½ cup water

2 cups half and half   ½ teaspoon salt

1 cup less 2 tablespoons sugar   1 teaspoon almond extract

I suggest you use the following: a cookie sheet, a small copper saucepan, a blender, and an electric ice-cream maker.

To make the praline: Preheat oven to 350°F. Toast almonds in oven in a single layer on a cookie sheet for about 15 minutes, or until light brown; keep near the stove.

Grease a cookie sheet lightly with vegetable oil.

Combine sugar and water in a small copper saucepan. Boil over medium-high heat, without stirring, until syrup turns light brown. Do not let it get too dark; it burns very quickly. Immediately drop in nuts. Pot holder in hand, pour mixture onto the greased cookie sheet. It will become hard as it cools. Break into small pieces and pulverize in a blender; set aside.

To make the caramel: Combine heavy cream and half and half and keep near the stove, along with a whisk. Combine sugar and water in a large saucepan. Boil over medium-high heat, without stirring, until sugar turns light brown. Immediately pour into combined creams, beating mixture with a whisk. Bring to a boil and whisk until sugar is dissolved and liquid is smooth. Remove from heat and let cool.

Mix in praline. Pour into bowl of an electric ice-cream maker and follow instructions. Freeze in a covered container.

NOTE: If you do not have a copper saucepan, use any heavy one.

COMPOTE OF ORANGE SLICES

A refreshing dessert when the citrus fruit is at its best. Serve it 6 SERVINGS
very well chilled.

8 medium navel oranges   Juice of ½ lemon, strained
2 tablespoons sugar

I suggest you use a large crystal or glass bowl.

With a vegetable peeler, remove very thin (almost transparent) strips of orange rind from 2 of the oranges and cut into very thin julienne shreds. Place in a small saucepan with water to cover. Boil, uncovered, for 10 minutes. Drain and pat dry with paper towels. Reserve for garnish.

Peel all the oranges with a sharp or serrated knife, removing all the white pulp and cutting as close to the flesh as possible.

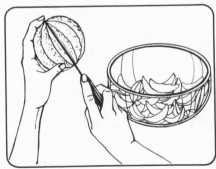

Hold oranges over a bowl to catch the juices and cut in between the membranes into thin sections. Place orange sections in a large glass bowl and squeeze over them all the juice left in the membranes. Stir in sugar and lemon juice without breaking up the orange sections. Sprinkle with reserved strips of rind. Cover with plastic wrap and refrigerate for at least 4 hours, or until very cold.

HOT LEMON SOUFFLÉ

Soufflés have a reputation for being difficult to make. This one 6 SERVINGS
is easy and foolproof. The soufflé, being flourless, is baked in a bain-marie, or hot-water bath, in a very low oven.

1 tablespoon unsalted margarine, at room temperature	2 to 3 tablespoons sugar
5 eggs, at room temperature, separated	Grated rind of 2 lemons
¾ cup sugar	¼ cup lemon juice, strained
	⅛ teaspoon salt
Boiling water	

I suggest you use the following: an electric mixer, a 6-cup soufflé dish, and a pan 3 inches deep, large enough to hold the soufflé dish.

Use half of the margarine and half of the sugar to grease and coat a 6-cup soufflé dish. (To hold the puff of the soufflé in bounds, you will need a foil collar, which will increase the height of the dish another 3 to 4 inches.) Cut a 26-inch sheet of foil and fold in half lengthwise; grease with the remaining margarine and coat with the remaining sugar. Wrap around top of soufflé dish and tie with a string.

Preheat oven to 325°F. In an electric-mixer bowl, at medium speed, beat egg yolks, adding sugar gradually and continuing to beat until pale and thick, about 10 minutes. With a rubber spatula, fold in lemon rind and juice until well combined.

Beat egg whites at high speed until foamy. Add salt and continue beating until stiff. With a rubber spatula, fold a quarter of the whites into lemon mixture until well combined. Now reverse the process, pouring lemon mixture over whites. Gently fold the two mixtures together, using a motion like a figure eight, until most of the whites have disappeared. Be careful not to overfold.

Place soufflé dish in an approximately 3-inch-deep pan and ladle soufflé mixture into it. Pour boiling water into pan to half the height of the soufflé dish.

Bake in center of oven for 45 minutes. The soufflé will rise and have a brown crust on top. Take out of oven, remove foil collar, and serve at once. (The soufflé will not fall if left for a few minutes in a turned-off oven with the door ajar.)

NOTE: You may have to adjust the timing, depending on your oven. The soufflé should be dry on the outside and soft on the inside.

FROZEN RASPBERRY MOUSSE

10 TO 12 SERVINGS

Although I don't always like to have a dessert after a full meal, I always find this one appealing. This cold mousse can be enjoyed all year, because it is made with frozen raspberries. Pre-

pare it a day ahead of time to chill properly. For a special dinner,
serve the mousse in Michel Fitoussi's Tulipes (page 210) over
a coating of raspberry sauce.

Three 10-ounce packages
  frozen raspberries, thawed
2 egg whites, at room
  temperature

2 tablespoons framboise
  (raspberry liqueur)

*I suggest you use the following: a 1-quart copper saucepan, a candy
thermometer, a blender, a mesh sieve, and an electric mixer.*

Drain raspberries over a 1-quart measuring cup. You should have about 2
cups raspberry liquid. Pour liquid into a copper saucepan and bring to a
boil. Cook briskly until a candy thermometer registers 220°F (you may wish
to leave the candy thermometer in the pan to gauge the temperature), about
35 minutes.
    In the meantime, puree drained raspberries in a blender. Strain puree,
in batches, through a mesh sieve, pressing on solids with back of a wooden
spoon to obtain as much puree as possible. Discard seeds. You should have
about 1 cup strained puree. Just before the syrup reaches 220°F, beat egg
whites in an electric mixer at low speed until foamy. Increase speed to high
and beat until stiff. With motor running at high speed, dribble in raspberry
syrup. Continue beating until outside of bowl feels cool to the touch.
Combine thoroughly with the strained puree and framboise.
    If you are planning to serve the mousse in tulipes, place it in a covered
container and freeze overnight. If not, place in a glass soufflé dish, cover
tightly with plastic wrap, and freeze overnight. Serve directly from the
freezer with Raspberry Sauce (below) on the side.

ORANGES IN RASPBERRY SAUCE

Serve this dessert very well chilled.
        6 SERVINGS

8 medium navel oranges
One 10-ounce package frozen
  raspberries, thawed

2 tablespoons Grand Marnier

I suggest you use a glass or crystal bowl and a blender.

Peel oranges with a sharp or serrated knife. Remove all the white pulp,
cutting as close to the flesh as possible.
    Holding oranges over a glass bowl to catch juices, separate into thin
sections by cutting in between membranes. Place orange sections in bowl
and squeeze over them all the juice left in the membranes.

To make the sauce: Puree raspberries in a blender until smooth. Strain through a mesh sieve, pushing with a wooden spoon. Discard residue.

Mix puree with Grand Marnier and combine gently with orange sections.

Cover with plastic wrap and refrigerate for at least 4 hours, or until very cold.

NECTARINES IN STRAWBERRY SAUCE

6 SERVINGS   A delightfully refreshing summer dessert. Prepare the nectarines and sauce a day ahead of time and chill.

6 medium ripe, unblemished nectarines

1¾ cups cold water

STRAWBERRY SAUCE:

One 10-ounce package frozen strawberries, thawed

⅓ cup sugar

1-inch piece vanilla bean or 1 teaspoon vanilla extract

1 tablespoon brandy (Cognac)

4 Amaretti cookies, crushed coarse (optional)

I suggest you use the following: an enameled saucepan large enough to fit nectarines in a single layer, a blender, and a glass or crystal platter.

Bring a large pot of water to a boil, drop in nectarines, and return to the boil. Drain nectarines and peel (if skins do not come off easily, briefly return to the water). Halve nectarines and remove pits.

In a large saucepan, bring water, sugar, and vanilla to a boil. Simmer for 10 minutes. Place nectarines in pan, cut side down, return to the boil, and turn fruit over. (They should be almost soft.) Remove from heat; nectarines will continue cooking while they cool. Cover pan with a lid or heavy foil and let cool completely. Refrigerate nectarines in their syrup.

To make the sauce: Pour off 3 tablespoons liquid from strawberries. Puree strawberries in a blender until smooth. Strain through a mesh sieve, pushing on solids with a wooden spoon. Discard residue. Refrigerate sauce in a covered container.

To serve: Arrange nectarines, cut side down, on a glass or crystal platter. Combine sauce with brandy (Cognac). Coat nectarines with sauce and sprinkle with crushed cookies.

NOTE: You can substitute peaches for nectarines and raspberry sauce for strawberry sauce. The sauce can also be flavored with any other liqueur.

Amaretti are Italian almond-flavored cookies and can be found in many specialty stores.

POACHED PEARS WITH SABAYON SAUCE

->>>

A favorite, elegant light dessert, which I like to serve after an elaborate meal. The pears can also be served in the poaching liquid without the sabayon sauce. The sabayon sauce can also be served with any berry.

6 SERVINGS

Juice of about 1½ lemons, strained
6 medium firm, unblemished ripe pears (Bartlett or Anjou)

About 1 bottle dry white wine
½ cup sugar
Water

SABAYON SAUCE:
4 egg yolks, at room temperature

¼ cup sugar
½ cup dry white wine

I suggest you use the following: an enameled saucepan large enough to fit the pear halves in a single layer, a double boiler, and a stainless-steel whisk.

To poach the pears: Combine 1 quart water and juice of 1 lemon in a large bowl. Peel pears and cut in half lengthwise. Scoop out center cores with a melon scooper. To prevent discoloration, drop immediately into lemoned water as soon as they are finished.

Combine wine, sugar, and juice of ½ lemon in a saucepan and boil for 5 minutes. Arrange pear halves, flat side down, in pan. Liquid should barely cover the fruit; if not enough, add more water and wine.

Bring to a boil, cover with a lid or heavy foil, and simmer for 3 minutes. Turn pears over, cover, and simmer for about another 3 minutes. Test with a sewing needle: The pears should be almost soft, since they will continue cooking while cooling. Uncover and let cool. Drain.

Pears can be poached earlier in the day, left in the syrup, and served at room temperature.

To make the sauce: Prepare a bowl of ice. In top part of a double boiler, beat egg yolks, sugar, and wine with a whisk until well blended. Set over simmering water and continue whisking until sauce doubles in volume and is thick enough to coat a metal spoon; it should look like a thin custard. Set at once over ice and whisk until sauce is cool to the touch.

Arrange drained pears in a shallow crystal or glass bowl and coat with sabayon sauce.

◆Sabayon sauce can be made earlier in the day and refrigerated. Before serving, whisk again.

POACHED PEARS IN RED WINE SAUCE

4 SERVINGS Serve this easy, refreshing winter dessert at room temperature.

1 cup dry red wine
2 tablespoons sugar
1-inch piece cinnamon stick

4 medium unblemished ripe
    pears (Bosc)

I suggest you use an enameled saucepan large enough to fit the pears in a single layer.

In a saucepan, bring wine, sugar, and cinnamon to a boil over high heat. Simmer, covered, for 5 minutes.

Peel pears and scoop out center cores from tops of pears with a melon scooper. Lay pears down in pan in a single layer and bring to a boil. Cover and simmer for 3 minutes. Turn pears over and simmer for about another 2 minutes. Test with a sewing needle. Pears should be almost soft, since they will continue cooking while cooling. Uncover and let cool. Serve with sauce.

SORBETS: KIWI, PINEAPPLE, STRAWBERRY, PEACH, PLUM, APRICOT

10 SERVINGS EACH Fresh-fruit sorbets are ideal endings to any meal, especially in kosher homes, where there is a limited selection of pareve desserts. Experiment with the fruits you like.

Make the sorbets a day ahead of time to freeze.

I suggest you use a blender or a food processor, a mesh sieve, an electric ice-cream maker, and a 1-quart soufflé dish (preferably glass).

KIWI SORBET:

11 to 12 medium ripe kiwi
    fruits
1¼ cups sugar

3 tablespoons fresh lemon
    juice, strained

Peel kiwi fruits carefully and quarter them. Puree very well, in batches, in a blender. Strain kiwi puree, in batches, through a mesh sieve, pushing with back of a wooden spoon to obtain as much puree as possible. Discard residue each time. Some of the black seeds will pass through the sieve, but don't worry about it: They add to the texture. You should have 3 cups strained puree. Stir in sugar and lemon juice. Pour into an electric ice-cream maker and follow instructions on the machine.

When sorbet is ready, place it either in a covered container or, if you are planning to serve it at the table, empty it into a soufflé dish, cover with plastic wrap, and freeze.

This sorbet freezes very hard. I suggest transferring it to the refrigerator about 30 minutes before serving, to soften it a bit.

PINEAPPLE SORBET:

1 medium to large ripe pineapple

1¼ cups sugar

3 tablespoons fresh lemon juice, strained

2 tablespoons kirsch

Peel pineapple and remove center core. Cut front into pieces and puree very well, in batches, in a blender. Strain pineapple puree, in batches, through a mesh sieve, pushing with back of a wooden spoon to obtain as much puree as possible. Discard residue each time. You should have 3 cups strained pineapple puree. Stir in sugar, lemon juice, and kirsch. Pour into an electric ice-cream maker and follow instructions on the machine. Pineapple sorbet does not freeze very hard; it must be served straight from the freezer.

STRAWBERRY SORBET:

2 to 2½ pints fresh strawberries, about 4 cups

1¼ cups sugar

3 tablespoons fresh lemon juice, strained

Rinse strawberries, hull, and pat dry with paper towels. Slice them and puree very well, in batches, in a blender. (I do not strain strawberry puree, but you may do so if you like.) You should have 3 cups strawberry puree. Stir in sugar and lemon juice. Pour into an electric ice-cream maker and follow instructions on the machine. Strawberries make a sorbet that freezes very hard, so transfer from freezer to refrigerator for about 30 minutes before serving.

APRICOT, PEACH, AND PLUM SORBETS:

6 to 7 medium ripe apricots, peaches, or plums

1¼ cups sugar

3 tablespoons fresh lemon juice, strained

Rinse fruit, pat dry with paper towels, and remove pits. Cut into pieces and puree very well, in batches, in a blender. You may strain if you wish. You should have 3 cups strained or unstrained puree. Stir in sugar and lemon juice. Pour into an electric ice-cream maker and follow instructions on the machine. These fruits make a sorbet that freezes very hard.

NOTE: Any of the sorbets can be served with natural fruit sauces, which you can make by pureeing and straining fresh fruit and flavoring with confectioners' sugar and liqueur.

Please follow sugar-to-fruit proportions carefully. Too little sugar gives a nonsilky texture; too much prevents freezing. There is, however, no way of predicting how a sorbet will freeze, for it depends on the acid-sugar balance of the fruit itself. Sometimes you can serve it directly from the freezer without softening it in the refrigerator.

Pastries
and Breads

PÂTE BRISÉE (SHORT-CRUST DOUGH)

>>>

I use this very flaky dough almost like puff pastry, as a base for both sweet and nonsweet dishes, such as the quiches, Tarte Tatin, and Mocha–Walnut Tart.

ONE 11-INCH SHELL

10½ tablespoons (1 stick plus 2½ tablespoons) sweet butter

⅛ teaspoon salt

1 cup plus 2 tablespoons unbleached flour

2 to 3 tablespoons ice water

1 egg white, lightly beaten

I suggest you use the following: a pastry blender; a straight French rolling pin; a 10- to 11-inch dark metal quiche pan with removable bottom; a thin, flat cookie sheet or foil oven liner; and about 3 cups aluminum pie weights or uncooked rice or beans kept expressly for this purpose.

Freeze butter lightly, for about 1 hour, before making dough.

Combine salt and flour in a metal bowl. Cut frozen butter into small pieces. Add to flour and mix rapidly with a pastry blender until mixture resembles coarse crumbs. Particles of butter will be visible. From time to time scrape sticky dough from pasty blender with a knife. Gradually sprinkle tablespoonfuls of ice water over mixture and blend until dough begins to hold together. It will still be crumbly, with visible pieces of butter. Clean pastry blender and combine dough with your hand until it sticks together. Turn out onto a sheet of wax paper. Press into a square with wax paper, wrap, and refrigerate for 2 to 3 hours.

Remove dough from refrigerator. If it is too hard to roll out, let rest for a few minutes to soften. Roll out between two lightly floured sheets of wax paper into an approximately 12-by-6-inch rectangle.

Lift wax paper and fold dough into three parts like a letter to be placed in an envelope. Turn dough so that it resembles a book with the opening on your right side. Repeat rolling and folding three or four times in the same fashion, each time dusting lightly with flour. Dough will become progressively smoother and the particles of butter less visible. Wrap in wax paper and chill for 30 minutes.

To roll out dough: Roll dough out, on both sides, between two overlapping lightly floured sheets of wax paper. You will need two sheets on the bottom and two on top, since a single sheet is not wide enough. Roll into a very thin circle, about 13 inches. Dough will spread more easily if you lift the papers and dust lightly with flour from time to time. Lift top sheets and place back on dough; turn dough over and remove what are now the top sheets. Roll dough loosely over rolling pin (1) and unfold over a 10- to

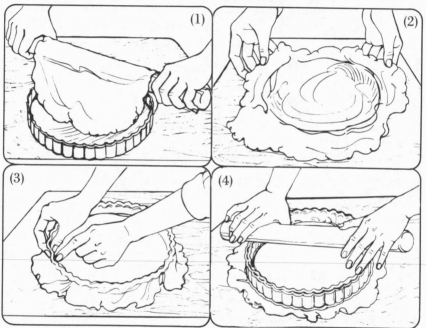

11-inch quiche pan with removable bottom (2). Press dough carefully into corners of pan and, with your thumb, shape sides so that they are thicker than the bottom (3). Make sure that a bit of dough extends over the rim. Roll pin over top pan to cut off scraps (4), but save these to use for patching. Prick bottom lightly with a fork to prevent dough from puffing up.

Chill for about 30 minutes.

To bake: Preheat oven to 375°F. Place quiche pan on a thin, flat cookie sheet or foil oven liner; it will be easier to handle. Line pie shell with lightly buttered foil, buttered side down. Press gently into corners and fold foil over rim. Fill bottom with pie weights, rice, or beans, distributing most of the weights around the sides.

Bake on lowest rack of oven for 20 minutes. Very carefully remove weights and foil. Brush dough lightly with egg white and bake in center of oven for about another 10 minutes, or until slightly golden.

NOTE: If you want to refrigerate the unrolled dough overnight, leave it at room temperature until it is malleable before attempting to roll it out.

CREAM CHEESE DOUGH

This is a flaky, versatile dough that is very easy to handle. I use it for both sweet and nonsweet recipes, such as Mushroom and Sole Tartlets and Pecan Pie.

ONE 11-INCH
PIE SHELL

8 tablespoons (1 stick) sweet
  butter, chilled

3 ounces cream cheese
1 cup unbleached flour

I suggest you use a pastry blender.

Cut butter and cream cheese into small pieces. Place in a bowl and combine thoroughly with a pastry blender. Add flour and continue blending until mixture resembles coarse crumbs. From time to time, scrape sticky dough from pastry blender with a knife. Turn dough out onto a pastry board and combine with your hand until you can gather it into a smooth ball. Particles of butter will be visible. Flatten ball, dust lightly with flour, wrap in wax paper, and refrigerate for about 6 hours or overnight.

    Remove dough from refrigerator and let it rest until malleable. Roll out on a lightly floured board with a lightly floured rolling pin, lifting dough and reflouring board and pin as necessary to shape and size your recipe requires.

◆This dough can be frozen successfully. Wrap it in wax paper and foil and place in a plastic bag. When needed, defrost in the refrigerator.

WHOLE WHEAT BREAD

This is the easiest method of baking. Dried yeast is combined with all the other ingredients to make a light, grainy bread that is wonderful toasted and buttered. This bread freezes very well and is nice to have on hand.

2 LOAVES

¾ cup milk
2 tablespoons sugar
4 teaspoons salt
¼ cup honey
6 tablespoons sweet butter, at
  room temperature
1½ cups warm water (100° to
  115°F)

2 packages active dry yeast,
  about 2 tablespoons
About 4½ cups whole wheat
  flour
2¾ cups unbleached flour

I suggest you use an electric mixer with a dough hook and two 9-by-5-inch loaf pans.

Heat milk to the boiling point, but do not boil. Just as bubbles appear at edges, stir in 1 tablespoon of the sugar, salt, honey, and 5 tablespoons of the butter. Let cool to lukewarm.

Pour warm water, yeast, and remaining tablespoon sugar into an electric-mixer bowl. Add milk mixture, 2 cups of the whole wheat flour, and all the unbleached flour. Knead with dough hook at low to medium speed for about 10 minutes, adding more whole wheat flour to make a firm dough. Turn dough out onto a pastry board and knead further with the heel of your hand, adding more flour as needed until dough does not stick to board or hands and is smooth and elastic.

Wash and dry mixer bowl. Grease with ½ tablespoon of the butter and place dough in it, turning to coat all sides. Cover bowl with a towel and set in a draft-free, warm place (80° to 100°F), such as a food warmer or lightly heated, then cooled-down oven, until double in bulk, about 1 hour.

Punch dough down and let rise again to the same bulk. Punch down a second time and divide into two equal pieces. Grease two 9-by-5-inch loaf pans with remaining ½ tablespoon butter. Shape pieces roughly on a board and place in pans. Cover with a towel and leave in a draft-free place until dough reaches top of pans.

Preheat oven to 375°F. Bake loaves in center of oven, without touching each other, for about 30 minutes, or until tops are golden brown. Let cool on a rack.

◆When completely cool, wrap loaves in plastic wrap, then in foil, and place in a plastic bag to freeze.

BREAKFAST RYE BREAD

2 FREE-FORM LOAVES

This is not the usual Jewish rye bread; it is not good for sandwiches. It has a light texture and a touch of sweetness. I love it toasted, buttered, or eaten with jam.

1 cup milk
3 tablespoons honey
1 tablespoon salt
1½ tablespoons sweet butter, at room temperature
¾ cup warm water (100° to 115°F)
1 package active dry yeast, about 1 tablespoon

1 tablespoon sugar
1 tablespoon caraway seeds (optional)
2½ cups rye flour
About 2½ cups unbleached flour

GLAZE:

1 egg white, lightly beaten and mixed with 2 tablespoons water

*I suggest you use an electric mixer with a dough hook and a
12-by-16-inch baking sheet.*

Heat milk to the boiling point, but do not boil. Just as bubbles appear at
edges, stir in honey, salt, and 1 tablespoon of the butter. Let cool to
lukewarm.

Pour warm water, yeast, and sugar into an electric-mixer bowl. Stir
gently, cover with a towel, and set in a draft-free place for about 15 minutes,
or until bubbles appear and liquid is foamy. Add caraway seeds, all the rye
flour, and 1 cup of the unbleached flour. Knead with the dough hook at low
to medium speed, adding more flour to make a stiff dough.

Turn dough out onto a pastry board and knead further with the heel of
your hand, adding more flour as needed until dough does not stick to board
or hands and is smooth and elastic.

Wash and dry mixer bowl. Grease with remaining ½ tablespoon butter
and place dough in it, turning to coat all sides. Cover bowl with a towel and
set in a draft-free, warm place (80° to 100°F), such as a food warmer or
lightly heated, then cooled-down oven, until double in bulk, about 1 hour.

Punch dough down and divide into two equal pieces. Form into two
oblong loaves and place them side by side, not touching, on a 12-by-16-inch
baking sheet. Let rise, covered, in a draft-free place until almost double in
size.

Preheat oven to 400°F. Brush loaves with egg white–water glaze. Bake
in center of oven for about 20 minutes, or until golden. Let cool on a rack.

◆When completely cool, wrap loaves in plastic wrap, then in foil, and place
in a plastic bag to freeze.

MARLENE'S MONKEY BREAD

This is more of a coffee cake than a bread. The recipe was given
to me by a Southern friend, who does not know the explanation
for the name.

1 GUGELHUPF
LOAF

It is meant to be pulled apart, not sliced, which is easy to do
since the bread is made of small circles.

I serve it warm for breakfast, with a dairy meal, or as a snack.
It freezes very well.

1 cup milk

2 packages active dry yeast,
   about 2 tablespoons

8 tablespoons (1 stick) sweet
   butter, at room
   temperature, quartered

¼ cup sugar

1 teaspoon salt

About 3½ cups sifted
   unbleached flour

4½ tablespoons sweet butter,
   melted

I suggest you use the following: an electric mixer with a dough hook, a 2-inch round cookie cutter, and a 10-inch gugelhupf mold.

Heat milk in a small saucepan until lukewarm (100° to 115°F). Add yeast, butter pieces, sugar, and salt. Stir; butter does not have to dissolve. Pour into an electric-mixer bowl, add 3 cups of the flour, and knead with a dough hook at low to medium speed for about 10 minutes, adding more flour as needed to make a stiff, elastic dough that does not stick to the bowl.

Grease a metal bowl with some of the melted butter and place dough in it, turning to coat all sides. Cover bowl with a towel. Set in a draft-free, warm place (80° to 100°F), such as a food warmer or lightly heated, then cooled-down oven, until double in bulk, about 1 to 1½ hours.

Punch dough down and cut in half. Roll out each piece into a 10-inch circle. With a 2-inch round cookie cutter, cut out as many circles as you can.

Grease a gugelhupf mold with some more of the melted butter, keeping remaining melted butter nearby. Dip each circle of dough in the butter, then place one on top of the other, buttered sides down, in the mold. Form scraps into a ball, roll it out, and repeat. The idea is to build up layers of circles. Cover with a towel and leave in a draft-free place to rise to an inch or so below the rim.

Preheat oven to 400°F. Bake bread in center of oven for about 25 to 30 minutes, or until top is brown. Test with a cake tester in the center; it should come out dry. Let cool on a rack until easy to handle. Invert and serve.

NOTE: Sift flour directly into the measuring cup.

◆When completely cool, wrap bread in foil and place in a plastic bag, then freeze. When needed, do not defrost, but place, partially wrapped in foil, in a preheated 350°F oven until heated through.

PUFF PASTRY (PÂTE FEUILLETÉE)

Puff pastry is time-consuming to make, but if you follow the rules, you will find it is worth the effort. Puff pastry consists of flour, margarine or butter, and cold water. Layers of dough are formed when the dough is rolled out six times and chilled in between. After the sixth time, the dough is ready to be rolled out into the shape you want. The result of all the rolling out, folding, and chilling is that the pastry, when baked, puffs up into many layers. You may refrigerate the dough for up to five days.

ABOUT
1½
POUNDS

About 1½ cups unbleached
  flour
½ cup cake flour
1 teaspoon salt

14 tablespoons (1¾ sticks)
  unsalted margarine, or 16
  tablespoons (2 sticks) sweet
  butter, chilled
About ½ cup ice water

I suggest you use the following: a marble surface, a dough scraper, and a straight French rolling pin.

To make the dough: Sift both flours together with salt. Set aside ¼ cup of the sifted flour. Spread remaining flour on a marble surface. Cut 3 tablespoons of the margarine or butter into small pieces and place on flour. Keep the rest refrigerated. Combine with a dough scraper into a coarse mixture. Make a well in the center and add ice water gradually (1), working

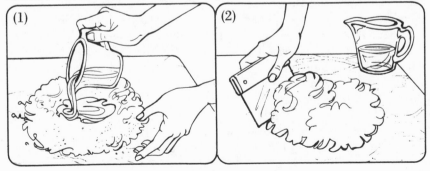

it with the scraper into the flour (2). (The exact amount of ice water will depend on the atmospheric humidity.) Dough will be crumbly.

Gather dough with your hands into a loose ball (3). To combine dry parts of dough with moist ones, cut dough with scraper into many pieces; turn dough over and do it again. Repeat cutting four to five times in the same fashion. Gather dough into a ball (it may be rough). Wrap dough in wax paper and freeze for 30 minutes.

Spread reserved ¼ cup flour on the cleaned marble surface. Cut remaining margarine or butter into quarters and place on flour. With the heel of your hand, press shortening into flour until all the flour is absorbed (4). Shape into a 5-inch square (5). Lift square with scraper, dust on both sides with flour, wrap in wax paper, and freeze for 30 minutes.

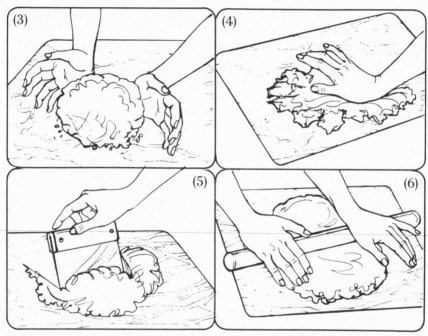

To roll out the dough: Lightly flour the cleaned marble surface and a rolling pin. Roll dough out into an 11-inch circle (6); it will not be smooth. Place cold square of shortening into center of circle, folding over sides of dough to cover completely, like a well-closed package (7). Turn dough over, seam side down. Start rolling dough from the center away from you, then again from the center toward you, leaving the edges untouched; roll into a 6-by-12-inch rectangle (8). If shortening breaks through dough, cover spot with additional flour. Try to keep sides of rectangle straight by adjusting them with rolling pin.

Starting with the short side nearest you, fold dough into three parts like a letter to be placed in an envelope (9). Give dough a quarter turn, so that open side is on your right. Reflour board and rolling pin and roll dough

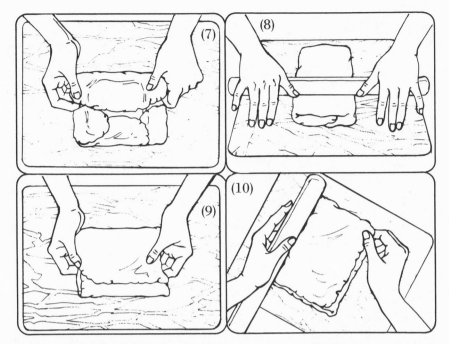

out into a 6-by-12-inch rectangle. Place rolling pin lengthwise and roll out edges lightly to the same thickness as the rest of the dough. Keep sides straight with the help of the rolling pin. If shortening breaks through dough, cover spot with flour. Fold again into three parts and stretch edges of dough with your hands to meet the corners (10). Make two indentations with your fingertips on dough as a reminder that it has been rolled out twice. Dust lightly with flour if necessary, wrap in wax paper, and chill for 2 hours.

Repeat two more times in the same fashion. Always remember the following rules as you work: (a) keep marble surface clean; (b) dust dough lightly with flour; (c) keep open side of dough on your right before rolling; and (d) keep sides straight and match corners.

Now make four indentations in dough. Wrap in wax paper, then in foil, and refrigerate overnight.

Now repeat the process twice more to complete six turns. If shortening breaks through dough, do not worry, just dust the spot with flour. The dough may even look messy up to the last turn.

Refrigerate dough for 3 hours more. It is now ready to be used or frozen.

NOTE: Puff pastry made with butter is easier to work with; the butter incorporates more easily into the flour. It also has a richer flavor and is flakier.

◆To freeze the finished dough, wrap it first in wax paper, then in foil, and place it in a plastic bag. Before using, defrost it in the refrigerator.

POTATO BREAD

This bread is good cut into very thin slices, toasted, and served with soups, pâtés, and cocktail spreads. It freezes very well.

1 large baking potato, about 9 ounces
1½ packages active dry yeast, about 1½ tablespoons
About 7½ cups unbleached flour

1½ tablespoons salt
1½ tablespoons caraway seeds
½ tablespoon unsalted margarine

I suggest you use an electric mixer with a dough hook and a baking sheet.

Wash potato well and place in a saucepan with 1 quart water. Bring to a boil, cover, and cook slowly until potato is soft. Measure 2½ cups of the cooking water and set aside. Peel potato and mash until smooth.

Pour ½ cup of the warm cooking water (100° to 115°F) into an electric-mixer bowl. Add yeast and 3 tablespoons of the flour. Stir lightly, cover with a towel, and leave in a draft-free place for about 15 minutes, or until bubbles appear. To this mixture, add the remaining 2 cups warm potato water, salt, mashed potato, caraway seeds, and 6 cups of the flour. Knead with dough hook at low speed for about 10 minutes, adding more flour as needed to make a stiff, smooth dough.

Turn dough out onto a board and knead with the heel of your hand, adding more flour as necessary to make a smooth, elastic dough that does not stick to hands or board.

Wash and dry mixer bowl, grease with margarine, and place dough in it, turning to coat all sides. Cover bowl with a towel. Set in a draft-free, warm place (80°F to 100°F), such as a food warmer or lightly heated, then cooled-down oven, until double in bulk, about 1½ hours.

Punch dough down and divide into two equal pieces. Form into two oblong loaves and place side by side, not touching, on a baking sheet. Let rise, uncovered, for about 25 minutes.

Preheat oven to 400°F. Brush loaves lightly with cold water, using a pastry brush. About 2 inches in from each end of the loaf, cut a cross with a scissor. Bake in center of oven for about 45 minutes, or until golden brown and crusty. Let cool on a rack.

◆When completely cool, wrap loaves in plastic wrap, then in foil, and place in a plastic bag.

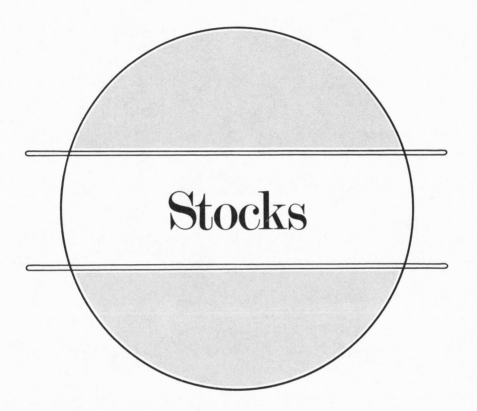

Stocks

BEEF STOCK

I use thick stock as a base for robust soups, such as Cabbage Borscht and Beet Borscht. The meat is delicious, too.

ABOUT 9 CUPS

3½ pounds lean chuck
15 cups cold water
3 ice cubes
1 onion, peeled

2 cloves garlic, peeled
1 bay leaf
20 black peppercorns

I suggest you use a very thin muslin towel or piece of thin cotton cloth.

Place meat in a large pot. Add water and bring to a boil over high heat. Add ice cubes, lower heat, and skim froth as it rises to the surface. Add remaining ingredients and simmer, half covered, for 3 to 4 hours, or until meat is tender. Remove meat and save.

Wet a cloth with cold water, wring dry, and over a large measuring pitcher or bowl; strain stock. (It takes a while.) At the very end, do not press cloth, or droplets of fat will get through. The thin cloth, unlike cheesecloth, strains the stock fat-free. Refrigerate or freeze in covered glass jars.

NOTE: If you refrigerate stock for a few days and then wish to freeze it, boil it first. This kills any bacteria that may have developed.

BROWN VEAL STOCK

I use this stock for most meat sauces.

6 TO 7 CUPS

6 pounds meaty veal shanks,
  sawed into 2- to 3-inch
  pieces
2 onions
3 carrots
3 cloves garlic, unpeeled

Bouquet garni: ¼ bunch
  Italian flat-leaf parsley with
  stems, 2 bay leaves, 10
  black peppercorns, 1
  tablespoon dried thyme,
  tied in a double cheesecloth
Water

I suggest you use a very thin muslin towel or piece of thin cotton cloth.

Preheat broiler. Pat shanks dry with paper towels and place in a roasting pan. Trim unpeeled onions and cut into quarters. Wash carrots, pat dry with paper towels, trim, and cut into quarters. Scatter onions, carrots, and garlic around bones.

Broil, not too close to heat source, until light brown, about 45 minutes. Turn each piece with tongs and transfer, as it is finished, to a stockpot; the vegetables will brown first.

Deglaze roasting pan with 1 cup water, scraping the brown bits clinging to the bottom and sides. Add these juices to the stock pot with enough cold water to cover bones by about ½ inch, about 3 quarts.

Bring to a boil over high heat. Skim froth as it rises to surface. Add bouquet garni. Simmer, covered, for 1 hour. Uncover and continue simmering for another 3 hours. Remove bones. Wet a cloth with cold water, wring dry, and drape over a large measuring pitcher or bowl; strain stock. (It takes a while.) At the very end, do not press cloth, or droplets of fat will get through. The thin cloth, unlike the cheesecloth, strains the stock fat-free. If you want a more concentrated stock, reduce it over high heat. Refrigerate or freeze in covered glass jars.

NOTE: If you refrigerate stock for a few days and then wish to freeze it, boil it first. This kills any bacteria that may have developed.

LIGHT CHICKEN STOCK

ABOUT 11 CUPS

I use this stock as a base for soups in which the flavor of the stock should not overpower the other flavors. Simmer the stock gently to ensure a crystal-clear broth.

5 pounds chicken parts: carcasses, necks, wings, legs, gizzards
Cold water

4 ice cubes
1 onion, peeled
2 cloves garlic, peeled

I suggest you use a very thin muslin towel or a piece of thin cotton cloth.

Rinse chicken and remove any dangling fat. Place in a stockpot with enough cold water to cover chicken by about 1 inch.

Bring to a boil over high heat. Add ice cubes, lower heat, and skim froth as it rises to the surface. Add vegetables and simmer, half covered, for about 2 hours, or until meat is soft. Remove chicken parts. Wet a cloth with cold water, wring dry, and drape over a large measuring pitcher or bowl; strain stock. (It takes a while.) At the very end do not press the cloth, or droplets of fat will get through. The cloth, unlike cheesecloth, strains the stock fat-free. Refrigerate or freeze covered glass jars.

NOTE: I do not use whole fowl for this purpose, because the stock cooks for so long that the meat would be overcooked.

If you refrigerate stock for a few days and then wish to freeze it, boil it first. This kills any bacteria that may have developed.

STRONG CHICKEN STOCK

→≫

This strong, flavorful chicken stock is the base for many soups, such as Mushroom–Barley Soup, Fresh Spinach Soup, and Chicken Soup with Watercress. Simmer the stock gently to ensure a crystal-clear broth.   7 TO 8 CUPS

5 pounds chicken parts:
  carcasses, necks, wings, legs,
  gizzards
Cold water
4 ice cubes

1 carrot, peeled
1 onion, peeled
5 sprigs Italian flat-leaf
  parsley

I suggest you use a very thin muslin towel or piece of thin cotton cloth.

Rinse chicken and remove any dangling fat. Place in a large stockpot with enough cold water to reach just below top of chicken parts.

Bring to a boil over high heat. Add ice cubes, lower heat, and skim froth as it rises to surface. Add vegetables and simmer, uncovered, for about 2 hours, or until meat is soft. Remove chicken parts. Wet a cloth with cold water, wring dry, and drape over a large measuring pitcher or bowl; strain stock. (It takes a while.) At the very end, do not press cloth, droplets of fat will get through. The cloth, unlike cheesecloth, strains the stock fat-free. Refrigerate or freeze in covered glass jars.

NOTE: I do not use whole fowl for this purpose, because the stock cooks for so long that the meat would be overcooked.

If you refrigerate stock for a few days and then wish to freeze it, boil it first. This kills any bacteria that may have developed.

Pareve

FISH STOCK

If you have a cooperative fish man, you should be able to get bones, heads, and trimmings from a variety of fresh fish. If not, buy whiting or other bony, nonoily fish.

4 pounds fresh fish bones,
  heads, and trimmings, or 4
  pounds bony fish
6 cups cold water
1 cup dry white wine
1 carrot, peeled and quartered
2 onions, peeled and quartered

2 bay leaves
1 teaspoon dried thyme
5 sprigs Italian flat-leaf
  parsley
7 black peppercorns
1 teaspoon kosher salt

I suggest you use an enameled stockpot and a very thin muslin towel or piece of thin cotton cloth.

Rinse fish well. Place in a stockpot along with water, wine, and all the remaining ingredients. Bring to a boil over high heat. Skim froth as it rises to surface. Simmer, partially uncovered, for 45 minutes. Let cool a bit.

Wet a cloth with cold water, wring dry, and drape over a large bowl; strain stock, pouring in entire contents of pot. Wring cloth to obtain all the liquid and flavor from the bones and vegetables. Correct seasoning.

If you want a more concentrated stock, reduce it over high heat.

Refrigerate or freeze.

NOTE: If you refrigerate stock for a few days and then wish to freeze it, boil it first. This kills any bacteria that may have developed.

Sauces and Salad Dressings

Dairy

TAMARA'S MOCK HOLLANDAISE

This is a nonclassic version of a hollandaise sauce, useful because it does not curdle and can even be made a day ahead of time.

ABOUT
1 CUP

1 cup milk	About 2 tablespoons fresh
3 egg yolks	lemon juice, strained
1 tablespoon cornstarch	Kosher salt
6 tablespoons sweet butter, at	White pepper, freshly ground
room temperature, cut into	
tablespoons	

I suggest you use a double boiler.

With a whisk, combine milk, egg yolks, and cornstarch in top part of a double boiler. Set over simmering water and whisk until thick and smooth. Remove from heat and whisk in butter, 1 tablespoonful at a time. Season to taste with lemon juice, salt, and pepper.

◆If you like, you can make this sauce a day ahead of time, refrigerate it, then reheat slowly in a double boiler, whisking all the time.

CRÈME CHANTILLY

Try to buy cream that is one to two days old and not the super or ultra-pasteurized variety. Day-old cream whips easily, since it thickens naturally as it stands in the refrigerator. If you want to make Crème Chantilly several hours in advance, you may have to beat it again before serving, and there may be some milky liquid settled on the bottom of the bowl.

1 CUP

1 cup heavy cream, chilled	1 tablespoon Grand Marnier
1 tablespoon confectioners'	or other liqueur
sugar	

I suggest you use a metal bowl and an electric hand mixer.

Before beating cream, put metal bowl in freezer for 30 minutes. The colder the bowl and the cream, the lighter Crème Chantilly will be. Beat cream at low speed, rotating beater around bowl. As cream begins to take shape, add sugar and continue beating at high speed until lightly whipped, or almost firm. With a rubber spatula, fold in Grand Marnier or other liqueur. Transfer to a glass bowl and refrigerate.

CREAMY LEMON DRESSING

ABOUT
½ CUP

This dairy dressing is a nice change from the basic vinaigrette. It keeps well, refrigerated in a covered glass jar.

1½ tablespoons fresh lemon
  juice, strained
About 1 teaspoon kosher salt
White pepper, freshly ground

¼ cup olive oil
¼ cup heavy cream, at room
  temperature

I suggest you use a blender.

Place lemon juice, salt, and pepper in a blender. With motor on, pour oil, then heavy cream in a slow stream through the opening in the lid. Season to taste.

Pareve

FRESH TOMATO SAUCE

→≫

I make quantities of this in September, the height of the tomato season, and freeze it in covered glass jars. It is a lot of work, but well worth it.

ABOUT
2 CUPS
THICK SAUCE

If flavorful, ripe fresh tomatoes are not available, use canned, drained, imported plum tomatoes with basil; they make a good substitute.

¼ cup olive oil
1 large onion, chopped fine
3 cloves garlic, chopped fine
2 pounds ripe plum or regular
   tomatoes or 2-pound
   3-ounce can Italian plum
   tomatoes, drained

½ bunch basil
½ bunch Italian flat-leaf
   parsley
Pinch sugar
Black pepper, freshly ground
Kosher salt

I suggest you use a large heavy saucepan and a food mill with a medium blade.

Heat oil in a large, heavy saucepan until hot and sauté onions and garlic over low heat until soft and transparent.

Wash tomatoes, cut out cores, and cut into large pieces. Remove basil stems and bottom part of parsley stems.

Wash the rest, spin dry, and chop coarsely.

Add tomatoes, basil, and parsley to onions, season with sugar and pepper, and bring to a boil. Cook slowly, covered, for about 45 minutes, or until tomato skin has separated from pulp. Stir from time to time. Puree sauce in a food mill. Return to saucepan and boil until thick, stirring from time to time to prevent scorching. Season with salt.

NOTE: Plum tomatoes, sometimes called Italian, have a firm texture, which produces a good puree.

If you like, you can chop onion, garlic, basil, and parsley in a food processor fitted with the steel blade.

If you are making this sauce with drained canned tomatoes, and fresh basil is unavailable, use dried basil instead, but rub it between your fingers to release extra flavor. Follow the basic recipe.

VINAIGRETTE DRESSING

ABOUT ½ CUP DRESSING, ENOUGH FOR A GREEN SALAD SERVING 6 TO 8

A basic lightly creamy dressing, which I use for most green salads. A good salad dressing depends on the ratio of oil to vinegar, the strength of the vinegar, and the type of oil; you must therefore taste it.

I like to make the dressing in a blender, combining all the ingredients thoroughly. You can make it a few days in advance and refrigerate in a covered glass container. If you are adding garlic or other herbs, do so at the last minute and shake the jar well.

2 tablespoons tarragon wine vinegar
1 teaspoon Dijon-type mustard
¼ teaspoon Madras curry powder

About 1 teaspoon kosher salt
Black pepper, freshly ground
½ cup olive oil or safflower oil, or a combination of both

I suggest you use a blender.

Place all the ingredients except for the oil in a blender. With motor on, pour oil slowly through the opening in the lid. Season to taste.

NOTE: This basic dressing can be flavored with garlic or fresh chopped herbs. You can also omit the curry powder and add a tablespoon of soy sauce or omit the mustard and curry powder and add soy sauce and tahini.

STRONG VINAIGRETTE DRESSING

ABOUT ⅔ CUP

About ⅓ cup tarragon wine vinegar
2 teaspoons Dijon-type mustard
About 2 teaspoons kosher salt

½ teaspoon Madras curry powder
Black pepper, freshly ground
½ cup olive oil

I suggest you use a blender.

Place all the ingredients except for the oil in a blender. With the motor on, pour oil very slowly through opening in the lid. Season to taste.

◆This dressing can be made several days ahead of time and refrigerated in a covered glass jar.

MAYONNAISE

→»»———————————————

This mayonnaise is lightly seasoned, making it a good base for other dressings. You can flavor it with garlic, more mustard, anchovies, capers, herbs, yogurt, sour cream, or chopped peeled, seeded tomatoes.

ABOUT 1¼ CUPS

It keeps for weeks, refrigerated in a tightly closed container. I don't think you will ever buy commercial mayonnaise again.

1 egg, at room temperature
¼ teaspoon dried mustard
   (Coleman's brand)
½ teaspoon kosher salt

½ cup vegetable oil
½ cup olive oil
1 tablespoon tarragon wine
   vinegar

I suggest you use a blender.

Place egg, mustard, and salt in a blender. Combine vegetable and olive oils in a measuring cup. Turn motor to highest setting and do not shut it off until all the oil has been added. With motor on, add vinegar through opening in the lid, then dribble in combined oil in a very slow stream. As the mixture begins to thicken, add oil faster until finished. The thickness of the mayonnaise will depend on how quickly the oil has been incorporated into the egg. Transfer to a glass container.

NOTE: It is easier to pour in the oil from a measuring cup. The spout makes the pouring easier to control.

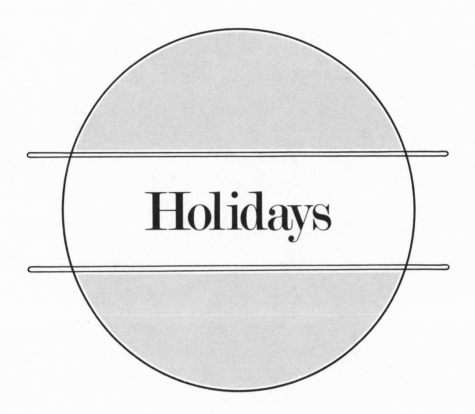

Holidays

Friday Night

CHALLAH

Challah is one of the delights of a Friday night or holiday meal. Don't be afraid to make it. You will be surprised how easy and enjoyable it will become once you familiarize yourself with the process. If you have children at home, they will be fascinated with the making of the dough, waiting for it to rise, braiding it, baking it, and inhaling the wonderful yeast aroma that permeates the kitchen.

4 MEDIUM BRAIDED LOAVES

2¼ cups warm water (100° to 115°F)

2 packages active dry yeast, about 2 tablespoons

⅓ cup plus 2 tablespoons sugar

2 eggs plus 1 yolk, at room temperature

1¼ tablespoons salt

¼ cup vegetable oil

2½ tablespoons unsalted margarine, at room temperature

About 8 cups unbleached flour

GLAZE:
1 egg yolk mixed with 1 tablespoon water

I suggest you use an electric mixer with a dough hook and two 12-by-16-inch baking sheets.

Pour warm water into an electric-mixer bowl; add yeast and 1 tablespoon of the sugar and stir lightly. Cover with a towel and leave in a draft-free place for about 10 to 15 minutes, or until bubbles appear. (This is called proofing the yeast to make sure it is still active.)

Add to this yeast mixture the rest of the sugar, eggs and egg yolk, salt, vegetable oil, 2 tablespoons of the margarine, and 7½ cups of the flour. Knead with dough hook at low to medium speed for about 10 minutes, adding more flour as necessary to make a firm dough. Turn dough out onto a pastry board and knead further with the heel of your hand, adding more flour as needed until dough does not stick to board or hands and is smooth and elastic.

Wash and dry mixer bowl. Grease with remaining ½ tablespoon margarine and place dough in it, turning to coat all sides. Cover bowl with a towel.

Set in a draft-free, warm place (80° to 100°F), such as a food warmer or lightly heated, then cooled-down oven, until double in bulk, about 1½ hours.

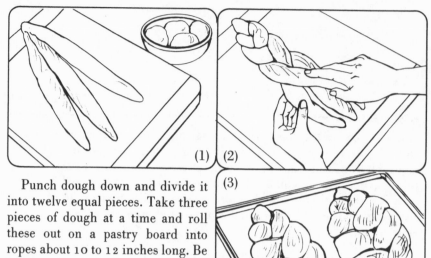

Punch dough down and divide it into twelve equal pieces. Take three pieces of dough at a time and roll these out on a pastry board into ropes about 10 to 12 inches long. Be sure to make ends thinner than center to give bread a better shape. Pinch ends of the three ropes together (1), braid to the other end (2), and seal well (3). Place two challahs on each baking sheet. Proceed in the same fashion with the remaining dough. Cover challahs with a towel and let rise in a draft-free place for about 35 minutes.

Preheat oven to 350°F. Brush challahs with glaze. Bake in center of oven for about 35 minutes, or until golden. Let cool on racks.

NOTE: If you like smaller challahs, divide dough into smaller pieces. On Rosh Hashanah, add raisins to your challah and make them round. For variety, sprinkle with poppy seeds.

To make challah with fresh yeast, dissolve crumbled yeast in lukewarm water (80° to 90°F) and proceed in the same fashion.

If you do not have two ovens, your second batch of challahs will have a lighter texture because the rising time will be longer.

◆To freeze, wait until completely cool, then wrap in plastic wrap, then in foil, and place in a plastic bag. Defrosting will not be necessary. Remove wrappings and place challah directly on rack of a 350°F preheated oven, for about 20 minutes, or until heated through.

Challah also keeps fresh for several days without freezing.

CLEAR CHICKEN SOUP

When I think of Friday night or holidays, I immediately think of crystal-clear chicken soup served with square noodles, Kreplach (page 287) and Knaidlach (page 303), and garnished with snipped fresh dill.

7 CUPS, ABOUT 8 TO 10 SERVINGS

About 6 pounds boiling chicken, quartered, or the equivalent in chicken parts: carcasses, necks, wings, legs, gizzards, or a combination	1 onion, peeled and cut into quarters
	4 sprigs parsley
	4 sprigs dill
	Kosher salt
Cold water	White pepper, freshly ground
4 ice cubes	
1 carrot, peeled and cut into quarters	

I suggest you use a thin muslin towel or cloth.

Rinse chicken parts and cut off any dangling fat. Place in pot with just enough cold water to reach just below top of chicken parts. Bring to a boil over high heat, add ice cubes, and lower heat at once (to stop soup from boiling rapidly). It is important to simmer chicken soup very slowly so that it will be very clear, not gray. Skim froth, add vegetables and herbs, and cook, uncovered, for about 2 hours, or until meat is soft.

Wet a cloth with cold water, wring dry, and drape over a large bowl. Remove chicken parts and strain soup through cloth. Toward the end of the straining, there will be fat left in the cloth: Remove it right away. (The cloth, unlike a cheesecloth, strains the stock thoroughly.) Return soup to the rinsed pot and heat gently until boiling. Correct seasoning.

NOTE: I do not recommend freezing chicken soup, unless you want to use it as stock; it loses some of its delicate flavor. The cooked chicken can be used for Mrs. Khazzam's Miniature Chicken Turnovers (page 6) or chicken salad or just eaten plain.

RACHEL NASH'S GEFILTE FISH

This is my mother-in-law's gefilte fish, which she learned from her mother in Cracow, before World War II. They are soft, pale in color, and delicately seasoned. They are traditionally served on Friday nights and most holidays and must be made a day ahead of time to chill sufficiently. Serve them with freshly grated white horseradish.

ABOUT 12 TO 14 SERVINGS

FISH OVALS:

About 3 pounds whitefish	About 1¾ tablespoons kosher salt
About 3 pounds pike	
2 medium onions, grated fine	About 1 tablespoon sugar
3 eggs, whisked until foamy	White pepper, freshly ground
About ¼ cup ice water	1 heaping tablespoon blanched bitter almonds, ground fine
2 tablespoons matzoh meal or flour	

STOCK:

Heads, skin, and bones from whitefish and pike	7 cups cold water
2 onions, sliced	1 tablespoon kosher salt
1 carrot, quartered	2½ teaspoons sugar
	10 peppercorns

SAUCE:

2 onions, cubed fine	About 2 teaspoons kosher salt
3 carrots, cut into thin rounds	About ½ teaspoon sugar
2 tablespoons blanched bitter almonds, chopped fine	White pepper, freshly ground

Horseradish root	Fresh lemon juice, strained

I suggest you use an approximately 12-by-18-inch enameled oval pan with lid to fit the fish in a single layer, a metal chopper, and a thin muslin towel or cloth.

To make the fish ovals: Have the fish man bone and fillet the fish and grind them together twice to obtain a very smooth texture. You will have about 2¾ to 3¼ pounds ground fish, depending on how fleshy they are. (Reserve heads, bones, tails, and skin for stock.)

Place the fish in a large, preferably metal bowl and add onions. Mix with a chopper, then pour in eggs in a slow stream and mix with chopper until they are very well combined. Do the same with the ice water and matzoh meal or flour, adding them 1 tablespoonful at a time. Be patient and continue chopping and combining for about 15 minutes to make the ground fish soft to the touch. Season with remaining ingredients and refrigerate for at least 2 hours.

You can cook stock and sauce while fish is chilling.

To make the stock: Place all the fish trimmings, onions, carrot, water, and seasoning in a large pan. Bring to a boil over high heat and boil gently, covered, for about 1½ hours. Let stock cool a bit.

Wet a cloth with cold water, wring dry, and drape over a large bowl; strain stock. Wring cloth well to obtain all flavor and liquid from fish. This stock will appear cloudy, but do not worry about it. Rinse pan and pour in strained stock.

To make the sauce and the fish: Add onions, carrots, almonds, and season-ings to stock. Bring to a boil. Mix ground fish again and correct seasoning and texture. It should be soft to the touch. Have a bowl of cold water nearby. Wet hands well and shape fish, 2 heaping tablespoonfuls at a time, into very smooth ovals. Drop them carefully into gently boiling fish stock and proceed in the same fashion with the rest. Be sure to wet your hands well each time.

Shake pan and cook fish gently, covered, turning them from time to time, for 1½ hours. Let cool and correct seasoning of sauce. Transfer fish to a tightly covered container and refrigerate. Stock will make a soft jelly. Serve with freshly grated horseradish on the side.

To make the horseradish: Peel the horseradish root and grate it by hand, moistening well with fresh lemon juice to prevent it from turning gray. (Sorry, you will be teary-eyed.) Place into a covered container.

NOTE: If you like a more robust gefilte fish, you may wish to add carp to it. Try the following proportions: 2 pounds whitefish, 2 pounds pike, and 2 pounds carp.

Bitter almonds are available in specialty stores and add an interesting flavor to the fish; they can be frozen. To blanch them, drop them into boiling water, bring water back to the boil, drain at once, and remove skins. Dry on paper towels and grate in a Mouli grater.

APPLE STRUDEL

Apple strudel is traditionally served on Friday night or on holi-days, especially in the winter, when there is a limited selection of interesting fruits, but apples are plentiful. Serve warm for best flavor.

2 STRUDEL STRIPS, EACH SERVING 6 TO 8

½ cup cornflake crumbs or unseasoned bread crumbs
Generous ½ cup light brown sugar
6½ tablespoons unsalted margarine, melted
5 medium apples (Cortland, Granny Smith, or greening)

½ cup seedless golden raisins
¾ cup walnuts, chopped coarse
1 teaspoon ground cinnamon
4 16-by-22-inch sheets strudel dough

I suggest you use the following: two damp dish towels, a pastry brush, and a cookie sheet.

Preheat oven to 400°F. Mix cornflake or bread crumbs with 3 tablespoons of the brown sugar.

Brush a cookie sheet with some of the melted margarine.

Have ready the melted margarine, a pastry brush, 2 damp towels, and a cookie sheet.

Peel, core, quarter, and cut apples into thin slices. Combine with raisins, walnuts, and cinnamon. (Do not add sugar until just before filling the leaves; if added earlier, sugar will melt and make strudel dough soggy.)

Spread a damp, not wet towel on a work surface. Unwrap one of the strudel sheets and place on towel. Keep the rest of the sheets covered with another damp towel. Brush dough lightly with margarine and sprinkle with some of the crumb-sugar mixture. Place a second sheet on top and repeat brushing and sprinkling.

Add remaining ⅓ cup sugar to apple mixture and place half of the resulting mixture along the edge closest to you, leaving a 1-inch margin, and fold in the shorter sides. With the help of the towel, roll loosely, jelly roll fashion, away from you to the end.

Slide strudel onto the prepared baking sheet and brush generously with margarine. Mark portions with a serrated knife. Repeat in the same fashion with remaining two sheets of dough.

Bake in center of oven for 25 to 30 minutes, or until golden. Serve warm.

NOTE: Have all the utensils and ingredients ready before uncovering the dough; it is delicate and dries out very quickly.

If you like, you can slice apples and chop walnuts in a food processor.

Strudel leaves can be found in specialty stores. Do not confuse them with phyllo dough.

◆Strudel can be made earlier in the day and reheated.

BAKED APPLES FILLED WITH WALNUTS

4 SERVINGS   A good winter dessert.

2 tablespoons unsalted margarine, melted	1 teaspoon ground cinnamon
2 tablespoons dark brown sugar	4 medium baking apples (Rome Beauty)
¼ cup walnuts, chopped coarse	½ cup dry white wine
	½ cup water

Preheat oven to 375°F. Combine margarine, sugar, walnuts, and cinnamon.

Rinse apples. Scoop out center core from top of apples with a melon scooper without piercing bottom. Prick skin with tip of a knife to keep it from bursting.

Fill centers with walnut mixture.

Place apples in a baking pan. Combine wine and water and pour over apples.

Bake for about 45 minutes, basting occasionally, until apples are soft, but retain their shape. Serve warm or at room temperature.

LUSIA'S CHOCOLATE–WALNUT TORTE

>>>

My aunt, Lusia, gave me this recipe. It is a wonderful party dessert—chocolaty, moist, and easy to serve. It stays fresh for many days refrigerated.

16 TO 18 SERVINGS

½ pound walnuts, about 2 cups

5 tablespoons unbleached flour

½ tablespoon unsalted margarine, at room temperature

½ cup boiling water

ICING:

¼ pound semisweet chocolate, broken into small pieces

2 tablespoons instant coffee powder

⅓ cup boiling water

8 tablespoons (1 stick) unsalted margarine, at room temperature

GARNISH:

Semisweet chocolate shavings (optional)

¼ pound semisweet chocolate, broken into small pieces

2 tablespoons instant coffee powder

8 eggs, at room temperature, separated

Scant 1½ cups sugar

2 egg yolks, at room temperature

2 tablespoons dark rum

Walnuts (optional)

I suggest you use the following: a food processor, a 12-by-2½-inch springform pan, and an electric mixer.

To make the torte: Preheat oven to 350°F. Roast walnuts in oven in a single layer in a baking pan for about 10 minutes. Let cool. Grind half of them fine and the other half coarser in a food processor fitted with the steel blade. Combine both with ¼ cup of the flour.

Grease a 12-by-2½-inch springform pan with margarine. Dust evenly with remaining 1 tablespoon flour. Invert pan and tap to shake off excess.

In a small bowl, place boiling water, chocolate, and coffee powder. Stir until smooth. Let cool.

Preheat oven to 325°F. In an electric-mixer bowl, at medium speed, beat egg yolks, gradually adding ½ cup of the sugar and continuing to beat until pale, thick, and bubbles appear, about 10 minutes. Add cooled chocolate and combine.

Beat egg whites at high speed until foamy, gradually adding remaining scant cup sugar until stiff. With a large spatula, fold half the nuts and a quarter of the whites into chocolate mixture. Repeat with remaining nuts and another quarter of the whites. Now reverse the process, pouring chocolate over remaining whites. Gently fold the two mixtures together, using a motion like a figure eight, until all the whites have disappeared. Be careful not to overfold.

Pour batter into the prepared pan and bake in center of oven for about 55 minutes. Test with a cake tester in the center; it should come out dry. Do not overbake. Let cool on a rack. (Cake will fall a bit.) Release sides with a knife and remove rim. Loosen bottom with a knife and unmold onto a serving platter to ice. Let cool completely or, if you like, cover with plastic wrap, then foil, and leave to ice the following day.

To make the icing: Place chocolate, coffee powder, and boiling water in top part of a double boiler. Cover and set over simmering water until melted. Stir until smooth. Remove chocolate from heat and whisk in 1 tablespoonful of margarine at a time until smooth. Whisk in egg yolks, one at a time, then rum. If icing is too thin, place in freezer for a few minutes.

To ice the torte: Stick pieces of wax paper under cake to catch icing driblets. Spread top and sides with icing. When it is beginning to set, decorate with chocolate shavings or extra walnuts if you like. Remove wax paper.

NOTE: I use Saint James dark rum, imported from Martinique.

This torte is equally good without the icing. It is easier to cut if all the nuts are finely ground, but I like the crunchier texture.

IDA'S POTATO KUGEL

8 SERVINGS   I had a very special aunt who was sick for a long time with a hopeless illness. To make the time pass faster, we often discussed my book. This is one of her "heirloom" recipes.

1 tablespoon vegetable oil	About 1 teaspoon kosher salt
6 medium baking potatoes	White pepper, freshly ground
3 eggs	¼ cup vegetable oil, boiling

I suggest you use a 9-by-9-by-2-inch ovenproof dish and a food processor.

Preheat oven to 425°F. Grease an ovenproof dish with oil. Peel and quarter potatoes. Place in a bowl of cold water to prevent them from discoloring.

Whisk eggs in a large bowl. Grate potatoes coarsely in a food processor fitted with the grating attachment. Add eggs and season to taste. Immediately add boiling oil (this keeps potatoes from turning gray), place in the prepared dish, and smooth the top. Bake for about 1 hour, or until bottom and top are crisp.

POT ROAST

Pot roast is a convenient holiday or party dish. It requires a minimum of attention, and it must be made a day ahead of time if you are to degrease it and slice it properly. The meat is first sautéed, then gently braised with vegetables, which are later pureed into a sauce. It is refrigerated overnight, sliced, degreased, and heated again. Do buy top-quality beef; it will taste and slice better.

12 TO 14
SERVINGS

½ ounce imported dried
   Italian mushrooms
¾ cup boiling water
7 to 8 pounds boned brisket
   of beef, bottom part only,
   trimmed of all but a thin
   layer of fat
1 tablespoon vegetable oil
2 leeks
3 cloves garlic
2 medium onions
2 carrots

½ bunch Italian flat-leaf
   parsley
6 ripe plum or 4 regular
   tomatoes
1 cup Scotch, heated
Bouquet garni: 1 bay leaf, 10
   whole peppercorns, and 1
   teaspoon dried thyme, tied
   in a double piece of
   cheesecloth
Kosher salt
Black pepper, freshly ground

I suggest you use an enameled cast-iron saucepan large enough to hold the meat, and a food processor.

Place mushrooms in a small bowl and pour boiling water over them. Let soak for 1 hour. Line a mesh sieve with a paper towel and strain mushroom liquid, squeezing mushrooms over strainer to extract all liquid; set aside. Wash mushrooms carefully; set aside.

Preheat oven to 300°F. Pat meat dry with paper towels. Heat oil in a large enameled cast-iron saucepan until hot. Sear meat over high heat on both sides (but don't burn), about 10 minutes. Transfer meat to a platter and sprinkle lightly with salt and pepper. There will be drippings left in the pan; leave them there to sauté vegetables.

Cut off dangling roots and all but 1 inch of green stems of leeks. Discard tough outer leaves. Cut leeks into quarters and chop coarsely in a food processor fitted with the steel blade. Empty leeks into a sieve and wash well under cold running water to remove sand. Drain and set aside.

Peel, quarter, and coarsely chop garlic and onions in food processor. Do the same with carrots.

Wash parsley with its stems and drain.

Remove core of tomatoes and cut into small pieces.

Sauté all the vegetables, except parsley and tomatoes, for a few minutes in the drippings in the saucepan. Place meat on the vegetables, pour on hot Scotch, and ignite. When flames die down, add reserved mushroom liquid, mushrooms, parsley, tomatoes, and bouquet garni. Bring to a boil, covering pan with a sheet of heavy foil and then the lid.

Place in oven and braise for about 1 hour. Turn meat over and continue braising for another 1½ hours. Meat should be semisoft. Make sure that it cooks very slowly; you may have to adjust oven temperature.

Let cool and refrigerate overnight in the saucepan.

The next day, remove hardened fat from top of sauce. Place meat on a carving board, trim fat, and slice thinly across the grain. You may have to rotate the meat in order not to lose the grain. Discard bouquet garni and puree sauce with vegetables in a food processor. Return sliced meat to saucepan with the pureed sauce. Bring to a boil and cook very slowly, covered, for about 1 hour, or until meat is soft. Season to taste.

NOTE: If you wish to make this dish on Passover, use red wine instead of Scotch.

◆Pot roast freezes very well, but be sure to defrost it in the refrigerator.

ROAST CAPON

6 SERVINGS The low-temperature method for roasting capon produces moist meat. The skin will not be crisp because the bird is covered with foil after roasting to permit the juices to flow back into the meat.

One 6-pound capon	2 teaspoons dried tarragon
Juice of 1 lemon	3 tablespoons unsalted
2 tablespoons thin Chinese soy	margarine, melted
sauce	¼ cup bottled orange juice
2 medium onions	¼ cup dry white wine

I suggest you use a roasting pan just large enough to hold the capon.

Preheat oven to 325°F. Rinse capon and pat dry inside and out with paper towels. Cut off excess fat or skin. Place in a roasting pan and season with lemon juice and soy sauce inside and out. Peel onions; quarter one and slice the other. Put onion quarters into cavity of capon. Rub tarragon in your fingers to release more flavor, then place in cavity. Scatter sliced onions around the bird and smear capon with margarine. Combine orange juice with wine.

Place capon on its side and roast in center of oven for 30 minutes. Baste with orange juice–wine mixture. Turn bird to other side and roast for another 30 minutes, basting frequently. Turn capon breast side up and roast for 15 minutes, then turn breast side down for another 15 minutes. The total roasting time is 1½ hours, or 15 minutes per pound. Capon is ready when drumsticks move easily in their sockets.

Remove pan from oven and cover tightly with heavy foil. Leave for 20 minutes before carving. If you like, degrease pan juices and serve sauce separately.

NOTE: Do not use freshly squeezed orange juice; it is too acidic.

Sabbath

CHOPPED CHICKEN LIVER

8 SERVINGS Chopped liver is not to be confused with pâté. It can be chopped either in a food processor or by hand. It can be made a day ahead of time and refrigerated.

About 1¼ pounds chicken liver, fresh or frozen

About ½ cup vegetable oil
4 medium onions, chopped
  coarse
About ¼ cup cream sherry

4 eggs, hard-boiled and cut
  into quarters
Kosher salt
Black pepper, freshly ground

I suggest you use a food processor or a wooden bowl with a chopper.

Preheat broiler. Line a broiler pan with foil. Remove and discard any green spots on livers (they are bitter). Place livers on foil and broil close to heat source, on both sides, turning with tongs, until dry.

In a large skillet, heat ⅓ cup of the oil. Sauté onions over medium-high heat until brown. Stir frequently so they don't burn. Let cool.

Chop some of the livers, onions with their oil, some of the sherry, and eggs medium fine in a food processor fitted with the steel blade. I do it in three batches, emptying each batch before placing in the next one. Adjust moistness and flavor with remaining oil, sherry, salt, and pepper. Refrigerate in a tightly covered container, but serve it at room temperature.

PETCHA

8 TO 10
SERVINGS
Petcha is a traditional Sabbath luncheon dish made of calves' feet. It is cooked for a long time. The meat is then removed from the bones, combined with the gelatinous liquid, and allowed to set.

2 to 2½ pounds calves' feet,
  cleaned and chopped coarse
4 cloves garlic, peeled
About 1 tablespoon kosher
  salt

Black or white pepper, freshly
  ground
1 or 2 lemons for garnish
  (optional)
White radishes, sliced thin

I suggest you use 10-by-2-inch glass or ceramic dish.

Rinse calves' feet and place in a saucepan. Add 2 cloves of the garlic, salt, and about 7 cups cold water. (Water should cover the bones by about 1 inch.) Bring to a boil, then simmer, covered, for about 5 hours.

Pour everything into a sieve to drain. Return stock to saucepan. Remove meat from bones and chop fine. Mince remaining 2 cloves garlic and add, along with meat, to stock. Boil for about 5 minutes. Season to taste and pour into a dish. Let cool.

Cover tightly with plastic wrap and refrigerate overnight.

If the top of the Petcha has any fat, blot it with paper towels. Cut into squares or wedges and serve with quartered lemon, if you like, and with radishes.

CHOLENT

The origin of the word *cholent* may come from the old French word *chald* or the modern French word *chaud*, meaning "warm." Cholent is a barley, bean, potato, and meat dish, which is cooked in a heavy pot in the oven until Sabbath lunch. This dish is particularly popular among Eastern European Jews, who have many versions of it.

4 SERVINGS
AS A
MAIN COURSE
6 SERVINGS
AS A
SIDE DISH

½ cup medium barley
½ cup small white, baby lima,
  or Great Northern beans
½ cup red kidney beans
6 small red potatoes
1½ to 2 pounds flanken,
  trimmed of fat and cut into
  large pieces

About 6 beef bones
1 onion, chopped fine
2 cloves garlic, chopped fine
Cold water
About 2 teaspoons kosher salt
Black pepper, freshly ground

I suggest you use a 3-quart enameled cast-iron saucepan with lid.

Rinse barley in a sieve under cold running water, until water runs clear. Rinse all the beans and pick them over.

Peel potatoes and cut into eighths.

Place barley, beans, potatoes, meat, bones, onion, and garlic in a large saucepan. Add 6½ to 7 cups cold water, or enough to cover, and bring to a boil over high heat. Season with salt and pepper and simmer for 1 hour. Skim froth as it rises to the surface.

Before lighting the Sabbath candles on Friday night, place the cholent in a preheated 225°F oven and leave to cook until the following day.

A few hours before luncheon, check cholent: If too moist, uncover and leave in oven to dry; if too dry, add some boiling water. Correct the seasoning.

NOTE: I prefer to buy beans in health food stores; they are fresher.

LOKSHEN KUGEL (SWEET NOODLE PUDDING)

8 SERVINGS   Kugel is traditionally served on Friday nights or on the Sabbath. I find it equally delicious served hot or at room temperature.

4½ tablespoons unsalted margarine, melted	2 large tart apples (Granny Smith or greening)
½ pound medium-wide egg noodles	2 tablespoons fresh lemon juice, strained
Kosher salt	⅓ cup seedless golden raisins
2 eggs	½ cup walnuts, chopped coarse
⅓ cup sugar	

I suggest you use a 9-by-9-by-2-inch ovenproof dish.

Preheat oven to 350°F. Grease an ovenproof dish with ½ tablespoon of the margarine.

Cook noodles in lightly salted water for about 5 minutes, or until *al dente.* Pour into a sieve, refresh with cold water, and drain well.

In a large bowl, beat eggs with sugar until well combined.

Peel apples, grate coarsely, and immediately sprinkle with lemon juice to prevent discoloration. Combine apples, noodles, raisins, walnuts, and remaining margarine with egg mixture. Pour into the prepared pan.

Bake for about 1 hour, or until top is golden.

MRS. LICHTENFELD'S SPONGE CAKE

12 TO 14 SERVINGS   This cake is traditionally eaten on the Sabbath and holidays. It is moist, very light, and is a good accompaniment to fresh or poached fruit and, of course, hot tea. It stays fresh for many days.

Unsalted margarine, at room
  temperature
10 eggs, at room temperature,
  separated
1½ cups sugar
Rind and juice of 1 large, ripe
  lemon (about ¼ cup),
  strained, at room
  temperature

Rind and juice of 1 orange
  (about ⅓ cup), strained, at
  room temperature
1½ cups sifted unbleached
  flour

*I suggest you use an electric mixer and a 10-by-4-inch tube pan
with removable bottom.*

Preheat oven to 350°F. Lightly grease the funnel part of a tube pan with margarine. Beat egg yolks in an electric mixer at medium speed, gradually adding ½ cup of the sugar until pale and thick (about 8 minutes).

Lower speed and slowly pour combined juices and rinds into yolks until well blended. With motor on, gradually add flour until combined.

Beat egg whites at high speed. As they begin to hold a shape, gradually add remaining 1 cup sugar and continue beating until stiff.

With a large rubber spatula, fold a quarter of the whites into the yolk mixture and combine well. Repeat with another quarter of the whites. Now reverse the process and pour the yolk mixture over the remaining whites. Gently fold the two mixtures together until all the whites have disappeared.

Pour batter into the prepared pan and bake in center of oven for 50 to 60 minutes. (Top should be golden and springy to the touch.) Test with a cake tester in the center; it should come out dry.

Turn cake upside down onto a cookie rack to cool completely. Loosen sides with a knife before unmolding.

NOTE: Sift flour directly into the measuring cup.

In some tube pans, the funnel part extends over the top of the mold. If you have one, do not be afraid to stand the cake upside down; it will not topple.

KICHLACH

Puffy, very lightly sweetened egg cookies, which are traditionally served on the Sabbath. Leave them, uncovered, in a cool
place to dry out, and keep in a plastic bag.

ABOUT
35 KICHLACH

3 eggs, at room temperature
3 tablespoons sugar

Vegetable oil
1 cup unbleached flour

I suggest you use a food processor and a cookie sheet.

Preheat oven to 325°F. Combine eggs and 2 tablespoons of the sugar in a food processor fitted with the steel blade. With the motor on, slowly add ½ cup of the oil, then flour, blending until smooth. Let batter rest for 5 minutes.

Grease cookie sheet lightly with oil.

Drop batter onto cookie sheet by ½ tablespoonfuls, slightly apart. Sprinkle lightly with remaining 1 tablespoon sugar and bake in center of oven for 20 to 25 minutes, or until lightly golden. Let cool on a rack.

MRS. LICHTENFELD'S HONEY CAKE

On Rosh Hashanah, the Jewish New Year, sweet dishes made with honey, raisins, and carrots are served in anticipation of a happy New Year. One of these traditional delicacies is honey cake (lekach).

2 LOAVES, EACH SERVING 12

Mrs. Lichtenfeld was good enough to share her heirloom recipe with me. It is not too sweet and stays moist and fresh for many days, refrigerated.

1 tablespoon unsalted margarine, at room temperature

2⅓ cups plus 1½ tablespoons sifted unbleached flour

1 teaspoon baking powder

1 teaspoon baking soda

2 eggs, at room temperature

Scant ⅔ cup sugar

1 cup dark brewed tea made with 3 teabags, cooled

⅓ cup vegetable oil

1 cup honey

½ medium ripe banana, thoroughly mashed

Grated rind of 1 orange

½ teaspoon ground cinnamon

⅛ teaspoon ground cloves

I suggest you use an electric mixer and two 9-by-5-inch loaf pans.

Preheat oven to 325°F. Grease two 9-by-5-inch loaf pans with margarine and dust with 1½ tablespoons of the flour. Invert pans and tap to shake off excess.

Sift flour together with baking powder and baking soda directly into a measuring cup.

Beat eggs in an electric mixer at medium speed, gradually adding sugar until pale and thick (about 10 minutes). Lower speed and add tea, oil, honey, banana, orange rind, cinnamon, and cloves, combining thoroughly.

With a rubber spatula, gradually fold in flour, combining it well after each addition; there should be no traces of flour visible. Divide batter evenly between the two pans.

Bake side by side, without touching, in center of oven for 15 minutes. Increase heat to 350°F and bake for about another 30 minutes. Test with a cake tester in the center; it should come out dry. Let cool on a rack. Loosen sides with a knife before unmolding.

◆If you want to freeze the honey cake, wrap it in wax paper, then foil, and place in a plastic bag.

TZIMMES

8 SERVINGS   Carrots are traditionally served on Rosh Hashanah, when you are supposed to eat sweet foods for a sweet year. When cut into round circles, they resemble coins, symbolizing prosperity as well.

10 medium carrots	3 tablespoons fresh lemon
3 tablespoons unsalted	juice, strained
margarine	Kosher salt
About 3 tablespoons honey	Black pepper, freshly ground
3 tablespoons brown sugar	

I suggest you use a food processor.

Rinse, peel, and trim carrots. Cut into rounds in a food processor fitted with the slicing attachment.

Place in a saucepan with margarine, honey, brown sugar, and lemon juice. Bring to a boil and simmer, covered, for about 1 hour, or until carrots are soft, but still crunchy. Season to taste.

Yom Kippur

KREPLACH

ABOUT
65 KREPLACH

Kreplach are half-moons of dough that are filled with a meat stuffing and usually served in a piping-hot, well-flavored chicken soup.

On Yom Kippur Eve, before the next day's fast, it is customary to eat lightly seasoned high-protein foods and to have a big, happy meal. It is traditional in Eastern European countries to serve kreplach with chicken soup, boiled chicken, and beef.

Kreplach are also traditionally served on Purim and on Hoshana Raba, one of the middle days of Sukkot.

FILLING:

1¼ pounds boneless fat-free chuck

2 small onions, peeled

About ¼ cup vegetable oil

Kosher salt

Black pepper, freshly ground

10 sprigs dill, snipped

DOUGH:

2¼ cups unbleached flour

¼ teaspoon salt

1 egg, at room temperature, lightly beaten

⅔ cup lukewarm water (about 100°F)

I suggest you use the following: a food processor, a pastry blender, a 3-inch round cookie cutter, a cookie sheet, and three damp towels.

To make the filling: Place meat in a small saucepan and cover with cold water. Bring to a boil, remove the scum, and add one of the onions. Cover saucepan and boil gently until meat is soft. Drain and let cool. (If you like, this can be done a day ahead of time, and the stock can be strained and used for soup.)

Chop remaining onion fine. Heat oil in a small skillet until hot and sauté onion over medium-high heat until light brown.

Cut meat into small pieces. Grind fine along with sautéed onion and its oil in a food processor fitted with the steel blade; remove to a bowl. Filling should hold together; if not, you may have to add some more oil. Season with salt, pepper, and dill. Let cool.

To make the dough: Mix flour and salt in a metal bowl. Add egg and mix with a pastry blender, gradually sprinkling on water until you can gather dough into a rough ball. (From time to time, scrape sticky dough from blender with a knife.) Turn dough out onto a board. Knead with the heel of your hand until dough is smooth and elastic. (If dough seems difficult to knead, let it rest for a few minutes to relax the gluten. To test if dough is fully kneaded, cut into it; if you see little holes inside, it is ready.)

To roll out the dough: Cut off a small piece (about one eighth) dough, keeping the rest covered with a damp towel. On a floured pastry board with a lightly floured rolling pin, roll dough out firmly on both sides (it is elastic) into a very thin circle. Cut out 3-inch rounds with a cookie cutter.

Place 1 teaspoon filling in center of each round and fold over to make

a half-moon (1). Fold edge over, then pinch to seal it tightly (2). (Do this carefully, or the dumplings may open while boiling.) Line a cookie sheet with a damp towel and place kreplach on it. Repeat in the same fashion with remaining dough. Save trimmings, form them into a ball, and roll out as well. Place another damp towel between layers of kreplach and cover with a third damp towel. Refrigerate until ready to boil.

To boil the kreplach: Bring a large pot of salted water to a boil. Drop in batches of kreplach, adjusting the size and number of the batches to the size of your pot. Return water to the boil and cook slowly, uncovered, till kreplach rise to the top (about 3 minutes). Remove with a slotted spoon to a bowl, cover with foil, and keep warm in a food warmer or over hot water.

If you are not serving them right away, place them in a saucepan with a little stock to keep them from sticking to each other.

To serve: Serve hot kreplach in heated soup bowls filled with piping-hot chicken soup, garnished with snipped dill.

NOTE: Leftover boiled kreplach can be fried and served with the main dish.

Sukkot

STUFFED CABBAGE ROLLS

Sukkot is the holiday of harvest. In ancient Palestine, it was the time of year when the first produce of the season was harvested.

In Eastern Europe stuffed cabbage rolls are traditionally served on the last days of Sukkot, probably because cabbage was a fall vegetable, and there was plenty of it.

There are many versions of this dish. Mine is sweet and sour, light, and not too spicy. I make it several days in advance to let the flavors blend.

This dish also freezes very well.

1 head cabbage, about 5 pounds

Kosher salt

FILLING:

1 small onion

1 clove garlic

1 medium potato

1 egg

¾ pound lean veal, ground, and 1 pound lean chuck, ground, then ground together twice

¼ bunch Italian flat-leaf parsley

3 tablespoons long-grain rice (Uncle Ben's converted brand)

2 tablespoons tomato paste

1 tablespoon black Chinese soy sauce

Kosher salt

Black pepper, freshly ground

SAUCE:

2 carrots

2 onions

1 tart apple (Granny Smith or greening)

¾ to 1 bunch Italian flat-leaf parsley

½ cup seedless dark raisins

2 ounces dried apricots, cut into small pieces

2-pound 3-ounce can peeled Italian plum tomatoes, undrained

8-ounce can tomato sauce

2 tablespoons tomato paste

About 2 tablespoons dark brown sugar

Juice of about ½ lemon

6 medium meaty beef bones

Kosher salt

Black pepper, freshly ground

¼ ounce kosher beef-flavored bouillon cube dissolved in ½ cup boiling water (optional)

I suggest you use a food processor and an enameled cast-iron saucepan large enough to fit the cabbage rolls in a single layer.

To prepare the cabbage leaves: Remove and discard bruised and discolored outer cabbage leaves. With a pointed knife, cut out some of the hard center core. Boil cabbage for a few minutes in a large pot of boiling water to which 2 tablespoons salt have been added.

Turn cabbage as it cooks. Lift out by piercing core with a large fork, then refresh with cold water to make it easier to handle.

To peel off leaves without damaging them, first cut them at the core, then remove. (When leaves are wilted, they are easy to remove. If not wilted, they will tear.) Return cabbage to boiling water and repeat in the same fashion; you may have to do this several times. The center cabbage leaves will be too small for stuffing, so shred them and save for the sauce.

To make the filling: Peel and quarter onion, garlic, and potato. Place in a food processor fitted with the steel blade. Add egg and puree until smooth.

Place chopped meat in a large bowl and add puree. Remove bottom half of parsley stems; wash the rest and spin dry. Chop coarsely in food processor. Add to meat along with rice, tomato paste, and soy sauce. Mix with your hands to combine well. (If you mix in one direction, it makes the filling fluffier.) Season with salt and pepper.

To make the sauce: Peel, trim, and quarter carrots and chop coarsely in a food processor. Do the same with the onions. Peel, core, and chop apple. Remove bottom half of parsley stems; rinse the rest and chop coarsely in food processor.

Place all but last three sauce ingredients in a medium saucepan and bring to a boil slowly, so that sauce does not burn. Simmer sauce, covered, while you fill cabbage leaves. Season with salt and pepper.

To fill the cabbage leaves: Preheat oven to 325°F. Spread a cabbage leaf and place about 2 tablespoons filling in the center. Roll halfway, fold the sides toward center, and continue to roll tightly to the end.

Place rolls, seam side down, close to each other in a large saucepan. Pour sauce over them, cover with shredded cabbage, and bring to a boil. Cover saucepan with a sheet of heavy foil, then a lid. Cook in oven for about 2 hours, turning rolls from time to time. Reduce heat to 300° and cook for another 30 minutes. Season to taste. If there is too little sauce, add dissolved bouillon until it is right.

NOTE: Ask your butcher to grind both meats separately, combine them, and then grind them again; it makes a smoother texture.

◆If you want to freeze cabbage rolls, defrost them in the refrigerator.

Hanukkah

LATKES (POTATO PANCAKES)

On Hanukkah it is traditional to serve dishes cooked in oil to commemorate the miracle of the oil that burned in the temple for eight days when there was only enough to last for one day. That's why Hanukkah is called the Festival of Lights.

ABOUT EIGHTEEN 2½- TO 3-INCH PANCAKES

3 large baking potatoes
2 eggs, separated
1 small onion, grated fine
1 tablespoon unbleached flour

¼ teaspoon baking powder
About 1 teaspoon kosher salt
Black pepper, freshly ground

½ cup vegetable shortening, such as Crisco or vegetable oil

I suggest you use a food processor and a large nonstick skillet.

Peel potatoes and grate fine in a food processor fitted with the grating attachment. Empty potato pulp into a mesh sieve and wash under cold running water until water runs clear. Drain well by shaking sieve. Empty potatoes into a bowl and combine with egg yolk, grated onion, flour, and baking powder. Beat egg whites until stiff and fold into potato mixture. Season well.

Preheat oven to 350°F. In a large skillet, heat some of the shortening, reaching to about ½ inch in the pan, until very hot. Drop full tablespoons of potato mixture into oil, flatten each mound slightly, and fry on both sides over medium-high heat until golden brown. Drain on paper towels, changing them frequently as they absorb the oil. Add more oil, and make sure that this oil is hot enough before you drop in more potato mixture.

To keep pancakes warm while frying the rest, place in oven on a rack set over a cookie sheet. Serve pancakes on a cloth napkin.

Purim

HAMENTASCHEN—DAIRY

ABOUT 50 TRIANGLES Purim is a joyous holiday, a time for exchanging gifts and sweets, particularly Hamentaschen, so called because they are supposed to resemble the wicked Haman's hat.

Hamentaschen are triangular sweets that are filled with poppy seeds or prune or apricot butters. In this dairy version, they are filled with poppy seeds. They keep for weeks in a covered tin box in a cool place.

DOUGH:

2 cups unbleached flour

⅛ teaspoon salt

⅓ cup sugar

10 tablespoons (1 stick plus 2 tablespoons) sweet butter, chilled, cut into tablespoons

Grated rind of 1 lemon

1 whole egg plus 1 egg yolk

¾ tablespoon distilled white vinegar mixed with ¾ tablespoon cold water

FILLING:

5 ounces milk

⅓ cup plus 1 tablespoon sugar

½ pound ground poppy seeds, about 2½ cups

2 tablespoons sweet butter

2 ounces semisweet chocolate, grated

½ cup seedless dark or golden raisins

GLAZE:

1 egg white, lightly beaten

I suggest you use the following: a food processor, a 3-inch round cookie cutter, and three cookie sheets.

To make the dough: Combine flour, salt, and sugar in a food processor fitted with the steel blade. Add butter and lemon rind and process until mixture resembles coarse crumbs. Add egg, egg yolk, and vinegar and combine until dough clings to blade, but before it forms a ball.

Turn dough out onto a pastry board and combine with your hands into a smooth ball. Dust lightly with flour, wrap in wax paper, and refrigerate for 30 minutes.

To make the filling: In a small saucepan, bring milk and sugar to a boil. Add poppy seeds and simmer for several minutes, stirring all the time with a wooden spoon. (Poppy seeds will expand.) Remove from heat and stir in butter, chocolate, and raisins. Let cool.

To make the hamentaschen: Preheat oven to 350°F. Cut dough into small pieces, but work with one piece at a time, keeping the rest refrigerated.

Roll out dough on both sides between two lightly floured sheets of wax paper until thin. From time to time, lift papers and sprinkle lightly with flour. Lift top sheet and place back on dough. Turn dough over and remove what is now the top sheet.

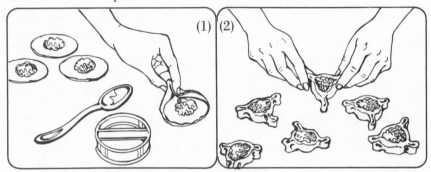

With a cookie cutter, cut out rounds. Place 1 heaping teaspoon filling in center of each circle. Pinch one end tightly (1), fold other two ends, and pinch tightly to form a triangle (2). Place on a cookie sheet.

Keep scraps refrigerated and continue in the same fashion, using all the dough and scraps, and changing the wax paper as needed.

Brush dough with glaze.

Bake in center of oven for about 20 minutes, or until golden. Let cool on racks.

NOTE: I grate such small amounts of chocolate in a Mouli grater or food processor.

◆If you wish, the filling can be made several days ahead of time and refrigerated.

HAMENTASCHEN—PAREVE

These are pareve hamentaschen, filled with prune or apricot butter. They also keep very well for weeks in a covered container in a cool place.

ABOUT 100 TRIANGLES

FILLING:

3 cups prune butter or apricot butter or a combination of both	1 cup seedless dark raisins or currants
	1 cup walnuts, chopped coarse
	Grated rind of 1 orange

Vegetable oil

DOUGH:

4 eggs, at room temperature

1 cup sugar

½ cup vegetable oil

Juice of 1 medium ripe lemon,
    strained, 3 tablespoons

Grated rind of 1 lemon

1 teaspoon vanilla extract

2 teaspoons baking powder

4½ to 5 cups unbleached
    flour

GLAZE:

1 egg, lightly beaten

I suggest you use the following: an electric mixer with a dough hook, a 3-inch round cookie cutter, and about four cookie sheets.

Combine filling ingredients and set aside.

Grease cookie sheets lightly, with vegetable oil.

To make the dough: Beat eggs in an electric mixer at medium speed, adding sugar gradually until thick and bubbles appear, about 5 minutes. With machine on, slowly pour in oil, lemon juice, lemon rind, and vanilla. Switch to a dough hook, lower speed, and add baking powder and enough flour to make a stiff dough. Turn dough out onto a pastry board and combine to make a smooth, stiff dough that no longer sticks to board or hands; if necessary, add extra flour. Cover dough with a towel.

To make the hamentaschen: Preheat oven to 350°F. Working with small pieces at a time, roll out dough on both sides between lightly floured sheets of wax paper until very thin. From time to time lift paper and sprinkle lightly with flour if paper is sticking. Lift top sheet and place back on dough. Turn dough over and remove what is now the top sheet.

With a cookie cutter, cut out rounds. Place 1 level teaspoon filling in center of each circle. Pinch one end tightly; fold other two ends and pinch tightly to form a triangle. (If ends do not stick together, moisten edges lightly with cold water.) Place on a cookie sheet. Continue in the same fashion with the remaining dough and scraps. Keep scraps covered, and change wax paper as needed.

Brush dough with glaze. Bake in center of oven for about 20 minutes, or until golden. Let cool for a few minutes, then release hamentaschen with a knife and let cool on a rack.

NOTE: Simon Fischer prune or apricot butter is available in most supermarkets. You will need two jars.

If you do not have enough cookie sheets, just clean what you have as you go.

Passover

HAZELNUT–CHOCOLATE LOAF

Nuts and chocolate are essential ingredients in Passover baking. 12 SERVINGS
What a wonderful combination! I make this Passover treat on
other occasions too. It is easy to make and stays moist for many
days, refrigerated.

1 cup hazelnuts
6 ounces semisweet chocolate
5½ tablespoons unsalted
   margarine, at room
   temperature
½ tablespoon potato flour

4 eggs, at room temperature,
   separated, plus 1 egg white
½ cup sugar
1 teaspoon almond extract

*I suggest you use the following: a food processor, an electric mixer,
and a 9-by-5-inch loaf pan.*

Preheat oven to 350°F. Roast hazelnuts in oven in a baking pan for about
15 minutes. Rub in a dish towel to remove skin. (Some skin will remain.)
Let nuts cool, but keep oven hot. Coarsely chop in a food processor fitted
with the steel blade; set aside.

Chop 2 ounces of the chocolate into small chips in food processor and
set aside.

Grease a 9-by-5-inch pan with ½ tablespoon of the margarine and dust
with potato flour. (If you are not making the cake on Passover, use regular
flour.) Invert pan and tap to shake off excess.

Place remaining 4 ounces chocolate, broken into small pieces, in top part
of a double boiler. Cover and set over simmering water until melted.
Remove top and whisk in margarine, 1 tablespoonful at a time, until smooth
and well combined; set aside.

Beat egg yolks in an electric mixer at medium speed, adding sugar
gradually, until pale and thick, about 10 minutes.

Lower speed and pour in cooled chocolate and almond extract, beating
until thoroughly combined; set aside.

Beat the 5 egg whites at high speed until stiff.

With a rubber spatula, fold half the nuts, the chocolate chips, and a quarter of the whites into the chocolate mixture. Repeat with another quarter of the whites and the remaining nuts.

Now reverse the process, pouring chocolate over whites. Gently fold the two mixtures together, making a motion like a figure eight, until all the whites have disappeared.

Pour batter into the prepared pan and bake in center of oven for about 55 minutes. Test with a cake tester in the center; it should come out dry.

Let cool on a rack. Loosen sides with a knife before unmolding cake.

Because the cake has a coarse texture, it is easier to slice it when it is completely cold. I therefore refrigerate it for a while first.

NOTE: If you do not use almond extract for Passover, just omit it.

HAZELNUT TORTE

12 SERVINGS   This easy-to-make Passover torte with a rich flavor of hazelnuts keeps fresh for many days, refrigerated.

¾ pound hazelnuts, about 2½ cups	¾ cup sugar
½ tablespoon unsalted margarine	Rind and juice of 1 large lemon, about ¼ cup, strained, at room temperature
1 tablespoon potato flour	
6 eggs, at room temperature, separated	Confectioners' sugar

I suggest you use the following: a food processor, an electric mixer, and a 10-by-2½-inch springform pan.

Preheat oven to 350°F. Roast hazelnuts in oven on a cookie sheet in a single layer for about 15 minutes. Rub hard in a dish towel to remove skin. (Some skin will remain.) Let nuts cool, but keep oven hot. Coarsely chop in a food processor fitted with the steel blade.

Grease a 10-by-2½-inch springform pan with margarine and dust with potato flour. Invert pan and tap to shake off excess.

Beat egg yolks in an electric mixer at medium speed, adding sugar gradually until pale and thick and bubbles appear (about 10 minutes). Lower speed and add lemon rind and lemon juice, beating until combined.

Beat egg whites at high speed until stiff.

With a rubber spatula, fold half the nuts and a quarter of the whites into yolk mixture. Repeat with the rest of the nuts and another quarter of the whites. Now reverse the process, pouring batter over whites. Gradually fold the two mixtures together, making a motion like a figure eight, until all the whites have disappeared. Do not overfold. Pour batter into pan and smooth top.

Bake in center of oven for about 35 to 40 minutes. Test with a cake tester in the center; it should come out dry. Do not overbake.

Let cool on a rack. (Cake will drop a bit.) Release sides with a knife and remove rim. Loosen bottom with a knife. Slide a large, wide spatula under torte and lift onto a serving platter. Sprinkle with confectioners' sugar.

NOTE: If top is too brown, invert cake and slide onto a serving platter.

BAKED GRATED APPLES WITH WALNUTS

A tart, refreshing Passover dessert.

10 TO 12
SERVINGS

9 medium tart apples
(greening or Granny Smith)
6 tablespoons unsalted
margarine, melted
½ cup sugar

Grated rind of 1 lemon
2 teaspoons ground cinnamon
1½ cups walnuts, chopped
coarse

I suggest you use a food processor and an 8-by-12-inch ovenproof serving dish.

Preheat oven to 375°F. Peel, quarter, and core apples. Grate coarsely in a food processor fitted with the grating attachment.

Grease an 8-by-12-inch ovenproof dish with some of the margarine. Combine apples with remaining margarine, sugar, lemon rind, cinnamon, and half the walnuts. Place mixture in dish, smooth top, and sprinkle with remaining walnuts.

Bake in center of oven for 25 minutes, or until apples are almost soft and still crunchy. Broil for a few minutes, not too close to the heat source, if you like the top to be brown.

MATZOH BREI

A favorite Passover breakfast treat.

1 TO 2
SERVINGS

2 eggs
Kosher salt
White pepper, freshly ground

2 matzohs
Boiling water
2 tablespoons sweet butter

In a small bowl, whisk eggs and season with salt and pepper.

Break matzohs into 2-inch pieces and place in a sieve. Pour just enough boiling water over them to dampen outer layer. Squeeze them with your hands and mix with eggs. (Matzoh needs to be moist to absorb the egg, but should not be soggy.)

In a skillet, heat butter until golden and fry matzoh for a minute, as though you were scrambling eggs. Fry until egg is firm. Serve at once.

NOTE: Matzoh brei can also be served sweet, by omitting salt and pepper and substituting sugar and cinnamon.

If you wish to make matzoh brei into a pancake, spread it in the skillet, fry until golden on one side, flip over to a plate, and slide back into the skillet to brown.

JEANETTE SCHAPIRO'S PASSOVER SPONGE CAKE

12 TO 14 SERVINGS

With the availability of timesaving appliances, it is possible to make wonderful Passover desserts without the use of flour or nonleavening agents.

This is one of those wonderful light desserts, which stays moist and fresh for many days.

Unsalted margarine
9 eggs
Scant 1½ cups sugar
Rind and juice of 1 large ripe
  lemon, about ¼ cup,
  strained, at room
  temperature

¾ cup cake meal and 3
  tablespoons potato starch
  sifted together

I suggest you use a 10-by-4-inch tube pan with removable bottom and an electric mixer.

Preheat oven to 350°F. Lightly grease funnel part of a 10-by-4-inch tube pan with margarine.

Beat eggs in an electric mixer at high speed for 6 minutes. Gradually add sugar and continue beating for 5 minutes. Lower speed a little, slowly pour in lemon juice combined with lemon rind, and beat for another 5 minutes. Slowly add cake meal and potato starch and beat for another 5 minutes. (The entire beating time is about 20 minutes.)

Pour batter into the prepared pan and bake in center of oven for 50 to 60 minutes. Test with a cake tester in the center; it should come out dry. Turn cake upside down onto a cookie rack to cool completely. Loosen sides with a knife before unmolding.

NOTE: In some tube pans, the funnel part extends over the top of the mold.

If that is the case, do not be afraid to stand the cake upside down. It will not topple.

MOCK EGG NOODLES

I once attended a Chinese cooking class taught by Florence Lin. <small>6 SERVINGS</small> She made these mock noodles as a garnish for a stir-fried dish. I immediately thought of Passover and chicken soup. Thin egg crepes are cut into narrow strips to resemble noodles and are served in piping-hot chicken soup, garnished with snipped dill. They can be made a day ahead of time.

2 eggs   Vegetable oil
Kosher salt

I suggest you use a 7-inch nonstick skillet.

Beat eggs with a fork until well blended. Season with salt to taste.

Grease a skillet lightly with oil and heat until hot. Wipe off excess oil with a paper towel. Lift hot skillet and pour in just enough egg to coat bottom by swirling it around. (The pan should be hot enough so that the eggs stick to it right away.) At once, tilt skillet over bowl of eggs and pour back any excess egg, no matter how little. (It is important to make the crepes as thin as possible.) Cook until pale, turn over, and continue cooking briefly. Remove to a plate. Repeat in the same fashion with the rest of the egg. When cool, pile crepes one on top of the other and cut into thin noodlelike strips.

IDA'S POTATO CHREMSEL (CROQUETTES)

These light croquettes are traditionally served on Passover. <small>12 CHREMSELS</small>

2 medium baking potatoes   Kosher salt
2 eggs, at room temperature,   White pepper, freshly ground
  separated

Peanut oil

I suggest you use a potato ricer or a food mill with a medium blade and a Dalkan form or a Danish pancake form with four to six cavities.

Boil potatoes in their skin until just soft; do not overcook. Peel potatoes and pass them through a ricer or food mill to make them smooth and fluffy. Add 1 egg yolk at a time and mix well.

Beat egg whites until stiff and fold into potato mixture. Season to taste.

Pour a little oil into each cavity of your pan and heat until very hot. Drop heaping tablespoons of potato mixture into each cavity. Fry over medium-high heat on both sides until lightly golden. Serve at once.

NOTE: Both the Dalkan form and Danish pancake form are available in kitchen equipment specialty stores.

ROAST TURKEY

12 TO 14
SERVINGS

Since most kosher turkeys are sold frozen, buy them from a reliable butcher and ask for a young turkey. Many experts maintain that slower thawing produces a more tender bird. I prefer unstuffed turkeys, but if you like the stuffing, serve it separately. I allow about 1 pound of uncooked turkey per person. Calculate 15 minutes of roasting per pound and 30 minutes of resting before carving; but do keep your own record as to how you like it.

1 young 14-pound turkey	2 onions
Juice of 1 lemon	5 tablespoons unsalted
Kosher salt	margarine, melted
Black pepper, freshly ground	½ cup bottled orange juice
1 tablespoon dried tarragon	½ cup dry white wine

I suggest you use a roasting pan large enough to fit the turkey.

To thaw the turkey: Place frozen turkey on a tray in the refrigerator. Partially open or puncture plastic bag and calculate 24 hours thawing time for each 5 pounds of turkey. In a pinch, the frozen bird may be thawed submerged in cool water in the unopened plastic bag for 5 to 6 hours. Change water frequently.

To cook the turkey: Preheat oven to 325°F. Rinse turkey and remove excess fat and skin. Pat dry inside and out with paper towels. Place in a roasting pan and season with lemon juice, salt, and pepper inside and out.

Rub tarragon between your fingers to release more flavor and place in cavity. Peel onions, quarter one, and cut the other into thin slices. Scatter sliced onion around bird and put onion quarters into cavity. Smear bird with margarine. Combine orange juice with wine. Place turkey on its side and roast for 1 hour, basting with orange juice–wine mixture. Turn turkey to the other side and do the same. Turn turkey breast side up and roast for 30 minutes. Baste. Turn turkey breast side down and do the same.

If the drumsticks begin to brown excessively, cover with foil. Turkey is ready when juices run clear instead of pink, when the thickest portion of the drumstick feels tender when pressed, or when a meat thermometer inserted in the thickest portion reads 180° to 185°F.

Remove from oven and cover pan with heavy foil. Leave to rest for 30 minutes to permit juices to flow back into meat. Carve. Skim fat from pan juices and serve this sauce separately. The roasting time plus the resting time should be about 3½ to 4 hours.

NOTE: If you are not making turkey for Passover, season it with 2 to 3 tablespoons black Chinese soy sauce instead of salt; it gives the bird a wonderful color.

STUFFED BREAST OF VEAL

Breast of veal is ideal for slow braising in wine and aromatic vegetables. The only difficulty is getting a young, pale, small-boned piece of meat. That kind of meat is not always available in American kosher markets. But you have two other alternatives. One is to have the meat boned and then stuffed, the bones added to the meat for extra flavor. The other possibility is to use any type of veal and ignore the size of the final carved pieces. Remember, it is the size of the bones that will determine how large or small the carved pieces will be. Either way this is a wonderfully tasty dish, which can also be prepared in advance and successfully reheated.

8 TO 10 SERVINGS

STUFFING:

¾ pound lean veal, ground, and ¾ pound lean chuck, ground, then ground together twice
1 medium onion, quartered
2 cloves garlic
1 medium potato, quartered

1 egg
½ bunch Italian flat-leaf parsley
1 tablespoon ketchup
1 tablespoon tomato paste
Kosher salt
Black pepper, freshly ground

About 10 pounds breast of veal with pocket for stuffing, surface fat trimmed
2 tablespoons unsalted margarine
2 tablespoons vegetable oil
Kosher salt
Black pepper, freshly ground

6 ripe plum or regular tomatoes, cored and cut into small pieces
10 medium shallots, chopped fine
2 cloves garlic, chopped fine
2 teaspoons dried tarragon
1½ cups dry red wine

I suggest you use a food processor and a 17-by-12-inch roasting pan.

To make the stuffing: Place chopped meat in a large bowl. Puree onion, garlic, potato, and egg until smooth in a food processor fitted with the steel blade; add to meat. Discard bottom half of parsley stems; rinse the rest and chop coarsely in food processor. Add to meat along with ketchup and tomato paste. Mix very well and season with salt and pepper.

Preheat oven to 375°F.

Pat meat dry inside and out with paper towels. Stuff pocket with chopped-meat mixture. (Depending on the size of the pocket, you may have quite a bit of meat left over; save it for the sauce.) Close opening by sewing it with heavy cotton thread and a thick sewing needle.

Heat margarine and oil until hot in a roasting pan. Sear meat lightly on both sides over medium-high heat. Sprinkle with salt and pepper and place, meaty side down, in pan. Scatter tomatoes, shallots, and garlic over meat. Rub tarragon between your fingers to release extra flavor and add to meat along with wine and leftover chopped-meat mixture. Cover pan tightly with heavy foil and braise for 1½ hours. Turn meat over, uncover, and braise for about another 2 hours; the meat should be soft and brown on top.

Remove from oven and let rest for a few minutes. Place, meat side down, on carving board. Remove thread and carve veal between ribs. Slices will depend on the size of the ribs. Keep meat warm while you boil down gravy to a sauce consistency. Skim off surface fat and check seasoning.

Arrange meat on a hot serving platter. Pour on some of the gravy and serve the rest in a sauceboat.

NOTE: Ask your butcher to grind the meat for you separately, then grind the two together. It improves the texture and flavor of the meat.

Be sure that the butcher does not cut through the edge of the meat when he cuts the pocket.

You can also make breast of veal without stuffing it. Have the butcher cut down the large bones and remove the fat. When there is no pocket, the support of the bones is unnecessary.

◆You can make this dish ahead of time. Before serving, combine meat and gravy and reheat in a preheated 350°F oven.

CHAROSES

10 SERVINGS   One of the Passover Seder dishes, charoses symbolize the mortar used by Jewish slaves in Egypt to anchor heavy blocks of rock and stone.

1 medium apple (McIntosh or
Red Delicious)
¼ pound walnuts, about 1
cup
About ⅓ cup dry red wine

½ teaspoon freshly grated
gingerroot
About 2 teaspoons sugar
½ teaspoon ground cinnamon

I suggest you use a food processor or a wooden bowl with a chopper.

Peel, core, and quarter apple. Chop apple, walnuts, and wine to make a semifine mixture. Season with sugar and cinnamon. Charoses should be moist enough to hold together and not too sweet.

◆Charoses can be made several days ahead of time and refrigerated in a covered container.

MRS. LICHTENFELD'S KNAIDLACH (MATZOH BALLS)

Passover immediately evokes the thought of matzoh balls and chicken soup. There are endless variations on how to make them and how to flavor them. They can be made with or without fat; they can be firm or light; they can be cooked in chicken stock or water. I like mine small, fluffy, and cooked in salted water. A lady in Florida shared her recipe with me. They can be cooked in advance and kept in a little stock for easier reheating. Serve in piping-hot chicken soup, garnished with snipped dill.

ABOUT 20
SMALL BALLS

6 TO 8
SERVINGS

3 eggs, at room temperature,
separated
½ cup plus 1 tablespoon
matzoh meal

About 1 teaspoon kosher salt
White pepper, freshly ground

½ cup to 1 cup chicken stock

Bring a large pot of salted water (or two smaller ones) to a boil and let simmer. (Matzoh balls need room to expand while cooking.)

Beat egg whites until very stiff. Add egg yolks and continue beating until very well blended. Gradually sprinkle small amounts of matzoh meal over top of eggs and gently combine with a rubber spatula, always reaching to bottom of bowl. Season with salt and pepper. Let mixture stand for 6 to 10 minutes, depending on how light or firm you like your knaidlach. (I leave mine for just 6 minutes.)

Have a small bowl of water ready. Moisten hands with water and shape full teaspoons of mixture into balls. Drop carefully into simmering water, cover, and cook gently for 15 minutes. Remove with a perforated spoon to heated soup bowls filled with hot chicken soup. Garnish with dill snipped to bits with scissors.

◆If you wish to make knaidlach in advance, place drained matzoh balls in a small saucepan along with chicken stock. When needed, reheat gently. Discard stock; it will be cloudy.

Shavuot

CHEESE BLINTZES

ABOUT 6
BLINTZES

Shavuot celebrates the giving of the Ten Commandments, the end of the barley harvest, and the offering of the first fruit at the Temple.

It is customary to eat dairy dishes on Shavuot, especially those made with cheese. There are many explanations of this custom. One of them is that the Jews did not have time to slaughter animals and kosher the meat after leaving the Sinai; another is that the Torah is like milk and honey; and another is that the period of May to early June is the spring harvest season, when more milk and cheese products are produced.

Cheese blintzes are therefore traditionally served on Shavuot. These are very light, not too sweet, and very convenient to make. The batter must be refrigerated for several hours or overnight.

BATTER:

2 eggs

3½ tablespoons unbleached flour

⅛ teaspoon salt

½ cup ice water

Sweet butter

FILLING:

½ pound farmer cheese

3 ounces cream cheese

1 egg yolk

½ teaspoon vanilla extract

Grated rind of 1 lemon

About 2 tablespoons sugar

Confectioners' sugar

Sour cream

I suggest you use the following: a blender, a 7- or 8-inch nonstick skillet, and a food processor.

To make the batter: Place eggs, flour, salt, and water in a blender and process at high speed until batter is very smooth. Transfer to a measuring cup; it is easier to pour from. Cover with plastic wrap and refrigerate for several hours or overnight.

To make the blintzes: Bring batter back to room temperature and mix well.

Heat a skillet over medium heat and butter it lightly. Sprinkle a drop of batter on it; if it sizzles, skillet is ready.

Lift skillet and pour in just enough batter (about 2 tablespoonfuls) to coat bottom by swirling it around. Immediately tilt skillet over measuring cup to pour off any excess batter, no matter how little. Cook blintzes on both sides until they are set.

To make the filling: Place farmer cheese, cream cheese, egg yolk, vanilla, lemon rind, and sugar in a food processor fitted with the steel blade. Combine until just blended, but not smooth.

To assemble the blintzes: Preheat oven to 325°F. Lay blintzes on a sheet of wax paper. Place about 2 tablespoons filling in lower center of each crepe. Fold over the edge closest to you, then fold in the two sides and roll to make an oblong package.

Heat skillet until hot and butter it lightly. Fry blintzes on both sides until golden. Serve sprinkled with confectioners' sugar, with sour cream on the side.

◆Unfilled blintzes can be prepared a day ahead of time and refrigerated with wax paper between the layers. The same is true of the filling. Or you can fill them and keep them refrigerated until you are ready to cook.

MRS. RAPP'S CHEESE KREPLACH

ABOUT
65 KREPLACH

These half-moons of dough that are filled with a cheese mixture and sautéed in butter are a wonderful dairy first or main course. I serve them often, not only on Shavuot.

FILLING:

1 pound all-purpose potatoes	About 2½ teaspoons kosher
3 tablespoons vegetable oil	salt
1 medium onion, chopped fine	Black pepper, freshly ground
½ pound farmer cheese	

DOUGH:

2¼ cups unbleached flour	⅔ cup lukewarm water (about
¼ teaspoon salt	100°F)
1 egg, at room temperature, lightly beaten	

Sweet butter

*I suggest you use the following: a food mill with a medium blade,
a pastry blender, a 3-inch round cookie cutter, and 3 damp towels.*

To make the filling: Boil potatoes in their jackets until soft. Peel and quarter.

Heat oil in a small skillet until hot. Add onions and sauté over medium heat until light brown. Strain potatoes with onions and farmer cheese through a food mill. Season well with salt and pepper.

To make the dough: Mix flour and salt in a metal bowl. Add egg and mix with a pastry blender, gradually sprinkling on water until you can gather dough into a rough ball. (From time to time scrape sticky dough from the blender with a knife.) Turn dough out onto a board. Knead with the heel of your hand until dough is smooth and elastic. (If dough seems difficult to knead, let it rest for a few minutes to relax the gluten. To test if dough is fully kneaded, cut into it; if you see little holes inside, it is ready.)

To roll out the dough: Cut off a small (about one eighth) piece of dough, keeping the rest covered with a damp towel. On a lightly floured board, with a lightly floured rolling pin, roll dough out firmly on both sides (it is elastic) until it is very thin. Cut with a cookie cutter into 3-inch rounds.

Place 1 teaspoon filling in center of each round and fold dough over to make a half-moon. Fold edge over, then pinch to seal it tightly. (Do this carefully, or kreplach may open while boiling.)

Line a cookie sheet with a damp towel and place kreplach on it. Repeat in the same fashion with the remaining dough. Save the trimmings, form those into a ball, and roll out as well. Cover kreplach with a damp towel and refrigerate until ready to boil.

To boil the kreplach: Bring a large pot of salted water to a boil. Drop in kreplach, in batches, adjusting the size and number of batches to the size of your pot. Return water to the boil and cook slowly, uncovered, until kreplach rise to the top (about 3 minutes). Remove with a slotted spoon to a towel-lined dish to absorb some of the moisture.

Heat butter in a skillet until hot and sauté kreplach until golden brown. Season with salt and pepper and serve hot.

◆If you like, you can boil kreplach earlier in the day and sauté them later. After draining, be sure to coat them with some melted butter to prevent them from sticking to each other.

You can also freeze kreplach before boiling. Freeze them on the tray and, when frozen, remove to a plastic bag. Do not defrost before boiling.

CHEESE KUGEL

8 SERVINGS   This is a light kugel, which can be eaten either hot or at room temperature.

½ pound medium-wide egg
   noodles
Kosher salt
1 tablespoon sweet butter,
   melted
1 pound pot cheese
¼ cup sugar

½ cup milk
½ cup bottled orange juice
½ cup seedless golden raisins
Grated orange rind of 1
   orange
2 eggs, at room temperature,
   separated

I suggest you use a 9-by-9-by-2-inch ovenproof dish.

Preheat oven to 350°F. Cook noodles in a large pot of boiling salted water for about 5 minutes, or until they are not quite cooked. Pour into a sieve, refresh with cold water, and drain well.

Grease an ovenproof dish with butter.

In a large bowl, mix pot cheese, sugar, milk, orange juice, raisins, orange rind, and egg yolks. Add noodles and combine. Beat egg whites until stiff and fold into noodle mixture.

Transfer mixture to the prepared dish and bake in center of oven for 20 minutes. Reduce heat to 325° and bake for another hour.

JUDY'S CHEESE KUGEL

8 SERVINGS   I prefer to serve this richer kugel hot.

½ pound medium-wide egg
   noodles
Kosher salt
4 tablespoons (½ stick) sweet
   butter, melted
1 cup sour cream

⅓ cup sugar
1 pound pot cheese
2 eggs, at room temperature,
   separated
½ teaspoon ground cinnamon

I suggest you use a 9-by-9-by-2-inch ovenproof dish.

Preheat oven to 350°F. Cook noodles in a large pot of boiling salted water for about 5 minutes, or until they are not quite cooked. Pour into a sieve, refresh with cold water, and drain well.

Grease an ovenproof dish with some of the melted butter.

In a large bowl, mix remaining butter, sour cream, 1 teaspoon of the salt, sugar, pot cheese, and egg yolks. Add noddles and combine. Beat egg whites until stiff and fold into noodle mixture.

Transfer mixture to the prepared dish and bake in center of oven for 50 minutes.

Sprinkle with cinnamon and bake for another 5 minutes. Serve hot.

Index

About the Author

HELEN NASH was born in Cracow, Poland, and now lives in New York City.